Economics of the Law

There is an ever increasing interest in the question of how and why legal norms can effectively guide human action. This compact textbook demonstrates how economic tools can be used to examine this question and scrutinize these legal norms. Indeed, this is one of the first textbooks to be based on civil law instead of the more usual common law, situating the study of both private and public law within the framework of institutional economics, with recommendations for further reading and a list of key terms in each chapter. Besides the standard economic problems in property, tort, contract, crime and litigation, areas covered include:

- new institutional economics
- public choice
- constitutional law
- public administrations
- regulatory impact analysis

This book will be essential reading for students in law schools and economics departments alike, particularly those engaged with the methodology of law and economics, applied economics and economic methods of legal policy.

Wolfgang Weigel is Associate Professor at the University of Vienna and Chair of the Joseph von Sonnenfels Centre for the Study of Public Law and Economics.

Routledge advanced texts in economics and finance

Economics of the Law

A primer

Wolfgang Weigel

Routledge
Taylor & Francis Group

LONDON AND NEW YORK

Originally published as *Rechtsökonomik – eine methodologische Einführung für Einsteiger und Neugierige* with Verlag Vahlen by C. H. Beck, Munich, 2003.

First published 2008 by Routledge
2 Park Square, Milton Park, Abingdon, Oxon OX14 4RN

Simultaneously published in the USA and Canada
by Routledge
270 Madison Avenue, New York, NY 10016

Routledge is an imprint of the Taylor & Francis Group, an informa business

© 2008 Wolfgang Weigel

Typeset in Times New Roman by
Keystroke, 28 High Street, Tettenhall, Wolverhampton
Printed and bound in Great Britain by
Antony Rowe Ltd, Chippenham, Wiltshire

British Library Cataloguing in Publication Data
A catalogue record for this book is available from the British Library

Library of Congress Cataloging in Publication Data
Weigel, Wolfgang.
  Economics of the law : a primer / Wolfgang Weigel.
    p. cm.
  Simultaneously published in the USA and Canada
    Includes bibliographical references and index.
  1. Civil law—Economic aspects.   2. Law and economics.   I. Title.
  K623.W45 2008
  340′.11—dc22   2007034653

ISBN10: 0–415–40104–6 (hbk)
ISBN10: 0–415–40105–4 (pbk)
ISBN10: 0–203–93077–0 (ebk)

ISBN13: 978–0–415–40104–3 (hbk)
ISBN13: 978–0–415–40105–0 (pbk)
ISBN13: 978–0–203–93077–9 (ebk)

Contents

List of figures

List of tables

List of boxes

Preface

You may have opened this book because you want to satisfy your curiosity about what makes it different from other introductions to the field of law and economics. Well, if there are any, then the peculiarities are threefold:

1   First of all, this book is based on a text that was originally published in German and which then was the first short and comprehensive introduction to the subject of the economic analysis of law in German-speaking countries.
2   Second, due to its origins, the text is not supposed to amalgamate views of common law and the toolbox of economists, but instead tends to discuss a civil law framework with some comparisons between civil law practices and common law.
3   Finally, it is the first book to contain a chapter on economic approaches to public law *apart* from criminal law, thus addressing various issues in constitutional law and administrative law.

Its other features are a digression on an interesting collateral development, 'regulatory impact analysis', which, from its original macroeconomic focus, has turned into an instrument now firmly rooted in welfare economics and cost–benefit analysis. Regulatory impact analysis is strongly advocated by the US government, the Organization for Economic Cooperation and Development (OECD), the European Commission and an ever increasing number of governments throughout the world. Despite its different origins, it shares many features with the current economic approach to law, as you will see in this book. Moreover, a brief overview of a critical appraisal of the economic approach to law is given by means of an exploration of the existing literature.

It is also noteworthy that in European countries, with very few exceptions, an economic approach to the law is much more controversial than it is in the United States. There are only a handful of law schools where it is taught as a standard approach. Although it is making progress, for many regions efforts to promote it resemble a campaign of conversion.

Given the state of the art of today, an undertaking such as the present book must be far from comprehensive. Bearing this in mind, I had to make some hard choices concerning focus. One is a strict restriction to economic aspects, the applicability of which is demonstrated in a few relevant fields of law such as property, nuisance, contract, dispute resolution and punishment. Another touches on the delicate problem that, in a sense, lawyers and economists should be offered a different text, each taking account of the special needs of the respective profession. However, such an ambitious undertaking may be possible on an advanced level, but once the scholars have reached this level, being aware of interdisciplinary approaches, they may no longer be in need of such differentiation. So the compromise here was to sacrifice some detail to aid readability.

The book, therefore, is intended to serve the needs of undergraduate students of economics and business as well as those in law. It may also satisfy the curiosity of scholars who are not acquainted with either of the issues at hand and of legal professionals and government employees engaged in the businesses of lawmaking and implementation.

A few remarks on the use of this book are in order. Those readers who simply want to become familiar with the essence of what usually is thought to comprise the economic approach to the law are invited to read Chapters 1 to 4. However, if you are interested in fields such as applications to labour law or corporate law, you are invited also to visit Chapter 6, which, moreover, includes the afore-mentioned notes on related approaches and a critical appraisal of the existing body of knowledge.

In order to get acquainted with the broad field of the economic analysis of public law, you are invited not to skip it but to read Chapter 5, eventually, since it is one of the innovations in textbooks such as this and, it is to be hoped, will trigger your curiosity.

Concerning references, the method used in this book slightly differs from standard rules inasmuch as you will be encouraged to consult additional materials as they occur in the course of my presentation, although they are repeated and summarized at the end of each chapter together with recommendations for further reading.

In order to attract attention, a list of key terms not only appears at the end of each chapter but also in bold at their first appearance in the text; moreover, in order to allow for short breaks in reading, questions for review appear in the text where I found it appropriate.

Before I turn to acknowledgements, I would like to share my surprise, which was immediately followed by pleasure, when Rob Langham of Routledge first contacted me to ask me whether I would consider a translation of my original text into English. Of course, it would be a challenge and the English edition will hopefully vindicate the trust that was put into this undertaking on behalf of the publisher.

Thanks are again due to Rob Langham for his support and patience as well as to Taiba Batool and her successor as editorial assistant, Thomas Sutton. Moreover, I am much obliged to Vahlen Publishers, who promptly endorsed the publication in English. I am especially grateful to Johnny Unger for refurbishing my English and also to Andreas Oeller, the technician in my department, who repeatedly helped with software problems. I received a great deal of support from my wife, Miriam, who is not only a professional graphic designer, but also fluent in English, since she was born in Scotland.

Last, the material in this book has benefited from the suggestions I received from students at the University of Vienna, but also from my audiences as a Socrates Exchange Professor in Hamburg. I hasten to add that any shortcomings are entirely my own.

I would like to conclude by saying that I would appreciate any feedback from readers.

Wolfgang Weigel
Vienna, July 2007

1 Looking at legal norms from an economic viewpoint

A very first look at the map

You are about to start reading an introductory text on the economic analysis of law. This has been and to some extent still is a controversial topic – particularly from the point of view of legal scholars. Therefore, some preparatory remarks might be in order. First, there is the self-evident observation that an economy cannot work without law. As you shall shortly see in a stylized example, economic action is embedded in legally defined entitlements, procedural rules and sanctions for misconduct, to mention but a few. Economists have not denied this, but in their reasoning they treat the legal framework as abstract most of the time (they take it for granted implicitly and moreover they seem to assume that the legal system works effectively and smoothly). There are economic scholars who believe that this is unfortunate. So schools of 'dissenters' have emerged, which are called 'institutionalists'. They will be introduced to you later (pp. 9–12).

An even more challenging relationship between economics and the law occurs when economics is brought into play as an instrument for a better understanding of the law. Sometimes economists are blamed for such application and they are labelled 'imperialists', because they intrude on foreign fields. However, it can easily be shown that such allegations are misleading. As economists and hopefully also lawyers will be aware in the course of reading this book, economics is not only an object of investigation, but also a distinct method for looking at things. Now, looking at the law from a historical perspective appears quite natural, as is looking at the law from a political perspective, so why not look at it from the sociological, psychological, philosophical or economic perspective? Each of these approaches uses a distinct methodology and each therefore can contribute to the better understanding of the issues at hand. One of the peculiarities of jurisprudence is the lack of a behavioural model of human action, by which the effectiveness (and failures, of course) of legal norms can be investigated. And it is one of the strengths of economics that it can provide such a model.

Through the application of economic model(s), economists can explain the ineffectiveness of legal norms and they can make predictions about effectiveness. They also have means by which they can develop recommendations toward the improvement of laws.

While these can definitely be beneficial for the people (society) at large, this requires the observation of these recommendations by the legislature (including bureaucrats engaged in drafting of laws) and the courts. There is a difference, however, in who is primarily addressed, which depends on the legal system in use in a given location. For the purpose of this book two types of legal system ought to be distinguished, namely **civil law** and **common law**. It should be pointed out that remarks on the differences in legal traditions are necessary since the original German edition of this book was written with a strong orientation towards civil law, this being the predominant system in German-speaking countries. With its focus on methodological questions the book is in principle applicable to all legal systems (including French or Roman Dutch law). However, as the economic analysis of law definitely falls within the domain of 'applied economics', one should be aware of the field of application. Although their distinctive features have been blurred in the course of time, the two systems may be characterized as follows:

- Civil law is characterized by codified sets of rules governing relation between persons (humans or legal personalities). Typical examples are family law, tort law, trade law and corporate law. Regulations contain statements about lawful and/or unlawful acts and their consequences. Courts are thus obliged to observe certain procedures but they are mainly concerned with comparing the (codified) facts of a case with the actual circumstances. The more detailed the facts the less discretion is left to the judge (obvious omissions notwithstanding which might call for decisions *per analogiam*).
- Common law, in turn, rests on procedural statutes that guide the courts to judge by comparing the evidence to previous judgements, thus stressing precedent, but also take guidance from principles of natural justice and fairness. Common law tends toward 'judge-made law' where no (matching) precedent is found. This being the underlying principle in a nutshell, it must not be overlooked that even with strong common law traditions an ever increasing number of issues is now codified.

The consequence of this very brief summary is that recommendations flowing from the economic analysis of law should be aimed at legislators in civil law countries, whereas the primary addressees are courts (judges) in the common law system.

Unfortunately, even for the vaguest principles there are exceptions. One such exception is that in civil law countries the economic analysis of law can be valuable for constitutional courts, for example in cases where the fundamental civil or economic rights of citizens are at stake (as is increasingly the case in Austria and Germany).

The situation is slightly different when it comes to **public law**. As you will have seen on the contents page of this book, there is a chapter devoted to public law – an innovation among introductory textbooks in this field. Normally, **criminal law** is seen as public law, since it deals with the codification of relations between individual wrongdoers and society (thus dealing with public affairs). Whereas criminal law has been a traditional subject of the economic analysis of law (in fact, it was among the first and enjoyed rigorous analysis by Nobel laureate Gary Becker in the 1960s), constitutional and administrative law have been much less so.

Constitutional law is primarily concerned with sets of rules designed to facilitate rule making. The purpose of a constitution following this definition is the stabilization of social interaction; it specifies rights and obligations that are (must be) observable and enforceable. The understanding of constitutional law has benefited much from 'positive political theory' or **public choice**.

Administrative law, in turn, comprises two interrelated areas: one dealing with the causes and consequences of bureaucratic action inside bureaucracies and the other focusing on external interaction, for example between legislators and the bureaucratic institutions comprising the executive branch, and also between these bureaucratic institutions and the citizens and enterprises, respectively. Research into the latter area is better known as research into regulation. The fields of administrative law are substantially covered by the economic theory of bureaucracy and the (law and) economics of regulation. Only more recently, in the course of public sector reform, issues such as labour contracts for civil servants, payment schemes and the like have caught the eyes of analysts. However, there is still much to do, as will be illustrated in Chapter 5.

For the sake of completeness, I would like to point out that in this introduction some very interesting areas cannot be covered, such as international treaties and codes stemming from organizations such as the United Nations or the World Trade Organization, canon law (the law of the church) and Islamic law, of course.

The idea of this first section was to have a look at the map before we start tracing our route, which we shall set off on now.

When law is allowed to enter the economy

When it comes to the introduction of basic principles, economists most frequently do this by drawing attention to how a market functions, preferably a market for a consumption good. A market is a distinct means of coordination for the supply of and the demand for some commodity. In the simplest form, exchange takes place, thus transferring a certain amount of the good at hand from the supplier to the consumer, when there is agreement about the unit price of the good. (We will consider the procedure in slightly more detail later.) I would like to demonstrate that it can be enlightening to bring into play the role of the law in actions like a market exchange. I promise that both lawyers and economists will be enlightened, although economists might be slightly more surprised.

Before we start, let us be clear about the scope of the economic analysis of law. Essentially, this deals with two questions:

1   How do legal norms affect human behaviour?
2   Are these effects socially desirable?

Of course, the second question entails two more, namely: If the effects are undesirable, why is that so? If one knows why they are undesirable, how can the situation be changed?

With this agenda in mind we can now turn to a closer examination of our market. Please be aware that this introduction cannot replace a primer in microeconomic theory and policy. (See 'recommended reading' at the end of the book for references.) It can merely serve as a reminder and as the basis for a fruitful discussion of legal norms. We turn to the market for an example: the soft drink *Fresh*, which is available in the familiar 33cl cans. The **law of demand** states that the number of cans bought will increase as the price per can goes down (other things remaining equal). Alternatively with an increase of the price, the number of purchases of cans will decrease proportionally. Thus, we have described *Fresh* as an ordinary consumption good. For the sake of completeness we should add that with consumers taste remaining constant and a fixed price, an increase in income (or in money for purchases) will lead to a (slight) increase in the level of consumption. A change of the price of competing soft drinks (of which a large variety are available) can also lead to a shift in the level of consumption of *Fresh* (up or down, in the opposite direction of the competitors' price changes).

The **law of supply**, in turn, states that the number of cans offered will be higher the higher the price per unit, which can be achieved – where as usual the marginal cost of an increase in production is assumed to be given. Note that for the time being we do not make a distinction between production, wholesale and retail. Also, we assume that the price per unit is always above the minimum price for which supply is definitely profitable. Short-term shifts in supply are possible by curtailing the capacity of the bottling plant. Long-term shifts of the supply are not possible in our framework, because this would require the installation of additional capacity (an investment, which is presumably not readily available at short notice).

A market emerges when demand and supply intersect (see Figure 1.1). The number of cans exchanged will be determined by the price at the point of intersection. It is said that the market is in **equilibrium**, since the amount sold and the amount purchased are equal. The equilibrium is stable inasmuch as it will not change as long as the conditions hold under which it was brought about. The result is conditional, however, on the rational behaviour of fully informed participants in that market (since these are essential prerequisites for the further development of our ideas, we will have to come back to this issue under the label of *homo oeconomicus*, pp. 14–22).

The situation is advantageous for both sides. Let us check why: following the line of demand, one can see that there are consumers of *Fresh*, who would have been willing to pay a higher price per can than what they were charged. In the point of equilibrium, however, that **willingness to pay** and the actual charge are equal. Those who are located to the left of the equilibrium point enjoy the additional advantage given by the vertical distance between the price line and the demand curve. The sum of all these advantages is termed **consumer surplus**.

For the supplier the sale at equilibrium price means that for the last can sold the price just matches the additional cost of providing that can. Note that beyond that

Price

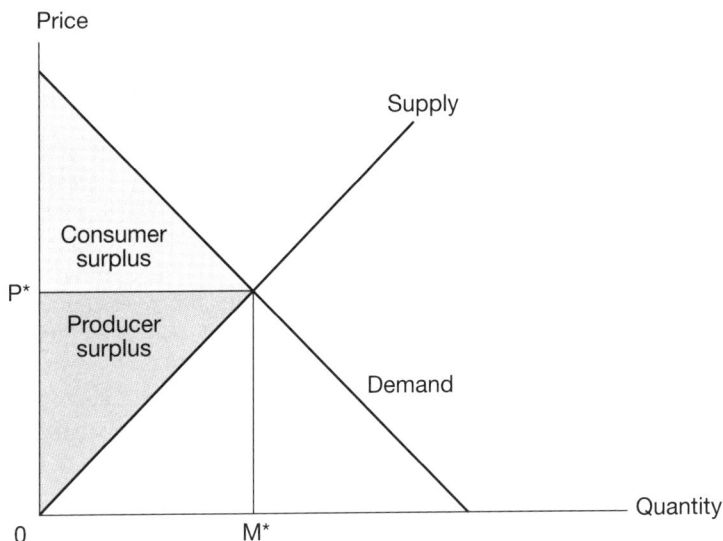

Figure 1.1 Market equilibrium and welfare gains

A partial market for a commodity: with no obstacles (transaction costs) the supply
schedule and the demand schedule intersect at equilibrium point P* and M*. Note that
the willingness to pay on behalf of consumers between 0 and M* is higher or just equal
to price P*. The accumulated gains are called 'consumer surplus' (the light grey
triangle); suppliers up to P* enjoy a welfare gain, since their marginal cost as reflected
by the supply schedule is – unless they are equal to P* – lower than the revenue, where
the total gain is the producer surplus (the dark grey triangle).

point sales would incur losses, since the marginal cost would be higher than the
attainable price. To the left of the equilibrium, however, the seller for each can
sold enjoys a positive difference between the attainable price and the marginal cost.
This is an additional profit, which becomes smaller the closer one gets to the
equilibrium point. The sum of all these additional profits (or, in more technical
terms: the area between the price line and the supply curve) is called the **producer
surplus**. Clearly a rational supplier of *Fresh* (or any other tradable commodity)
will maintain this offer so as to maximize surplus (rent) – unless there is no more
promising alternative in sight.

Thus, under the ideal conditions of our example, both sides extract maximum
advantages out of their position in the market for the soft drink *Fresh*.

Why might our findings be questionable?

What do you think about the following reservation? How come both sides of the
market are trading peacefully? Why is it that they are evidently trading cans for
money voluntarily? Does such activity not presume entirely unreal behaviour? If

– as has been stated already – participants in the market are guided by trying to gain an advantage for themselves, then consumers who want a soft drink could steal cans or rob the supplier. What keeps them from doing so in our ideal market? Or did we make an implicit assumption, which should be made transparent in our discussion?

To illustrate, let me quote from an Austrian newspaper headline from around Christmas 2000 (at this time of the year in Austrian cities one finds stalls all over the place where roasted chestnuts are sold for one euro a dozen): 'Snubbed customer had a knife. Criminal procedure for two hot chestnuts'. Conversely, the suppliers could satisfy their desire for money by force or guile.

Given such observations we will now set out to see whether there are forces at work that create sufficiently strong incentives to make trade in our market as peaceful as we have depicted it.

We are making progress! Let us pick up the conjecture that markets, in order to work appropriately, must be embedded in a legal and institutional framework. By tracing this conjecture further we are relating economic and legal issues to one another. We thus enter the domain of law and economics.

To be more specific with our example and the market for *Fresh*: in order for peaceful exchange to work the participants in the market must acknowledge **private property**, but possibly do so only in principle. This means that there must be effective institutions that enforce the observation of private property rights (see Box 1.1).

Box 1.1   Losses due to shoplifting

Let us stop for a moment and recall an event in the Austrian parliament, during a question time session in which the Federal Minister of Justice was asked his opinion on the likely consequences of the fact that, in 1998, losses due to shoplifting amounted to €545 million (an equivalent of 2 per cent of the GDP).

In his lengthy answer, the minister essentially stated that commerce must be designed in such a way that the incentives of perpetrating and the opportunities to perpetrate crimes were reduced. He was aware, he pointed out, that the then prevailing §42 of the Austrian Criminal Code provides a waiver for sanctions if an act lacks a certain type of offence.

Source: Minutes of the 152nd session in the 20th term of legislature, 5 December 1998.

As scholars of the economic analysis of law we can take this example as a starting point for the discussion of how economics can contribute to a better understanding of underlying problems and of how to take steps towards resolving them – exactly what we have stated at the beginning of this chapter as the essential questions our approach can help to answer!

Thus, from our observations (regarding the existence of private property as well as institutions for enforcement), two rather interesting and important questions emerge. First, what motivates people to acknowledge private property? And, second, how can such a fundamental agreement be accomplished? Shaping answers to these questions means delving into the world of economic order and, more specifically, constitutional order from the perspective of individual decisions. Moreover, the accomplishment of such fundamental rules can no longer be approached by means of a market. The fundamental rules at hand are *res extra commercio* by nature (although we will learn in the chapter on public law that this inherent property of rules can be violated!). The rules at hand are principally established by democratic vote, which is one type of coordination through non-market decisions (others being command or bargaining, norms, traditions and others).

Our market for *Fresh* as we have represented it in Figure 1.1 does not reveal whether any frictions arose in the course of the purchase, although we must admit that, in the present example, frictions or obstacles to the deal are much less likely than in the case of durables such as refrigerators, shoes or cars. Therefore, let us explore the kind of difficulty that may occur. In order to do this, we will first explore the example of our beverage and then move on to durables. Note that in order to accomplish our task we will look at purchases case by case, thus departing from the more general and abstract presentation as summarized in Figure 1.1. Furthermore, we will concentrate on problems related to economic efficiency. Although important or even essential in a legal sense, issues of justice or fairness are not our concern here, but we will pick up these questions later on (pp. 16–19), after we have explored the notion of efficiency in more detail.

What are the problems customers could face in purchasing a can of *Fresh*?

First of all, a customer wants to be sure that the product has the expected properties: in case of a soft drink, its taste, temperature, consistency and that it be untainted. She will therefore seek ways and means to secure these properties. However, such an undertaking requires some effort in terms of time and other resources. The cost our consumer will have to bear for the beverage will thus very likely exceed the market price for the drink. Fortunately, there is relief for our consumer. She may trust that the desired properties ('quality') are warranted through the brand name of the product, *Fresh*.

But now the seller comes into play: why should she be interested in offering untainted beverage with a certain taste? If the customer had chosen our seller randomly then it is very unlikely that the purchase will be repeated. Hence the seller (producer) might not be interested in good performance. The customer in turn might shun the additional effort of complaint or even lawsuit, when, after inspection, she finds the product unacceptable, since the effort for such activities most likely by far exceeds the value of the purchase. The seller in turn will anticipate such reactions. Note that our reasoning follows from the underlying assumption that every individual is rationally acting to her own advantage. Under such circumstances a solution can be found in a general rule that makes the seller bear responsibility for deceiving consumers. Such rule is called a liability rule and it essentially creates an incentive for good conduct through the threat of a penalty in case of misconduct.

There is another side to that problem, however, which we have already mentioned: the challenge of shoplifting by consumers. Again, there are rules in use, which ultimately should keep customers from wrongdoing, this time for the benefit of the sellers (recalling the quotation from the minutes of the Austrian parliament).

Things are most likely more complicated when something other than a quick purchase of a beverage is at stake, for example a durable consumer good such as a refrigerator or a pair of shoes. Here, there will be a lengthy and resource-absorbing process involving the gathering of appropriate information about available alternatives and about properties and conditions of sale, possibly some bargaining over price or discounts, warranties and so on. It will end with the signature of a 'contract', which hopefully contains all relevant contingencies for the deal – and if not, trouble is likely if the good at hand has a hidden defect.

As a matter of fact (and as lawyers are fully aware) contracts are a major issue in both law and economics. Likely sources of flaws are identified and means to prevent or at least remedy them are sought by legal economists. The interesting thing about these activities is that economics is salient in two distinct ways: as you are by now perfectly aware, purchasing a durable good may incur considerable 'time and trouble' cost (a more technical term for this is 'transaction costs'). So by shaping the conditions for the market of consumer durables, adjusting incentives accordingly and by other measures, the legal economist can help save a lot of the aforementioned 'time-and-trouble' cost. However, the necessary analyses and adjustments are made using typical economic methods, for instance, the model of human behaviour labelled *homo oeconomicus*. We can trace the presence of economics even further: it has a lot to say about conflicts leading to trials as well as alternative means of conflict resolution.

You may ask what the essence is of such considerations. The answer is here that in its most common form the economic analysis of law is oriented toward efficiency, more specifically 'social efficiency', which comprises the efficient allocation of resources so that they are used economically and at the same time give maximum satisfaction.

These aspects are combined in the principle of 'Pareto efficiency'. We will soon see, however, that this principle gives rise to some tricky problems of application, which have led, on the one hand, to harsh criticism and, on the other hand, to quite sophisticated 'workarounds' to make it work.

Now that you have examined some of the ideas behind an economic analysis of law, we can start our introductory tour in more detail. In doing this, we should be aware of the features of our methodology. The economic approach can be used for descriptive and explanatory purposes. To illustrate, we might ask why the prevailing legal remedies for shoplifting are ineffective? An investigation of this type involves the development of models and empirical testing. Nowadays, experimental economics is becoming increasingly widespread, where a selected group of people is observed under certain conflicting conditions. (By way of illustration, one experiment of this type will be reviewed in Chapter 3 (pp. 50–60). This was carried out in order to check the validity of the 'Coase theorem', a milestone in the economic analysis of law.) In addition to such positivistic analysis, economics is also used in a normative sense, that is to say in the design or achievement of socially desired states, which are generally characterized by the Pareto efficiency mentioned earlier. Although this textbook covers both applications, it emphasizes the normative approach.

Setting the stage: the economic analysis of law forms part of 'new institutional economics'

It is not just coincidence that, for several decades, legal norms have aroused the curiosity of economists. For some time economists whose work originated in the analytical approach of mainstream economics took an increasing interest in **institutions**. One reason for this may be rooted in the high degree of abstraction of mainstream economics, which is the price to be paid for the vast advantages in the application of mathematical tools in economic analysis. Strangely enough, very strong support for the better understanding of the upswing of institutional economics comes from Ragnar Frisch (a scholar whose writings are not associated with our topic normally). Back in 1959 he pointed out that two types of restriction (constraint) to human action ought to be observed:

- obligatory constraints, which are given by nature, for example short supply of crude oil)
- facultative constraints, which are designed by humans and therefore are open to both change and violation.

(See Frisch, 1959, 39–92.)

The two types of constraint have distinct features, both in terms of their effectiveness and their origin and potential for alternation. Let us look more closely at some of these features in order to learn more about the peculiarity of an 'institutional' approach to economics.

Obligatory constraints are the ones economists usually envisage, since economics is generally understood as the science of humankind's handling of scarcity. Those constraints are binding, at least in the short run. Clearly, for specific particularly scarce resources there are substitutes of some kind, temporarily at least. Moreover, research and development provide the means for overcoming tough constraints (such as the possibility of extracting crude oil from oil shale in case crude oil in situ runs out). It is very interesting, however, to learn that the economic historian Douglass North (Nobel laureate 1993) has convincingly shown that new inventions such as techniques of extraction are only rewarding when the conditions for the generation of a return from such activities have been adapted so as to give **incentives** and security beforehand! Obviously, such institutional preconditions fall into the category of facultative constraints. (It is worth reading North, 1981.)

As far as facultative constraints are concerned, one can ignore them if one is not afraid of sanctions (again, recalling the discussion on shoplifting in the Austrian parliament), one may attempt to move out of their geographical limits or one might like to try to change them (which would require acceptance by a sufficient number of other affected people). Essentially, facultative constraints can be thought of in terms of property rights, obligations and/or liabilities and more generally as a combination of these forming so-called 'institutions'.

Various definitions of institutions are in use. For our purpose, institutions are understood as systems of rules, which serve as guidelines for human action. This in turn requires mutual consent, willingness to comply as well as to impose sanctions for violation and to acknowledge sanctions on oneself in case of violation.

Clearly there is a huge variety of institutions, which can be more or less stringent. Institutions are present within families and on the global level.

The adherents of 'new institutional economics' argue that it is institutions that ultimately determine the use of scarce resources. Therefore, it is entirely inappropriate to look at them merely as a given framework for investigations into the economy – as is customary among mainstream economists (see Box 1.2 for quotations). Consequently, institutional economists devote themselves to the analysis of the rise, stability and change of institutions and to this end they apply the toolbox of economics.

Economic analysis of law can thus be seen as part of a comprehensive research program, which in a certain sense challenges the 'orthodox' point of view of economists.

Box 1.2   New institutional economics

'The governmental and institutional framework should be set aside, along with tastes and technology, as matters which economists have traditionally chosen not to consider within their province' says Pearson in her book *Origins of Law and Economics* (1997, 1), quoting from Paul Samuelson's seminal *Foundations of Economic Analysis*, Cambridge, MA, 1947.

'Die zentrale Idee des ökonomischen Denkens ist eine in einem sehr fundamentalen Sinn soziologische Idee: nämlich die, dass sich die Produktion und Verteilung der Güter in einem durch juridische Sanktionsmechanismen abgestützten System von kommerziellen Beziehungen zwischen den Personen und Gruppen einer Gesellschaft quasiautomatisch in einer für die Bedürfnisbefriedigung der betreffenden Individuen relevanten Weise regelt'. [The essential idea of economic reasoning is basically a sociological idea: the production and distribution of goods take place in a system of commercial relations that is supported by a mechanism of legal sanctions. Thus, the satisfaction of the needs of the individual members of a society is more or less automatically regulated in an appropriate way (my translation)]. This is what the distinguished economic philosopher Hans Albert stated in his seminal essay 'Modell-Platonismus' (the quotation follows Topitsch, 1972, 421).

What is noteworthy about institutions is the fact that they appear to be systems of rules shaped by people, but the prevailing shape must not always be viewed as the result of planning and cooperation: besides such institutions, which are consciously and purposefully designed and implemented, there are also ones that are based on tacit consent, have evolved from spontaneous action because people have independently discovered their advantages (more precisely, we are referring to Friedrich August von Hayek's famous notion of 'spontaneous order' here; for details you might consult his *Constitution of Liberty*, Tübingen, 1971).

A look into the history of some institutions can tell us that there are cases where a currently codified set of rules originally emerged spontaneously. Conversely, some codified institutions developed in a deviant manner later on, thus departing substantially or even entirely from the original intent. (One good example is the history of the Sicilian Mafia; 'institutionalized corruption' is an another example quite familiar to observers of both developing countries and some transition economies; the idea of legalizing the well-established black markets in post communist Russia for the sake of making the market economy work is similar.)

Moreover, it is institutions that allow the realization of values and *Weltanschauung* in the economy and society. Thus, ideas about equality and protection contained in the 'social market economy' are captured in specific institutional structures. An analogy can be found in the so-called *Katholische Soziallehre*, in which the values established in a blueprint for a distinct social order entail institutions such as the 'principle of subsidiarity' (as established in the encyclica *quadragesimo anno* by Pope Pius XI in 1931 and much later adopted in article 5a of the EC treaty), which attempts to limit rampant paternalism in central governments.

In summary, inasmuch as values and *Weltanschauung* find their way into legal orders via political implementation, the economic analysis of law tends to be treated as something like evidence in applied social philosophy. Bearing in mind our focus on normative views of law and economics, we are quickly approaching the inter- section between institutions and ethics here, where ethics means the tenet of a correct life, that is, of doing the right things, having the right habits and customs.

There is naturally a close relation between institutions and organizations. Organizations may be seen as the material precondition in terms of personnel, their functions and common goals for the establishment and safeguarding of institutions.

By now you should have become aware of the fact that the economic analysis of law is part of a broader scientific approach, a specific way of thinking about a framework for human action. Such scientific approaches, which find support from a fairly large number of scholars, are called paradigms (after Kuhn, 1996). Thus, the economic analysis of law is part of a specific paradigm in economics.

However, we must be very careful not to mix up different 'brands' of institu- tionalism here!

What we are talking about is, in fact, the economic approach that by no means refutes the methodology of neoclassical economic theory. It merely challenges its focus, which is to concentrate on human action and to take the constraints as given and – most of the time – unspecified. This brand has eventually been labelled 'new institutional economics' (see Furubotn and Richter, 1998). This is the case because (not surprisingly!) there is an 'old' institutionalism, which goes back to the nineteenth century, where it marks the hostile reactions of a group of economists (primarily in Germany, e.g. Gustav Schmoller and Adolph Wagner) to the rise of classical economics (mainly associated with the names of Wilfredo Pareto, Leon Walras, Friedrich von Wieser). The opponents held that the historical and – in some sense 'evolutionary' – view of economics must be observed. In the USA, John R. Commons and Thorsten Veblen were the standard bearers of this view. They claimed that not analytically founded predictions but rather contingent historical perceptions were the first source of insight. This view – perhaps somewhat softened with respect to methodology – is still current. The leading organ is the *Journal of Economic Issues*. Furthermore – importantly – since the group around Schmoller or Commons was then labelled 'Institutionalists', their more recent successors are called 'neo-institutionalists', in order to make clear which group is relevant for our economic analysis of law, the 'new institutional economics'.

Now that we have started discussing some historical facts it is time to complete our introduction with a short historical overview.

A glimpse at the origins of law and economics

Let us start with a piece of sophistry. The joint treatment of 'law and economics' has a much longer tradition than the 'economic analysis of law'. Let me also hasten to add that in the past this joint treatment was not felt at all to be something so peculiar that it needed special emphasis. To illustrate: early scholars of economics such as the *physiocrat* François Quesnay (1694–1774) approached the law in the manner typical of lawyers and moral philosophers. The principles of law were seen as evident. Where they seemed not to be entirely clear they were made the subject of thorough reasoning. Abstraction, logic and empirical evidence were not in use in the early days. However, approval of a more analytical approach can be found in the writings of Jeremy Bentham (1748–1832). Interestingly, the otherwise renowned representatives of *cameralism* do not appear to have explicitly considered law and economics (*cameralism* is the German equivalent of *mercantilism*, the dominant economic policy of the seventeenth and eighteenth century; its focus was agriculture and population growth and this was extensively maintained by the state and by means of a competent central public administration). As always, exceptions can be found, one being Joseph von Sonnenfels (1732–1817), who wrote a textbook in two volumes on *Administration, the Market and Finance* (an approximate translation of *Von der Polizey, den Handlungen und der Finanz*). During the nineteenth century a substantial change took place. One reason was that the rise of economics as a standalone discipline was mainly borne out by lawyers, who were in some senses 'entrepreneurs', in that they specialized in economics and subsequently succeeded as university professors. Eugen von Böhm-Bawerk anticipated the ideas that later became part of the notion of property rights (see Chapter 2) in his monograph *Entitlements and Relationships from the Viewpoint of the Tenet of Commodities* (published in Innsbruck in 1881). Emmanuel Herrmann in turn wrote a *Theory of Insurance* (1897), which gets close to the so-called Coase theorem, a widely held cornerstone of modern law and economics (see Chapter 3). Two more pioneers need to be mentioned here. Victor Mataja developed the theory of liability rules in his *Liability Law from an Economic Perspective* (1888) and Karl G. Wurzel published the seminal book *Jurisprudence as a Social Science – Legal Thought and the Social Dynamics of the Law*, a reprint of which was published in Vienna in 1991.

The emphasis on early Austrian writers does not mean that there were no important contributions from other countries. However, it is intended to show that the subject of our concern here is deeply rooted in what could be labelled the early days of political economics.

Now to turn to America. There two issues are seen as relevant to the emergence of an economic analysis of law: issues of antitrust in the 1920s and later, in the 1950s, a motion for the reform of accident insurance for automobiles. One must not forget, however, that by this time Joseph Schumpeter (1883–1950) had already imported the core ideas of an economic theory of democracy to Harvard, where he had a chair from 1932 onwards. These ideas became one of the roots of public choice (the theory of non-market decision making, sometimes labelled 'positive political theory'). The related issues of bureaucracy, a traditionally more institution-oriented 'public finance' (as distinguished from the now popular theory of optimal taxation) and the rise of institutional economics also have their share in the stimulation of the newly emerging economic analysis of law.

Here are the first 'blockbusters' in this area: Guido Calabresi's Some thoughts on risk distribution and the law of torts, *Yale Law Journal*, 70, 1961, 499–553 and Ronald Coase's The problem of social costs, *Journal of Law and Economics*, 3, 1960, 1–44. These papers were quickly followed by the development of the notion of property rights by Harold Demsetz (Towards a theory of property rights, *American Economic Review*, 57, 1967, 347–73), as well as a thorough elaboration of the concept of transaction costs by Armen Alchian (Some implications of recognition of property right transaction costs, in K. Brunner (ed.) *Economics and Social Institutions*, Boston, 1979, 233–52). The culmination of the first period of modern law and economics was definitely the publication in 1973 of Richard Posner's book *Economic Analysis of Law*. Because of the trend-setting formal treatment of the subject and its elegance, a book by Steven Shavell (*Economic Analysis of Accident Law*, Cambridge, MA, 1987) deserves mention here. This does not mean that there are no other outstanding writers. Still those who have been named here established the landmarks. (If you are interested in a more comprehensive review of the history of ideas in this area you are referred to Pearson, 1997.)

To round up our historical tour at this time: with respect to modern law and economics the civil law countries somewhat lagged behind the common law countries. In merry old Europe, on the continent, the departure started with Michael Adams's *Economic Analysis of Security Interests* (1980). Soon Hamburg became a hotspot in law and economics, when Peter Behrens's book *Economic Foundations of the Law* came out in 1986, immediately followed by Hans-Bernd Schäfer and Claus Ott's *Textbook of the Economic Analysis of Civil Law*.

The consolidation into a European school was achieved when the European Association of Law and Economics was founded in Lund in 1984. It is noteworthy that the USA followed only in 1991, when the American Association of Law and Economics was founded in a meeting in Urbana-Champaign, Illinois. Famous scholars such as Robert Cooter, Tom Ulen and George Priest (to name but a few) were the promoters of this event. It is interesting to give a thought to the likely reason for that delay. Contrary to Europe in the USA since the 1960s several schools had emerged (which we will briefly review in Chapter 6) and it obviously took some time to unite them into one organization.

The rapid further development is documented in two comprehensive volumes. The first is the *Bibliography of Law and Economics* edited by Gerritt de Geest and Boudewijn Bouckaert of Ghent in 1992, which lists the then relevant literature in 667 pages. This volume was followed by the *Encyclopaedia of Law and Economics* in five volumes, again edited by de Geest and Bouckaert, which has appeared from 2000 onwards.

Nowadays, the economic analysis of law can be regarded a well-defined paradigm centred on new institutional economics.

It is now high time to have a close look at the analytical foundations!

The economist's prerequisites for the analysis of law

Let us revisit the question in the introduction: what are the consequences of legal norms on the behaviour of affected people?

In order to answer such a question we need to have a clear idea about typical behavioural patterns of the individual. Note that we do not need to gain insights into the multiplicity of characters and lifestyles; what we require is a behavioural pattern that allows for predictions with a sufficient degree of likeliness. Such patterns are provided by a theory of decision making and actions. The underpinning of such a theory is that all people show similar reactions, so that a representative standard model can be developed. It is worth noting in passing that without this kind of theory all further investigations into our subject would be futile; even the collection of a huge amount of data from observations would give us only apparent correlations.

We have an appropriate model at our disposal, which has become known as *homo oeconomicus*. In the mainstream of law and economics, this model is the most widely used one. And as this is intended to be an introductory text, we will stick to that standard. However, bearing in mind the advances in science and research, we will have a brief digression to characterize departures from the standard model and recent trends.

As a first step we will characterize *homo oeconomicus* as not facing any uncertainty or risk. Thus our representative individual selects from given alternatives, which at a given time are all known to her, that one which gives her utmost satisfaction (pleasure, **utility**) under prevailing circumstances. To make this model work, tastes or preferences are assumed to conform to a subjective existential orientation. They are assumed to be unalterable. Accurate selection is geared by constraints, which are effectuated through (opportunity) costs, which means that the individual asks herself whether it is worth sacrificing a certain choice. In other words, our representative individual does a cost–benefit analysis. The yardstick is provided by money terms, which accrue to the benefits and cost in each and every situation. That is to say, while the cost–benefit calculation is essentially individualistic and subjective, we assume that it can be made measurable and thus comparable by the assignment of units of pound, euro or US dollar or any other currency.

Generally, the model applies to the individual and holds for individuals in whatever social role, as a consumer, entrepreneur, politician, judge, bureaucrat. That is, the individual becomes the essential unit for investigations. Therefore it is said that the economic analysis of law rests on 'methodological individualism'. However, there are exceptions to the rule in cases where the consideration of an individual as the smallest unit of decision making is inappropriate. This may be the case when a household, an enterprise or firm, a committee or board are at stake. Note that the reference to such aggregates only makes sense when it can be assumed that the unit at hand is sufficiently homogenous internally.

We have stated that the purpose of the economic analysis of law is to study human reactions to legal constraints and to seek adjustments of legal norms where the reactions are evidently not the desired ones. The desire is to bring about a situation that is socially (and economically of course) optimal. How can such a desirable state be explained in the presence of methodological individualism? It must somehow reflect the individual wellbeing of each of the individuals at hand! An appropriate scale is provided by the 'Pareto optimum'. According to this scale a situation is optimal when it is no longer possible to improve the (economic) situation of even one single affected individual when at the same time the situation of another would have to be worsened (an illustrative example using our earlier example of the soft drink *Fresh* will follow).

Frequently the analyst faces the problem whether an improvement is possible given a certain initial condition. Improvement here typically would mean a 'better law'. In this situation, a 'Pareto improvement' is sought. Unfortunately, the search for a 'Pareto improvement' frequently comprises the delicate problem that the change of a situation finds winners and losers. According to our scale this must not be allowed.

So a solution must be found in order to overcome the likely problems of unequal distribution and justice in the presence of winners and losers. The solution which has become standard for this type of problem is called the **Kaldor-Hicks test** (sometimes also named a compensation test). The gist of this test will also be presented in an example using our beverage *Fresh*. For the moment, however, we must be aware that such a test contains a sense of pragmatism, since from a strictly theoretical viewpoint massive objections can be raised. This has something to do with the aforementioned subjectivist approach to human action, which simply does not allow for any subjective comparisons. However, a hint for how to escape from such problems has already been given. It is the use of money terms as a proxy for the subjective appreciation of a situation. This holds in particular for consumers, where the 'willingness to pay' (as distinguished from the ability to pay) is seen as the proxy for the unhampered valuation of a unit of a commodity. We will soon expand this notion to that of property rights, where physical entities are no longer at stake but rather the various ways of disposing over goods are. It is only then that we will turn to a much debated and widely used concept of law and economics – **wealth maximization** (you might have heard about this already; particularly if you have ever heard about the approach advocated by Judge Richard Posner of Chicago!).

Let us turn to **Pareto optimality** first (note that occasionally the term Pareto efficiency is used; this indicates that it is not just the optimal situation for users of goods which is sought but also the economically optimal way of providing these goods in terms of efficiency in production and allocation).

Imagine there are ten people who are thirsty. Imagine further that for some reason there are 15 cans of *Fresh* available. These 15 cans could now be distributed in the following way: each member of the group gets one can and then a second round of distribution starts until the stock of cans is exhausted. Now each member of the group has one can and five enjoy one more. The result matches the earlier defined Pareto optimality. However, it could contradict a common sense of justice in distribution. For instance, we could have distributed the second can according to need. Unfortunately, by choosing the way of distribution we already have used, we slammed the door for a Pareto optimal correction of the initial distribution. It is easy to see this. If we took away one can from one of those who had two cans and gave it to someone else (who claims to be extremely thirsty), the move is in contradiction to Pareto optimality: the improved situation of one member of the group has been enabled by a sacrifice of another member.

Sadly, it is definitely no exaggeration to state that in practice the presence of winners and losers is the norm. Does this suggest that the joint accessibility of optimality and **distributive justice** is impossible? Well, the answer to this question obviously is of great practical importance. So let us see where we get. Before we start, however, let me point out that no objective scale for justice exists in the sense that it is remains valid independently from the will of those who are affected – note that we are talking about distributive justice and not commutative justice, although the latter is usually much more in line with legal thinking.

The first way out of the dilemma would be that the distribution of cans is Pareto optimal and just if no person envies one of those who are better off because of what they possess. **Envy** here means that I would prefer another person's assets to my own. Another possibility would be altruism: in this case my pleasure (utility) increases with the increasing happiness of someone else. The approach most used in practice is the following: assume that each member of the group originally was willing to pay ten units of some currency for one can. Those who enjoy owning a second can value this at five each. In turn, those who have just one can would have valued an additional can at only three. Given these circumstances, a redistribution could not lead to a Pareto improvement. The original situation is thus Pareto optimal.

Now let us revise the original situation by assuming that those who have two cans value the second can at three, whereas those who have just one can would value another one at five. In this case a Pareto improvement is possible. To see why, consider that a value of three means that three units of money in exchange for a can of *Fresh* leaves the person exactly as happy as before, whereas the person who has sacrificed three receives the equivalent value of five, thus enjoying a net gain of two! The cans thus would follow the highest willingness to pay! For the moment our puzzle seems to be solved. But before we lean back in relief we have to scrutinize our findings. In doing this we may first ask whether the emerging Pareto improvement would have been achieved by a vote on behalf of the group members. The act of voting would have solved the distributional problem by one shot whereas in our example two steps were necessary to get the envisaged result.

Ask yourself what intuition would tell you before you continue reading. The correct answer: there need not be just one standard of justice! We will pick up this point later on. Another problem which ought to be addressed is that of possible obstacles to the smooth processing of the redistribution of cans.

The issue of justice is extensively discussed. One of the most influential ideas about a generally acceptable standard of distributive justice comes from Rawls (2005). However, Rawls 'theory' cannot be illustrated by the straightforward expansion of our previous setting. The gist of this theory is the 'difference principle'. And the rationale of a group (or even society at large) to adopt this principle deserves a special setting.

The difference principle states that people are willing to adapt to following rules (both of law and of economics!) under certain circumstances: when in some initial situation there are people who are worse off than others then their assets should be increased more than that of those who are initially better off.

Why could this be acceptable?

If, in the initial state, people are separated from the future by a veil of ignorance (an opaque curtain) they will not be able to foresee whether they will be worse off or better off once they have passed that veil, provided that the people have the following characteristics:

1   They act in their own interest, knowing their own preferences and being capable of valuing their actions as well as those of their fellow people.
2   The needs and interests are similar (thus reducing the likeliness of disintegration).
3   The capabilities and powers are so close that cooperation is preferred to the achievement of a dominant position.
4   They are not envious.

Given all these circumstances the adoption of the difference principle is the best thing this group of people can do.

Consider a vertically integrated plant with six different stages of production and 60 employees. The total wage is 600,000 and the basic wage 10,000. Now, there are two bottlenecks where four and six employees are busy, respectively. They would be induced to increase their efforts so as to diminish the bottleneck if their salaries were increased from 10,000 to 15,000, say. But this would require additional revenues of 50,000. How could the necessary funds be raised?

As a consequence of the diminished bottlenecks, imagine three different cases: an increase in revenues of under 650,000, 650,000 exactly or more than 650,000.

In the first case, the 50 employees outside the bottlenecks must forego part of their salary for the benefit of the remaining ten, which they will hardly agree to. In the second case the salaries of 50 will stay the same, whereas the other ten are beneficiaries. While the former will be indifferent, the latter will be in favour of the solution. In the third case, an 'inequality surplus' will be left over, which could be distributed among the 50. Now, if characteristic four applies, then the 50 would enjoy a slight increase in their wages but the ten working in the bottlenecks would receive a considerably higher pay rise. That is to say, the gain of the 50 will be relatively smaller than the gain of the other ten. This solution will be accepted by all of them – and this example illustrates the difference principle.

This is not the end of the story, however. Rawls himself has elaborated on his original thoughts in *Justice as Fairness* (2001) and there is an abundance of explanations, exegeses and criticism to be found in most libraries! We will meet John Rawls once more in Chapter 5 (economic analysis of constitutional law), because the methodology he uses contains a key to understanding that analysis.

We now turn to our simple example of how to allocate cans of *Fresh* optimally. Let us start by changing the setting somewhat in order to demonstrate a possibly surprising but practically important insight.

Assume that our group parts, after having received their share of cans, returning to their home or workplace without having taken advantage of a round of Pareto-improving exchanges of cans for money. Assume further that return to the place of distribution would be so costly that no net gain would be possible if the cost of the return is taken into account. We then find a situation where there is an obstacle to the Pareto improvement, which makes the original distribution the optimal one despite the fact that there is still a potential improvement, which only could be effectuated, however, if there were means to reduce the cost of mobility. This not being the case, the status quo is the logically preferable situation. We can now go one step further and investigate a situation where beneficial exchanges are merely hypothetical from the outset. To this end we adopt a slightly stylized routine problem. Imagine a landfill site that ought to be remediated. The cost to taxpayers is 30,000. The beneficiaries of the remediation are the citizens of communities adjacent to the landfill site, consisting of 10,000 people in total. These people value the reduction of environmental risks at five each. Being a public good, it would be difficult or perhaps even too costly to finance the remediation directly from the beneficiaries. Issues of modern financing notwithstanding, the total benefits are then 50,000. Now assume that the beneficiaries and taxpayers are perfectly separable groups of citizens. Evidently there are losers and winners in this situation. Hence the straightforward application of our optimality criterion fails. However, the gains are so high that there would still be a net gain if the losers were compensated by the winners. Such compensation must not necessarily take place. As a matter of fact our finding here matches the test, which is carried out hundreds and thousands of times to find out whether a policy that cannot be effectuated via a market is worth being carried out at all. In a nutshell, it is a cost–benefit analysis.

Since in our example the compensation of losers does not take place although it would be possible in principle (or 'potentially'), it passes the test, which has been named after the economists Nicholas Kaldor and Sir John Hicks. In other words, a Pareto improvement is *potentially* possible if the benefits are so high that the beneficiaries could in principle compensate the losers and still enjoy a net advantage.

There are some inherent problems in a Kaldor-Hicks test. The most prominent of these defects is the following: imagine that the environmental authority has decided to crosscheck their calculation. In doing this they could learn that the beneficiaries, who valued receiving security from environmental risks at five each, are now only willing to sacrifice two each after seeing the remediation of the landfill taking place. That is to say, the test could very well lead to a different result once it is turned around. And at that time the test would not justify the undertaking. This is a well-known inconsistency which has caused much concern. The reason is that in compensation tests the willingness to pay and the **willingness to accept** can fall apart. We will come back to this problem in our discussion of the Coase theorem in Chapter 3.

Such weaknesses notwithstanding the Kaldor-Hicks test will be a companion throughout this book, although it will be in the background most of the time. You will have noticed that we expressed the value of benefits in money terms. This is a utilitarian element in our reasoning. What we are doing here is to approximate the subjective values of goods or actions by the amount of money people are willing to forego. Sometimes we use the same trick to find out how much people expect to receive in money terms for suffering some form of harm. However, we ought to take a closer look at these measures, which are obviously very important for our purposes. We are concerned about measures for:

• the individual valuation of goods
• the socially optimal arrangement of goods among people.

The clarification of both issues is in fact essential for the economic analysis of law, since it is rights which determine the availability of goods – as we have already demonstrated in the introductory example about the soft drink *Fresh*. If we want to say something about the effectuation of rights, we need to express this using an appropriate measure.

Let us start by discussing the concept of utility. Utility is an ordinal measure of individual pleasure or welfare. Talking of an ordinal measure means that degrees of utility can be ranked but not measured on a scale. We can say that the utility a person derives from a certain amount of a good increases with the amount of that good at a diminishing rate (in technical terms, in the standard textbook approach marginal utility is positive but decreases relative to the amount of the good at hand). Since the valuation is subjective, interpersonal comparisons are not possible. We should note in passing that Pareto optimality takes account of that, since it is logically correct that the welfare of all people affected increases as long as utility is tied to some positive asset (the size of the asset influences the marginal utility only). Unfortunately the straightforward application of this concept would not allow a quantitative statement about well-being. Observations or – as is becoming customary – experiments could help. But this appears not to be very helpful for an assessment of the properties of legal norms on an operational level, as it is characteristic for an applied approach such as the economic analysis of law.

One way out of the difficulties has been suggested by Richard Posner and it is labelled 'wealth maximization'. Among scholars this approach is quite popular, although it definitely has certain problems. What we mean by wealth maximization is that commodities (or property rights pertinent to commodities, as we will see in more detail in the following chapter) always (ought to) go to the location where they cause the highest utility. A quantitative expression for utility is the individual willingness to pay, which we have already mentioned. The willingness to pay must not be confused with the *ability* to pay! This is the case because it does not take into account any considerations of distributional justice; thus earnings or budgets are assumed not to have any impact on valuation. The best thing we can do is to look at an illustrative example: imagine that for an excursion to Utopia (or some other pleasant place) there is space for one more participant. The trip is offered at a sensational price of 10,000. A wealthy family considers the excursion as a gift to their only child, who just has successfully completed her master's degree. The parents are willing to pay up to 13,000 for the gift. There is another family, less well off than the first one, which has three children. The utmost desire of the oldest one is to go to Utopia. The family is willing to sacrifice 10,000 for this heart's desire. According to the principle of wealth maximization the spare place is given to the wealthy family, since they have the highest willingness to pay. By sacrificing 10,000 they would even enjoy a consumer surplus (recall Figure 1.1) of 3,000, which counts for wealth. The latter fact needs to be emphasized!

Willingness to pay here exceeds the mere purchase value of a good. It also comprises all amenities associated with a good (or, which we will discuss later, property right), such as satisfaction about the bargain and other 'intrinsic' values. In Posner's own terms (1998, 16) wealth includes opportunities for self-expression and self-realization, this being instrumental to the maximization of utility. He continues (1998, 17): 'Wealth as used by economists is not an accounting concept; it is measured by what people would pay for things . . . not what they do pay for them. Thus leisure has value and is a part of wealth, even though it is not bought and sold. We can speak of leisure as having an implicit or shadow price' (see Box 1.3).

The change from (traditional) utility maximization to the principle of wealth maximization aims at solving some problems arising from the need for an operational form of our analysis. However, we are not yet in a position to step back in order to see how the concept will now work out. We are left with one more rather fundamental problem: that of uncertainty and **attitudes towards risk**.

Recall the notion of 'decreasing marginal utility'. We have stated that individual utility or welfare will increase with the increase in wealth, but at a diminishing rate. Wealth may be viewed in money-terms or be the sum of property rights as in our earlier digression.

Box 1.3   Wealth maximization

The idea underlying the principle of wealth maximization can more formally be summarized as follows:

Let R be the set of all negotiable property rights of person j; let p be the price, explicit or implicit, one could get by selling a property right in a competitive market (where p means the subjective and voluntary valuation of a marginal unit if R).

It follows that:

$$\Sigma R_i^j p_i \equiv W^j$$

$$i \neq j$$

the total wealth W

According to the normative approach to the economic analysis of law underlying the argument so far, the law is supposed to serve the maximization of wealth in the sense just stated.

This point is both demanding and controversial. More can be found in Veljanovski (1981, 5) and Windisch (1985).

Now there is a serious problem. A decreasing but positive marginal utility is associated with a certain attitude towards risk. Risk reflects the attitude of people towards success or failure of an action, the result of which is associated with a certain probability. More specifically, people to whom a utility function with a decreasing but positive marginal utility applies are said to be risk averse! We will illustrate this by the following simple example. Imagine a €10 note. You need not spend this money at all, consequently facing neither a gain (in utility) nor a loss. Alternatively, you could insert it into a slot machine and – let us assume – get a return of either €0 or €20 with a 50:50 chance. If, under these circumstances, you prefer to keep your note, you are risk averse (you prefer to be on the safe side). Had you inserted the note you would have been risk loving.

Such attitudes towards risk play an enormous role when it comes to the assessment of the (ex ante) effectiveness of legal norms. Moreover, wherever issues of insurance against risk are at stake, the fact that people are risk averse plays an essential role in the analysis, since they tend to buy insurance under certain circumstances (you will learn a little more about these issues in Chapter 3).

Unfortunately, adopting such attitudes towards risk in an expository presentation of fundamentals would quickly make the presentation barely digestible for the newcomer. Therefore we will adopt a third possibility, located between risk aversion and risk loving, which is called 'risk neutrality'. Adopting the euro note example again, risk neutrality means that you would be indifferent whether you keep the banknote or insert it into the slot machine with the 50:50 chance to gain 20 or lose all (in the first case you definitely end up with €10, and in the second case you face odds of ½ (€20) + ½ (€0), which 'on average' gives a gain of €10; therefore, whatever option you pick, the result would be the same).

Now, we should look at the consequences of such attitude towards risk: the marginal utility of any money or wealth stops decreasing. Rather, the relationship between the increase in utility and the increase in the amount of wealth is linear. This avoids some difficulties without a substantial loss of insight. Since the concern of this book is to make you familiar with law and economics in a digestible way, we will stick to the assumption of risk neutrality most of the time.

Epilogue: what is the sacrifice to truth in applying the *homo-oeconomicus* model?

Our model of human action is built on the assumption of rational behaviour. That means that the individual maximizes a target function (usually her utility function) subject to constraints (obligatory, facultative) in pursuit of her self-interest. For a very short review of the agenda, let us first clarify that self-interestedness must not be confused with selfishness. The basic model has been extended so as to cover 'extended sympathy' (I believe it will be 'good for you') or altruism (my own utility rises with the increase in your well-being). Despite these modifications, the underlying model for quite some time can be criticized for containing excessive demands on the capability of human beings. Nobel laureate Reinhard Selten calls this 'empirically questionable'. Human beings have only limited cognitive capabilities, he says, which is quite in line with an ever increasing number of writers.

Several strands of research can be reported here as a reaction to the discontent with models of rational human action. They should be mentioned here in order to provide some information on the state of the art as well as possible helpful suggestions for further investigation.

Most critical work goes back to Herbert Simon (Nobel laureate 1972), who introduced us to **bounded rationality**. According to this most influential theory, people have limited capacity of mind and thus lack knowledge of all alternatives open to them in decision making. Therefore, they rely on investigations, heuristics (mental shortcuts) and rules of thumb. The performance of the heuristics and rules of thumb largely depends on the structure of the environment; clearly they prove their worth better the more stable the structure of the environment.

However, problems such as **framing** effects point to the difficulties one quickly gets into when a more realistic explanation of human action is sought. Framing refers to the fact that two logically equivalent situations need not lead to the same result, since this might depend on circumstances that are not effective as binding constraints. Thus, framing is one of two influential effects that have been summarized under the common label of 'situationalism', referring to the fact that people tend to isolate their decisions and give too much weight to immediate aspects of the situation or to longer term concerns.

The emerging behavioural approach to law and economics also takes into account, besides limited knowledge, limited volition as well as limited self-interestedness. It is strongly influenced by psychology. Nowadays even the roots in biology or more specifically neuroscience are explored.

Bounded rationality or more generally behavioural approaches make excessive use of experiments. Consequently, experimental economics is a quickly developing and powerful branch of economics.

It is definitely true that the research reviewed here can give valuable insights into human behaviour, specifically with respect to legal constraints and related restrictions to human action. It is also true that some of the standard results of the economic approach to law are very likely challenged by these theories. However, the insights you will be made familiar with in the remainder of this book are by no means obsolete, although they are derived from more standard methods of analysis.

Key terms

attitudes toward risk
bounded rationality
civil law
common law
commutative justice
consumer surplus
criminal law
distributive justice
envy
equilibrium
framing
homo oeconomicus
incentives

institutions
Kaldor-Hicks test
law of demand
law of supply
Pareto optimality
private property
producer surplus
public choice
public law
utility
wealth maximization
willingness to accept
willingness to pay

Recommended reading

Frisch, Ragnar, On welfare theory and Pareto regions, *International Economic Papers*, 9, London and New York, 1959, 39.

Furubotn, Eirik and Richter, Rudolf, *Institutions and Economic theory*, 2nd edn, Ann Arbor, MI, 1998.

Hey, John D. (ed.) *Experimental Economics*, Heidelberg, 1994.

Jolls, Christine, Sunstein, Cass R. and Thaler, Robert, Behavioral approach to law and economics, *Stanford Law Review*, 50, 1998, 1471.

Kuhn, Thomas, *The Structure of Scientific Revolutions*, 3rd edn, Chicago, 1996.

Morgan, John, *Experimental and Behavioral Economics*, Amsterdam, 2005.

North, Douglass, *Structure and Change in Economic History*, New York, 1981.

Pearson, Heath, *Origins of Law and Economics*, New York and Melbourne, 1997.

Posner, Richard, *Economic Analysis of Law*, 5th edn, New York 1998.

Rawls, John, *Justice as Fairness*, Cambridge, MA, 2001.

Rawls, John, *A Theory of Justice*, Cambridge, MA, 2003.

Robson, Arthur J., The biological basis of economic behavior, *Journal of Economic Literature*, XXXIX, 2001,11.

Rose-Ackerman, Susan, Altruism, nonprofits, and economic theory, *Journal of Economic Literature*, 34, 701.

Topitsch, Ernst, *Logik der Sozialwissenschaften*, Cologne, 1972

Veljanovski, Cento, Wealth maximization, law and ethics – on the limits of economic efficiency, *International Review of Law and Economics*, 1, 1981, 5.

Windisch, Rupert, Vermögensmaximierung als ethisches Prinzip?, *Beiträge und Berichte Nr.7 der Forschungsstelle für Wirtschaftsethik an der Hochschule St. Gallen für Wirtschafts- und Sozialwissenschaften*, 1985.

2 The law and economics and property rights

Property rights: an example and a generalization

In this chapter, the notion of **property rights** is at stake. In other words, we are dealing with actions following from decisions we are either explicitly allowed to take or which are generally tolerated and which we are free to do entirely unhampered. For those readers who are lawyers, a comment on usage appears useful at the outset. The term 'property rights' as I will use it here is slightly more general than the same term as used in property law and extensions. It is used in an all-encompassing way, thus including real assets as well as intellectual work and the creation of artwork. I will trace the origins of property rights as well as the reasons for their acceptability, I will examine how they operate, and will also turn to some special issues such as property rights when held in small groups or teams.

The first step in carrying out our plan is to leave behind the space of goods and their usual arrangement by quantity and quality. Since we are interested in the desired as well as the effective operation of norms (and all kinds of related facultative constraints such as habits and customs), it is fruitful to look at the various ways in which goods can be disposed of other than by amount and their properties. It is the multiple uses of goods which are captured by the term property rights. I will illustrate the basic idea by means of a simple example and then continue with a generalization.

Imagine an ordinary item such as a pencil. Offhand, the following uses for this pencil come to mind: writing, drawing, as a bookmark, as a paperweight for a single sheet, as a substitute for a ruler, as a substitute for a missing spoon for my coffee and (somewhat mischievously perhaps) as a missile.

Some of these uses are common sense, but some of them are the result of discovery, intuition, creativity . . .

Assuming that we have just one pencil at our disposal and given the set of possible uses, we can make the following observations. First, not all the uses are possible at the same time. This implies that one picks that use that instantly serves the most urgent need (since we still assume a *homo oeconomicus*). Then, for the time being, another use must be foregone. But that is exactly what economists call an opportunity cost. So, alternative uses are ordered according to the opportunity cost involved. However, there might also be other sources of costs. Consider the pencil as a substitute for a spoon. The producer of the pencil might not have taken into consideration such a strange application and it might contain a toxic substance! Being uninformed, I am therefore at risk of using my pencil in a health-threatening way! Leaving aside the question whether a producer must have foreseen such strange uses we must be aware that diversion from **common use** bears some risks, which are, broadly speaking, a cost. If the producer had anticipated this kind of harmful use, she might have attached a note to the pencils saying 'Not for use as a spoon'. (There is an anecdote that has become quite famous, among scholars of law and economics at least: a kitten died because it was dried in a microwave after a bath. After that, stickers started to be put on microwaves saying 'Unsuitable for the drying of small animals'.) Note that I am not saying that there is no risk whatsoever associated with common use. For example, the pencil could splinter thus hurting my fingers while in use exactly for the intended purpose – writing! However, this is something that we could presumably have expected the producer to anticipate and thus make provisions for safe use. She can be supposed to act economically, after all!

Another type of cost is associated with the use as a missile. While for me this uncommon use causes the opportunity cost mentioned earlier, use as a missile has the potential to hurt someone else. If someone else's well-being is impaired while I derive a benefit (entertainment value!) then a so-called 'negative **external effect**' is present (for a more technical treatment of this term, please, be patient until Chapter 3). Even such an ordinary item as a pencil contains the potential for detrimental misuse. And is seems quite natural that such misuse is forbidden. However, it would obviously be irrational to abolish the use of pencils altogether. Although this seems to be common sense, it gives rise to two quite important lessons. The first lesson is that we could not have separated harm*less* from harm*ful* uses without the turn to the notion of property rights (which supplements the step we have already taken). The second lesson is that we have just discovered the vehicle by which legal norms can be brought into play: where harmful uses (that is to say, uses that contain the potential of negative external effects) are to be restrained, this can be maintained by norms. These could carry the threat of liability for harm or they could even outlaw certain uses. In the remainder of the book, I will elaborate on these ideas. However, we must not overlook that, under certain stylized circumstances, no norms are required at all (this view will be discussed in Chapter 3).

Towards a definition

The important lesson from our contemplation about pencils is the following: it appears reasonable to make a distinction between possible uses in general and a subset of uses which are unobjectionable or legally defensible!

While all potential uses depend on our knowledge, intuition, skill or even physical strength, the subset of mutually accepted uses – property rights – depends on consent concerning the restraint of harmful effects. From that, it is only a small step to the definition of property rights.

Here are the two most widely used definitions:

> Property rights are the sanctioned behavioural relations among men [sic] that arise from the existence of things and pertain to their use.
>
> (Furubotn and Pejovich, 1974, Introduction)

> An owner of property rights possesses the consent of fellow men [sic] to allow him to act in particular ways. An owner expects the community to prevent others from interfering with his actions, provided that these actions are not prohibited in the specification of his rights.
>
> (Demsetz in Furubotn and Pejovich, 1974, 31)

From both definitions it follows that property rights are a societal phenomenon. To illustrate this point: as long as Robinson Crusoe stays alone on the island, there is no need for property rights. However, this situation immediately changes when Man Friday arrives on the island!

The introduction of property rights as an economic phenomenon might be surprising for lawyers, despite the fact that they are acquainted with property rights as part of their work. For the economists I hasten to add that, in the remainder of this book, I will mostly stick to the area of property rights, first transforming commodity space into the space of possible actions and then isolating the subset of rights or entitlements. However, every notice of intent has a caveat! Recall that I justified the need for the establishment of property rights by looking at the attempt to stop such potentially harmful uses of the pencil as a missile. That type of use would be sanctioned following mutual consent about legitimate and tortuous acts, but an exhaustive list of all property rights is not the only way of demarcation between these different acts. First, it is very important to observe that the task of compiling such a list is a hopeless undertaking when it comes to the invention of new and formerly unknown and therefore unanticipated uses. How can one specify rights, when the act to which they ought to refer is not yet known?

Alternatives?

Being aware of the shortcomings of a world with exhaustively defined property rights opens the avenue to an alternative way of managing the problem at hand. Where does it lead us? To a regime where there is no property rights specified *a priori*, that is to say all perceptible actions are admissible at the outset! What human beings ought to observe is that they are liable for harm to third parties resulting from their own actions. Such a liability rule is meant to induce us to act in a sufficiently careful manner so as to avoid harm.

In a nutshell then, there are two perceptible regimes, the property rights regime and the liability regime.

Clearly, they are not mutually exclusive alternatives in practice. In the world we live in they are present in a certain ratio instead. Which of the two appears to be the more appropriate one in a certain situation or, in more familiar terms, which promises to be more efficient, can be judged by applying a Kaldor-Hicks test.

It is important to note, however, that the totality of human action is not encompassed by formally specified property rights or **liability rules**. An ever increasing number of customs, habits and other **informal norms** have emerged in the course of time. They can serve to fill the gap where no legal provisions exist (e.g. commercial practices) or complement existing orders (a good example being a dress code, which makes a person identifiable as member of a distinct group; another example is queuing at bus stops as a selection mechanism or 'Women and children first', a widely known principle reported to be used on vessels in case of emergency).

I will touch on such informal rules eventually.

Another viewpoint is worth mentioning before we delve into a more detailed examination of property rights: property rights in general and legal norms building on property rights are subject to change. Change is a consequence of interaction with newly emerging substantial constraints, inventions, conflicts and other dynamics with a substantial impact on society.

The most prominent writer applying the toolbox of property rights theory to economic history is Nobel laureate Douglass North (whose work is worth at least having a look at: North and Thomas, 1973). The dynamics of the law is treated in an enlightening manner by the Professor of Legal Philosophy of the University of Graz, Peter Koller, in his *Theorie des Rechts* (Theory of Law), 1997.

Property rights classified

Property rights serve a large variety of purposes. Consequently, several classifications of property rights are in use depending on what kind of analysis is intended. For example, the main purpose could be to guide someone's actions so as to secure one's own property rights against the greediness of third parties. By contrast, the sole purpose could be to regulate the transfer of authority to induce people to act in a certain way.

Let us start with types of right characterizing a person's various positions in society. The list is taken from Hohfeld (1966):

- **claim rights** (pertaining to a thing or stipulation against someone else)
- **privileges** or liberties (e.g. in the formation of things or events)
- **powers** (legitimate authority and competence)
- **immunities** (claims to protection etc.).

Alternatively, we could look at the ways in which one can dispose over some commodity. Thus, we get the following familiar distinctions:

- *usus* (the entitlement to use)
- *usus fructus* (the entitlement to the fruit or yield flowing from some commodity, such as the apples from an apple tree)

- *abusus* (the entitlement to change the substance of the commodity up to its destruction, but also to do away with it, by exchange for example).

This distinction gives rise to the possibility of characterizing comprehensive and universal property rights. Such rights will not be limited by even the slightest qualification! Consequently, they would induce the holder of the rights to act in a particular way; for example, with no qualification a holder could use the right even if this causes harm for third parties! However, she would at the same time be very careful not to destroy or lose the good to which she is entitled since she would have to bear the whole loss, since otherwise this would have to be specified somehow – which is also an immediate consequence of unhampered disposition. In practice, unhampered disposition does not frequently apply and thus a 'property right in substance' is rarely observed!

As a matter of fact, most property rights are restricted in one way or the other. To illustrate: in the earlier example, the pencil must not be used as a missile (restricted *usus*) and a refrigerator must not be disposed of by dropping it in a remote area in the woods, so *abusus* is limited. The fact that the overwhelming number of cases pertain to distinct rights only is reflected in the notion of 'functional property rights' as a contrast to aforementioned 'property rights in substance'.

Another viewpoint comes into play when we return to the disposal of the refrigerator. Nowadays, this kind of *abusus* is only allowed when a specialized service is employed. We can therefore say that the rights contained in *abusus* are 'attenuated'. If we wanted to get rid of the fridge we must employ someone who is entitled to do so.

Note that **attenuation** is a widely observable phenomenon, not only when it comes to the intended disposal of unwanted goods by an individual. Attenuation is also present in teams, boards and committees, since such entities are typically allowed to take decisions jointly only. In other words, the property right concerning *abusus* is shared among the members (with the underlying purpose of delimiting the discretionary competences of each of them).

Property rights and 'coordination mechanisms'

When I demonstrated the rationale for the law by means of the demand for and supply of the beverage *Fresh*, the coordination happened via a market. However, markets are only one means of coordination in society. In markets, the participants act on the entitlement to *abusus* by exchange. Other means of coordination are:

- vote
- command
- bargain, etc.

Each of them can again be cast in terms of the endowment with the appropriate property rights.

For voting, it is characteristic that the relevant entitlement to take part in the ballot cannot be sold, that is, it is not transferable; the same holds true for command, which is characteristic for all types of hierarchy (including headquarters of corporations and government agencies); someone who is entitled to give orders is usually not allowed to sell this entitlement to someone else and to delegate it only under very special conditions, if at all!

Bargaining is different inasmuch as it mostly precedes transfers of rights, thus reflecting the entitlement to make and take offers concerning the amount of rights, their value and the conditions for exchange.

I would like to draw your attention to an interesting feature of this taxonomy. The right to vote as well as the right to give orders are rights of the second order, so to speak. Their entitlement and use depends on a prior determination, which in turn will follow distinct rules, if it did not emerge spontaneously (in the sense that has been emphasized repeatedly by Friedrich August Hayek). Thus the entitlement to command must be decided on in a more general level. So we can say that in the model just presented a kind of hierarchy of institutions is at work. Note that the same applies for exchange, since things can be declared *res extra commercio* thus abolishing the right to transfer entitlements (as is the case with certain drugs, such as cocaine and, even more important, the trade of people, as in slavery).

We know of course that legal norms form a quite complex institutional structure, but here we get a glimpse on why this is so. The specification of property rights may well have as a prerequisite that property rights are established on a higher or a more general level.

Building on the peculiarities noted earlier, let us turn to one more useful classification of property rights and then look at the intended economic effects associated with the establishment of property right schemes. The classification is as follows. There are:

- exclusive and alienable rights (which are typically given with marketable goods but also with **gifts**, **donations** and the like)
- exclusive rights that are not alienable (typically the rights of bureaucrats to release passports or the rights of police officers to arrest someone; the right of a professor to mark your exam is of the same kind)
- non-exclusive and inalienable rights (such as walking on common land or enjoying the view on a mountain range; the famous story about 'the man who tried to sell the Eiffel tower' fits nicely into this class, for reasons that should be apparent!).

(Intended) efficacy of property rights

You may by now rightly ask what the rationale is behind the establishment of such a relatively complex system of rights. A first although quite general answer is that this complex system is required to effectuate and secure social welfare. Let us look at how this might work:

- Specifying property rights is an attempt to create incentives for people to act in a distinct way. For example, comprehensive rights exclude the possibility of recovery in case of loss or destruction of a good thus creating an incentive to act carefully. Careful disposition over scarce goods in turn secures efficient disposition.
- The clear specification of rights allows for both their use and optional transfer via exchange without conflict. To illustrate: in the case of the purchase of some good this should mean inquiries about the entitlements of uses of that good are unnecessary, since such inquiries constitute a cost, which in turn creates an inefficiency. Moreover a clear specification of rights is a precondition for the identification of receivers of stolen goods. In the parlance of law and economics then the clear specification of rights helps avoid 'transaction costs' (you will learn more about this important term in Chapter 3).
- A third important aspect of well-specified property rights is that of interference with risks. To see this let us revert to the example of the fridge, which by assumption has now been dumped next to a remote pond. If it was not specified whether the property rights over the fridge included its disposal next to or even into a pond, then there will be a lack of clear assignment of who has to bear detrimental side-effects of the action at hand (a 'negative externality'). A specification of the right that clearly does not comprise *abusus* in the sense just described helps save costs for innocent third parties (who could be hurt by corrosive refrigerant). Again the rationale of the specification of rights proves to be in the interest of achieving efficiency!

From these considerations, it is evident that the specification of property rights does not only determine 'liberties', but by the same token delineates 'responsibilities'.

The rationale behind all this is that our conscious and self-interested *homo oeconomicus* will make use of her liberties in a way which is most beneficial to her. Alas, our assumptions about the nature of *homo oeconomicus* imply that she will try to achieve the benefits at minimum costs. Keeping costs at a minimum might induce her to shift their burden to someone else, where possible. Human beings exhibit, as Oliver E. Williamson has put it, **opportunism** – although they might be guided by morality occasionally, which is a different story, of course.

What we have seen is that the clear specification of property rights comprises the clarification of who is to bear the costs of certain actions, including wrong decisions, which the person regrets afterwards. This insight is exactly what I wanted to communicate in my introductory example about the market for the beverage *Fresh* . . . so now we can look at the details.

Some thoughts on the formation of property (rights)

Let us start with a little elaboration: the formation of property can be seen as an act by which a group, a people or a society subject themselves to common rules in the sense of the definitions which you should remember. (Task: try to commemorate these definitions before you proceed.) The formation of property can also mean that we are dealing with the conditions for the (legitimate) acquisition of something found, or the entitlements to the result of an act of creativity. Obviously both aspects are important. The first, however, falls into the category of constitutional acts, which makes it a case for 'public law and economics' (see Chapter 5). Nevertheless, we will have a glimpse at the relevant theory here. The second view deserves a more comprehensive treatment, since it comprises such diverse cases as gathering mushrooms in the woods and the entitlement to copyright for a novel.

Let us have our glimpse at the roots of property rights, the theory by which the acknowledgement of private property is explained.

Two questions should come to mind here:

1   Why is the opportunistic *homo oeconomicus* willing to acknowledge (and respect) private property?
2   Why do economic institutions such as markets perform peacefully, in general at least? What is it that keeps them stable under normal circumstances (for instances of irregular circumstances you will remember the pictures of large-scale looting in situations such as the war in Iraq or the evacuation of flooded New Orleans)?

Answers to both questions are offered in the theory by which the rise of a **protective state** is explained together with the transition into a subsequent **productive state** (see Buchanan, 1975). I shall summarize the theory since it conveys the way in which institutional restrictions are analytically derived.

Property rights, the contractarian viewpoint

Imagine an island with just two inhabitants, who both live on coconuts. In doing this they do not follow any rules or principles as such. They are – as usual – rationally acting utility maximizers, thus deriving increasing utility from a growing number of coconuts consumed, although at a diminishing rate. However, does this not imply risk aversion, as explained (and ruled out) at the end of Chapter 1? Yes, it does, but for the moment we ought to stick to that assumption in order to demonstrate an essential feature of the model we are following here; if we abolished our assumption we would face the problem of deriving reaction functions for our two inhabitants and would fail to see what an equilibrium solution would look like.

In order to harvest coconuts, both people have to spend part of their limited effort (and time), which causes a disutility for them. The more effort they put into harvesting the higher the disutility (in analogy to the level of utility for the coconuts). But since our inhabitants act opportunistically, they are aware that one can use effort and time not only for harvesting but also for stealing one another's coconuts.

However, this is possible only by sacrificing the effort spent on their own harvest. Moreover, since both act reciprocally, they will also have to use some of their resources to defend themselves from theft. What we get is an economic image of a state of **anarchy**.

Now it is obvious that the situation is associated with considerable losses of welfare on both sides, even if there is something like equilibrium of effort diverted to theft and defence as the mutual reaction to the efforts undertaken by the other side. The loss can be avoided if both sides agree to acknowledge private property. Such an agreement requires two prerequisites. First, there must be willingness to cooperate, which will materialize after the second prerequisite, which is that neither side expects to be able to subdue (enslave) her opponent. A cessation of hostility and the acknowledgement of property rights over coconut trees (and their *usus fructus*!) will eventually emerge. And consequently the welfare of both will increase due to the effort (and its associated disutility) saved. This is an example of a Pareto improvement, so the Kaldor-Hicks test need not to be applied here.

The next question which emerges is whether the solution will be stable. The question is far from trivial since the agreement has not necessarily caused the persons to relinquish their opportunism. In fact, our theory about human nature leads us to predict that the lesser loyal will try to trick her more naive neighbour. In economic terms, the loyalty of one person gives an incentive to the other person to violate the agreement, provided that the cost of doing so is sufficiently low. Therefore, a deterrent seems to be necessary for the sake of stability of the agreement to private property rights. This can be accomplished by the threat of punishment. However, such a threat will only be credible if it can be enforced and thus will not be credible unless a police officer is monitoring the situation and ensuring compliance to the newly established rules. Police – and subsequently the courts – thus come into play. However, the police and court services need to be organized and their staff paid appropriately. All at once some of the essential features of a state are present. Under the prevailing assumptions about human behaviour these features are indispensable for the stability of basic agreements on property rights. Needless to say, the benefits and costs of such provisions must be balanced in order to be justified from the economic point of view. Note that I did not want to go into details about 'public goods' and problems of finance by taxation at this time. At stake were only the considerations concerning the benefits of property rights and the likely steps to secure these benefits.

Let me point out that the emergence of property rights and an appropriate legal framework have been identified as driving rods for the *Rise of the Western World* (title of the seminal 1973 book by North and Thomas, which has been mentioned already) from the perspective of economic history. The authors argue that the emergence of private property on a large scale has contributed to the decline of feudalism in most parts of Europe, followed by a sharp rise in growth and welfare.

This contrasts with but does not contradict the logically derived theory of the transformation from a state of anarchy into an orderly state of private property, as presented by James Buchanan and others, who work in the tradition of Thomas Hobbes (1588–1679) and other 'contractarians'.

Incidentally, when reviewing the theory regarding the transition from a protective state to a productive state, we have implicitly come across a fundamental concept of law and economics. It is the main focus of the law and economics approach to look at conditions for compliance to existing norms ex ante, but not the question of how to deal with harm caused by disobedience to the law ex post, although our approach nevertheless has a lot to say about the latter problem (see Chapter 4 for further discussion).

Types of property and adoption and problems of possession

How to obtain property

Property (bundles of property rights) can be obtained in several ways:

- by the retrieval, acquisition or **adoption** of unowned things
- by invention and creative acts
- by way of exchange or donation.

Which of the means of obtaining property applies depends partly on the nature of the object at hand. It could be a material thing or **intellectual property**. The need to obtain property follows from the requirement of efficiency, from the economic viewpoint at least, although definite property rights are also a need for justice and societal stability.

Property for physical things

Fishing, hunting, mining or treasure seeking are costly in terms of time, effort and equipment. Therefore the question of the optimal amount of resources to be spent on exploration and exploitation arises. We can see this by imagining that someone can become the owner of a physical thing in an unrestricted way so that the finder automatically becomes the owner with comprehensive property rights. The consequence of such a rule would be that far too many resources were devoted to exploration and exploitation, that is to say, an inefficient result. Moreover success would be influenced negatively, since with limited things to be acquired, the average gain per party would go down. This is a well-known phenomenon (and is appropriately contested) in the case of non-renewable resources!

As a consequence of highly likely overinvestment in exploration and exploitation, limitations on the activities are determined, which take the form of entitlements assigned by some central authority. The organization of mining rights is an obvious example. Similarly, manganese deposits on the seabed have been a subject of international treaties mainly in order to avoid inefficient (and hostile) races to the deposits.

It is a well-known phenomenon that overexploitation follows once something previously unowned has been detected. Hence there is need for institutional mechanisms to prevent overexploitation. Since our starting point was so far unowned things and the efforts to retrieve and exploit them, at this point two ostensibly different cases ought to be distinguished. Fish, deer, mushrooms and gemstones are examples where inefficient overinvestment in exploration and overexploitation are most likely. However, all these items can be privately owned and therefore exclusive alienable property rights can be assigned, although their enforcement can pose some difficulties. The modern possibilities of regulation and enforcement in the very problematic field of overfishing are impressively demonstrated by the US National Marine Fisheries Service (see www.fakr.noaa.gov/).

Note that in the case of deep-sea fishing a difference must be made between the sea as such and the animals living in it. With respect to exploring and exploiting it is the fish, and not the sea, which are our concern here. The reason for this is that despite severe difficulties it is the fish to which alienable property rights ought to be assigned by way of **harvest limitations**, for example. The consequence of successfully enforced harvest restrictions are shares in fish which give rise to processing and trade. Alternatively one could try to assign more or less comprehensive property rights to parcels of the sea and then allow for full-fledged utilization. This is difficult to maintain, although zoning via satellite is a serious option nowadays, but the main problem is the fish, which travel around in huge shoals. Consequently, the attempt to assign fishing rights to fish is more reasonable. The problems, which have been dealt with briefly here, are well known in law and economics. Two seminal articles on the topic are by Gordon and Cheung respectively (note that both are economists). However, there are cases where there are no such problems as roving fish. One example worth mentioning here is common pastures. These are characteristic for property rights, which are non-exclusive and non-alienable. At the same time they are exhaustible resources. To picture this, imagine a herd of sheep grazing the common ground. As the number of sheep is increased because of expected profits from meat and wool, they will consume so much of the grass that it will not renew itself from a certain point on. Consequently, the animals will not find enough nutrition and will lose weight, leading to a *decrease* in revenues from sales of their meat.

It has been noted that the solution to this kind of problem can be solved by transferring the ownership of the pasture to a single owner, thus creating a monopoly. Clearly the monopolist will seek to maximize profits, which she will accomplish by reducing the number of animals allowed on the pasture, but also by extracting rents from fellow farmers due to her monopoly position. Thus, the solution most likely is not what it ought to be, namely welfare enhancing.

Alternatively the pasture can be divided into plots, which are then left to different farmers. Since now the *usus fructus* will depend on thoughtful use of the plot, the solution is promising in terms of welfare. However, there are examples of effective self-control concerning utilization of a common property resource that show that processes like that outlined for the emergence of property in a former anarchic environment can be effectuated under certain circumstances! Thrainn Eggerttson has pointed out that self-control leads to an efficient use of common pastures – the so-called *affretir* – in Iceland (unfortunately, the essay Analyzing institutional success and failures: a millennium of common mountain pastures in Iceland has as yet only been circulated as a mimeograph but not yet been published).

Let us have a look at some other issues in property that are open to considerations of efficiency: for example, why is it that property rights are preserved in case of loss?

Well, it would be very troublesome to recover an item if anyone could claim 'finder's keepers' instead of making attempts to find the legitimate owner. Even worse, this would even create an incentive to steal, since the proof of the claim to rightful **possession** would be very expensive for the victim of the theft. We can note in passing, however, that efficiency considerations are obviously linked to notions of order and justice. You can try your reasoning skills on the following question: why it is that the right of possession is registered, as it is the case for plots of land or a yacht? Another interesting example is found in cases of adverse possession. Here one might at first think of an additional cost imposed on the property owner, since she will be constrained to see that the prescription does no harm to the property. Conversely, adverse possession could be efficiency enhancing in the sense that some use of a higher order is brought about tacitly, if the owner has no inclination to sell the estate or to use it, if the property is viewed as long-term asset, for example.

Closely related to adverse possession are easements or **servitudes**. They play a big role in tourism, for instance, since the right of way in the countryside quite often takes the legal form of a servitude on a different person's land. While servitudes have historical reasons their function in terms of efficiency can be seen as aimed at preventing the fragmentation of estates while at the same time intensifying their use, thus enhancing welfare.

Donations and gifts can be tricky forms of alienated property rights. Consider first an innocuous act such as transferring the right of possession of my garden to my grandchild. This act will hopefully increase both the happiness and the wealth of my grandchild and give me the intrinsic utility of having pleased her. Now consider the gift of a model railway. No problem? What if the grandchild was expecting a personal computer? The gift then creates harm instead of joy. The question emerges of whether it can be legitimate to refuse the gift, that is to say, to disagree with the alienation of property rights by way of a donation. Does this require the existence of an established right? Is there a need for an efficient way of handling such cases? Conversely, what about the suability of a promise? The withheld right of possession of the garden, the personal computer and any promised gifts constitute detained wealth. The law might be required to help to meet justified expectations, since disappointment can go along with opportunity costs. To illustrate: imagine that you have missed a bargain for a personal computer because you believed in the promise that you would be given one by a relative.

Such examples notwithstanding, gifts and donations can cause immediate duties and charges for the recipient. At the same time they might exonerate the donor from taxes, to name just one rather relevant example. In such cases the donation or gift will become the matter of a contract (contracts will be extensively treated in Chapter 3). This calls for enforcement concerning the public interest in tax revenues!

For the sake of brevity, I ought to stop here although at this point the issues have been treated only tentatively.

Incorporeal goods, information

It seems that concerns about rights in incorporeal goods are steadily increasing and, more specifically, about rights related to **information**. The economic handling of information covers a huge range of applications from advice given by a tourist office employee or a vendor to more difficult cases such as **patents**, **copyright** for a typescript, trademarks, examples and everything that falls within the category of 'intellectual property'. The underlying problem common to all examples can be called 'asymmetric information'. The notion can only be outlined here, since it refers to a particular and expanding field of economics (for a more comprehensive introduction you should consult Pindyck and Rubinfeld, 2005, for example).

By information, I mean a change of valuable knowledge after receipt of a verbal, acoustic or visual signal. A peculiar feature of the information contained in a signal is that the message cannot be withdrawn, once it has been emitted – provided that the recipients of the message are aware of it! That is to say, as long as the message has *not* been emitted, the information contained in that message is purely private. As soon as it has been released the information contained in the message becomes public: everybody who is capable of making use of the piece of information may do so without interference from someone else. The information has turned into a pure collective good, since there cannot be rivalry in its use and it is hard to exclude someone from the reception. Now let us explore why this has very important consequences from the law and economics perspective.

First of all, please note that for a person who wants to value a piece of information it is difficult to assess the value contained in a message before it has been released. Therefore, if some payment is to be decided on that depends on the information contained in the message, it is hard to assess how much money to pledge ('willingness to pay') as long as the value of the information is not known. Hence the expenses for the request of information will most likely fall short of an efficient level.

The suppliers of information are not in an enviable situation either. Once the information has been spread, the recipients become most unwelcome rivals, since the information is received at no cost and can be immediately utilized. However, acquiring the original knowledge, before it can be turned into valuable information, can be very costly. Thus, such information is revealed at the risk that its cost can never be recovered. This is a first hint as to the rationale behind patents on can openers or the protection of an innovative design for a surfboard. Compared to such activities the transfer or distribution of information is very cheap (think about the difference in cost between first of all writing an article, and then distributing it by mass mailer).

The common problem behind all these cases is that under the circumstances given already property rights cannot be specified unambiguously. Consequently, the market is unable to do what it is supposed to be best equipped to do: direct property rights to their most valuable and exclusive use.

Let us elaborate on this underlying idea by looking at two typical problems with intellectual property. First of all, there are the efforts taken to protect copyright and subsequently those to secure compensation for the utility drawn from use by extracting **royalties**! For example, imagine a successful novel and an instructive textbook. Only a few copies of each will be sold if circulation by way of photocopying is cheap. The same holds for works of music, which nowadays can easily be digitalized and then dispersed via the internet at almost zero cost. Popular recordings are particularly affected. Clearly such practices have an immediate impact on the revenues of both composers and musicians. Moreover, commercial trade in compact disks will be substantially affected sooner or later. Given these circumstances, it is easy to predict that the amount of creative work will be inefficiently small, as long as there are no provisions for appropriate protection. From this the very unpleasant prediction follows that there will be a general shortage of new pieces of music, as well as recordings, pleasant designs of fabric or enjoyable books.

There are cures against such inefficiencies, of course. More specifically, the public authorities could step in and:

- either take over promulgation of artwork (information) directly
- or protect private provision by granting exclusive rights to the artists.

I am sure you have immediately recognized that the second case refers to copyright law. However, patents follow the same line of reasoning, as do trademarks and trade samples. In all cases, legal norms are indispensable and render possible the provision of efficient levels of output. Nevertheless, they will not automatically accomplish their task. In order to be effective they must create appropriate incentives. One way of doing this is to establish a claim to royalties (thus opening the possibility of a lawsuit for the artist, for example, which with certainty will be favourable for her and therefore induces users of a piece of art to observe the property rights ex ante, since it would become very costly for them otherwise – we will come back to this kind of individual cost–benefit calculus in Chapters 3 and 4). Note that we are still dealing with 'intellectual property', which allows us to examine three more quite important aspects of the issue at hand:

1   It is noteworthy that copyright for works of art lasts for extremely long periods. This implies that the artists (authors) are conceded longlasting monopolies, which at first glance conflicts with economists' understanding of efficient rules. However, the long periods of protection are claimed to be indispensable to give the artist (author) the possibility of recovery of the cost expended on the act of creation of the piece of work – which can, in fact, take quite long. By the same token, the incentive to create new work is reinforced. There is another interesting argument, which states that longlasting copyright is a much cheaper way of keeping records about property rights than some sort of central register!

2   It is also noteworthy that sometimes the prices for the purchase of creative work are differentiated depending of characteristics of customers. For example, institutional customers such as libraries or associations are charged more for academic journals than are individuals. One explanation is that the availability to a larger number of people justifies a multiple of the price of the individual purchaser.

3   The third point is a little more sophisticated: it is widely held that in the fine arts artists have a claim to a certain share of the sales revenue, every time the ownership of the painting or sculpture changes. This is called the *droit de suite*. What could be an argument in favour of that special kind of royalty? Well, pieces of art, which are not reproducible, normally realize only a fairly low price when they are offered in the market for the first time. The reason is that

the popularity of the artist is low when she first appears on the scene, but then increases in the course of time, as does the market value of the artists' work. This will allow the seller to extract a rent and a *droit de suite* therefore allows artists to get their fair share of the profit. It has also been claimed that the *droit de suite* matches the situation of a successful author, whose income increases with the number of copies of a book sold (as I write this, it is in the news that 2 million copies of the first print run of the German edition of Volume 6 of *Harry Potter* are being distributed).

This topic is not yet exhausted. In fact, the present brief introduction can only highlight some of the major issues. Hopefully, your curiosity has been aroused and you will have a look at some of the recommendations for further reading at the end of the chapter.

Bundling and splitting property rights

Let us start by recalling the distinction between the use, the entitlement to the returns and the alienation of things. We might wish to see all three ways of dealing with things together, certain qualifications concerning externalities aside (remember the use of a pencil as a missile!); however, there are instances where the three ways should be kept separate; finally, there are some mixed structures for the arrangement of rights to things.

The separate possibilities for disposing of things must be carefully distinguished from **splitting rights** in the sense that they are shared by several people, as is the case where a board makes decisions, that is to say, they share rights in a certain sense.

Consider bundling first. An intuitive example for the feasibility of bundling is a decision over an investment. If one was not allowed to decide on the use of, acquire the returns from and deliberately replace equipment, there would hardly be an appropriate incentive to invest at all.

Next we turn to splitting: the essential feature of many services is the separation between use and the appropriation of returns. Consider a car rental for private use, where the right to use is an alienable but commercial use and thus the appropriation of returns is excluded. However, in the case of custodianship over a person, the ward is given the right of use of a room, but not its alienation. Finally, in the German laws covering the transplant of human organs, the responsibility for the extraction of a kidney, for example, is separated from its procurement. These examples can be argued on grounds of efficiency as well as justice, inasmuch as risks (externalities) may be associated with the different ways to dispose of things, which give rise to protective provisions ex ante.

More complex structures of rights pertaining to things can typically be found in the specification of rights to decide, on one hand, and those of monitoring and control, on the other hand. It is here that unbundling and sharing a right among several people both occur. The board of directors of some enterprise may serve as an illustration here. Note that we have thus entered the vast and rapidly growing field of **corporate governance**, since this can be seen as a systematic way of arranging property rights to enable the best outcome, given the risks of failures in decision making, the cost of finding solutions and likely externalities. Once a certain design (arrangement) of property rights is found it can then be implemented by means of contracts (one of the main topics in Chapter 3).

We may note in passing that some of the precursors of law and economics have contributed to the field of corporate governance, among them Ronald Coase, the Nobel laureate to whom we will pay tribute in Chapter 3, who initiated research in the field by his paper On the theory of the firm in 1937(!). The ramifications of this became apparent with a considerable 'recognition lag' only in the 1960s! The issues at hand are not only relevant for private enterprises; of course they also apply to the state as well as not-for-profit organizations (as we will see in Chapter 5).

As far as legal norms are concerned, the structure of property rights is reflected in typical blueprints for firms, as laid down in trade law and corporate law, where you find 'joint stock companies', 'limited liability companies', public utilities or even cooperatives. The relevant legal norms mostly contain an abundance of rules related to governance.

On exclusive and inalienable rights

These types of right do not receive the attention they deserve. To illustrate, I will once more turn to an example from everyday life. Let's assume that you need a passport. Passports are issued by authorities, that is to say, in the domain of public administration. The civil servant is entitled to issue the passport according to a code of official duties. You might say 'so what?' – the crucial point here is that our civil servant must not transfer the entitlement to someone else. An attempt to sell that right or to employ a lay assistant would immediately lead to disciplinary action.

Civil servants are vested with exclusive and inalienable (or non-transferable) rights. But this type of right is not found in public administration alone. For example, administration of the licence for the use of a new type of aircraft (the Airbus A360, say) in Austria is in the hands of Austro Control, a limited liability company. Some of the employees are entrusted with the right to issue such licences. Neither they personally nor their company are allowed to sell this particular entitlement. If they did, they might quickly be suspected of corruption.

From an economic viewpoint, the entitlement to decrees and directives is meant to solve certain selection problems or problems of **sorting** in an efficient manner. To illustrate by means of the release of a passport: why is such a release excluded from trade, why is it *res extra commercio*? Simply, because it is the only effective way to guarantee the identity of a person. If it was the willingness to pay (or the ability to pay) which determined which identity one could assume, this would have disastrous consequences for trustworthiness in the assignment and use of property rights! Of course, there is a market for counterfeiting passports. Although I have no idea about the going rate for a fake passport, I can imagine that the price is quite high because disguising one's true personality can be very valuable under certain circumstances and at the same time the release of a counterfeit is a risky undertaking that requires a large amount of – costly – precautions (at this point your attention is drawn to Chapter 4, where issues of criminal actions are at stake).

Exclusive, inalienable rights are obviously valuable. Still we could imagine substitutes! Think about the entitlement of Austro Control to assign a certain route to aircraft. Instead of command we could imagine an auction. Why not? Companies would make offers for the route best suited for a particular journey and the sorting problems can thus be solved. But such a procedure will not automatically minimize the probability of a collision. Thus a system of licences appears to be less costly overall.

The peculiar rights we are dealing with here cannot be effective without a prerequisite, some institution by which the rights are assigned or removed. This institution must necessarily be of higher rank than that which forms the entrusted authority. Inalienable rights are thus dependent on a distinct hierarchical (vertical) structure of institutions. A natural example is the distinction between procedures that lead to constitutional laws and the subsequent emergence of federal laws. Note that the identification of such vertically structured institutions raises a large number of economic issues such as the well-known relations between a 'principal' and an 'agent', where the principal is entitled to entrust the expert agent with the performance of duties, but she might be unable to monitor the agents' activities at a reasonable cost. You will certainly have realized that this is a standard problem in public administration. However, the problem is present in any vertically structured organization such as an enterprise or a not-for-profit organization. Therefore, as we proceed, we will come back to this type of problem several times.

Inasmuch as civil servants are entrusted with special rights or entitlements, the principal–agent problem just noted implies the engagement in the question of how the agent can best be guided to observe her duties. This can be done for example by including appropriate incentives in her labour contract (Chapter 6 contains an outline of the underlying problem).

As has been noted, a serious problem – and a typical one for exclusive and inalienable rights – is corruption. The agent feels unobserved by her master (the principal) and therefore accepts, for example, bribes in exchange for illegitimate benefits to a client. However, not only the agents but also the principals have deficiencies. The **discretionary power** of principals, for example, is one of the main roots for the economic theory of bureaucracy. In both cases legal norms are urgently needed that effectively constrain the actions of civil servants appropriately and to the benefit of citizens.

Splitting rights

These results can now be rounded up by a final note on the splitting of rights: the misuse of power and the susceptibility to misconduct can partly be precluded by splitting a certain entitlement among a small group of people. Thus a decision can only be taken jointly according to some procedure. Clearly, this is a way of reducing opportunities for misconduct and the cost inflicted on society. Alas, such splitting of rights entails an opportunity cost inasmuch as the procedure of decision making may be time consuming and may thus narrow the capacity of some authority and at the same time cause lost opportunities for the client, who has to face delays.

I shall stop here, hoping that the crucial importance of the notion of property rights for an economic analysis of law has by now become clear.

Key terms

abusus	intellectual property
adoption	liability rules
anarchy	opportunism
attenuation	patents
claim rights	possession
common use	powers
copyright	privileges
corporate governance	productive state
discretionary power	property rights
donations	protective state
external effect	*res extra commercio*
gifts	royalties
harvest limitations	servitudes
immunities	sorting
inalienable rights	splitting rights
informal norms	*usus*
information	*usus fructus*

Recommended reading

Buchanan, James, *The Limits of Liberty: Between Anarchy and Leviathan*, Chicago, 1975.
Cheung, S., The structure of a contract and the theory of a non-exclusive resource, *Journal of Law and Economics*, 13, 1970, 49–70.
Eggerttson, Thrainn, *Analyzing Institutional Success and Failures: A Millennium of Common Mountain Pastures in Iceland*, research paper, mimeo.
Furubotn, Eirik and Pejovich, Steve (eds) *The Economics of Property Rights*, Cambridge, MA, 1974.
Gordon, H.S., The economic theory of a common property resource: the fishery, *Journal of Political Economy*, 62, 1954, 124–42.
Hohfeld, Wesley N., *Fundamental Legal Concepts*, New Haven, CT, 1919.
Koller, Peter, *Theorie des Rechts* [Theory of Law], Vienna, Cologne and Weimar, 1997.
Landes, William M. and Posner, Richard A., An economic analysis of copyright law, *Journal of Legal Studies*, 18, 1989, 325.
North, Douglass C. and Thomas, Robert Paul, *The Rise of the Western World*, London, 1973.
Pindyck, Robert S. and Rubinfeld, Daniel L., *Microeconomics*, 6th edn, Upper Saddle River, NJ, 2005.
Shleifer, Andrej and Vishny, Robert W., A survey of corporate governance, *The Journal of Finance*, 52, 2, 1997, 737–83.

3 Conflicts caused by accidents, damages, failed negotiations and broken contracts

Preparing for disturbances in the use of property rights

Before we can set out to study nuisance, accidents and contracts in detail, that is to say, cases where the possession and the use of property rights are impaired, we ought to develop some tools. Essentially, there are two such tools we need to consider here. The first is labelled 'externalities'. An externality obtains whenever a beneficial activity by one person interferes with the activities of third parties in a way which causes harm. We will see later, however, that the interference could also be beneficial, but we are more concerned about harm here. Interestingly we can distinguish two cases: one is the typical situation, where the victim can be identified ex ante; to illustrate, this holds in the case of smoke from a barbecue party creeping over the neighbour's garden, thus causing nuisance to her. The other situation is such that a victim cannot be identified beforehand, as is the case in an accident because of reckless driving (hitting a certain person on purpose falls within a different category of action, namely that of a criminal offence). Both cases of (negative) externality show obstacles to overcoming them or acknowledging them by means of compensation. With the victim known ex ante, negotiations could be hampered by the unwillingness of one or both sides to comply, because of the power they have compared with the opponent. When the victim is not known ex ante then negotiations can hardly take place. Note that there are obstacles in both cases that fall into the category of 'transaction costs'. We will deal with these types of problem in the first part of this chapter.

When two or more parties meet in order to carry out some business that entails an exchange of property rights, this is called a contract. Unfortunately, contracts can turn out to lead to controversies. One partner might not perform in the agreed way or in the course of processing it might turn out that the parties have overlooked contingencies such as responsibility in case of delay and so forth.

Under ideal circumstances such problems can quickly be settled, but this need not be the case. As a result, grievances emerge that are a consequence of transaction costs and this type of problem will be studied in the second part of this chapter.

What externalities and failed contracts have in common are transaction costs. In the third part of this chapter, we will therefore study in more detail whether the presence of transaction costs can be avoided by an unequivocal specification of property rights. In answering this question, we set out to construct a model by which an ideal state can be depicted and thus a benchmark can be created against which the reasons for obstacles to negotiation or settlement, respectively, can be studied. As an upshot our model will explore the need for legal acts. That miraculous benchmark or point of departure for the study of all kinds of failures in human interaction has been labelled 'Coase theorem'. Let us start!

Nuisances and accidents: externalities and a first approach to transaction costs

First, we ought to clarify the notion of an externality in some detail. We will start by making the – ostensibly sophisticated – distinction between 'technological' and 'pecuniary' externalities.

Technological externalities

We talk about a negative externality when a person makes use of property rights in a way that increases her utility (or profit), and in doing so creates a side-effect that lowers the utility of another person without that person's help or prior consent. Conversely there can be a positive externality if the utility of the third party is increased by someone's activity. Note that it is not essential to know whether the negative externality has been brought about by clumsiness, nuisance or playfulness (a flowerpot can fall down, can be dropped unintentionally or can be thrown deliberately). Likewise, a positive externality can be the result of coincidence or purpose (a vaccination against influenza creates protection against infections unintentionally, whereas fireworks can cause pleasure on purpose).

Externalities are not restricted to people in certain social or economic functions, that is to say they may occur between consumers and consumers (neighbourhood effects like the smoke and smell from the barbecue); producers and consumers (smell and noise from a plant in a neighbouring residential area) as well as consumers and producers (forest fires started by a cigarette); producers and producers (when chemicals decontaminated by a factory into a river accelerate the corrosion of the hull of commercial vessels in service on that river).

It is noteworthy that even government agencies can cause externalities, leading to the interesting situation where one authority takes action against another authority.

What all these cases have in common is that ultimately changes in the utility of the parties involved are brought about by changes in the stock of rights pertaining to things. In the case of negative externalities the affected party suffers from opportunity cost, but involuntarily (a simple but common example being a delay due to a traffic jam); in the case of positive externalities, there will be unanticipated cost savings (since there is no charge for watching a fireworks display, the money is left over for an additional drink).

Pecuniary externalities

As the term indicates, the impact of activities on third parties is effectuated via the price system here. A typical example is the economic effect of a newly opened steel mill on a nearby plant producing railway tracks. The low transportation cost from the former to the latter will cut the cost of input for the rails, which in turn increases revenues (ceteris paribus). Note that revenues or profits replace the explanatory variable for utility in the case of a firm.

Similarly, the increase in value of a house after a nearby stop for the new underground line opens is an example of a pecuniary externality, where easier access brings about the change of relative prices.

These cases ought to be distinguished from a case such as the following: opposite a sushi bar, another restaurant opens and for some reason a couple of customers switch from the first to the second place. In this case, relative prices are not necessarily affected and the only effect is a shift in money outlays – an instance of redistribution. As you can see, so-called pecuniary externalities are quite an important phenomenon. However, we will not trace this type of externality further unless it proves useful in certain special cases.

(If you would like to learn more about the two types of externality, I recommend reading Heller and Starrett, 1976; also see Posner, 1998.)

For a deeper understanding of the economic analysis of law a theory about the handling of technological externalities by people is essential. To illustrate, let us have a look at an everyday situation: while taking a nap on a sunny Sunday afternoon, you are disturbed by your neighbour's lawnmower. Now, if you are on good terms with your neighbour, you will hardly rush off to check the civil code to see whether she is allowed to do so, but will, rather, go over to talk to her. As a result, she may stop mowing. However, she may also argue that friends are coming over for a round of boccia and so the lawn urgently needs to be cut. So, whatever the outcome is, it will incur a loss: either to you or to your neighbour. Either you will have to defer your nap or she will not be ready for a game with friends. Having not (yet) employed legal remedy, who ultimately bears the cost will depend on success or failure in bargaining, but the situation could be defused if your neighbour offers you some compensation for your disturbance.

Irrespective of the outcome both sides will have had to expend effort; this kind of effort has been labelled rather accurately as 'time and trouble costs'. And they can be most frustrating if no agreement can be reached after all.

Note that in the case of our example there was at least a fair chance of reaching an agreement so that the efforts or time-and-trouble costs were not spent in vain after all! However, assume that your nap is disturbed by the takeoff and landing of noisy aircraft. In this case, an attempt to start bargaining with the originator of the noise would be superfluous. In more economic terms, the time-and-trouble cost would be prohibitively high.

Transaction cost

The lesson from these two examples is that whether one has to suffer from a negative externality or not depends on the subjectively perceived amount of effort that needs to be incurred in order to bargain over a resolution of that type of conflict.

It is time to generalize and discuss the idea behind our examples. The proper term for effort or time-and-trouble cost is *transaction cost*. These are the costs of establishing, enforcing and transferring (alienating) property rights. Transaction costs must not be mixed up with the resource costs entailed in things or the present value or trade value entailed in property rights. What transaction costs reflect are the frictions that emerge in the handling of property rights. Note that these frictions are subjective in nature, which is why I described them earlier as the 'subjectively perceived amount of effort'. The upshot is that because of being subjective in nature, they cannot be shared. That is a marked difference from transportation cost. The cost of transportation can be shared. 'Postage paid' or 'free on board' are standard forms of cost sharing of transportation costs. Clearly transaction costs can be influenced by certain actions, such as voluntary signals to comply or an acceptable offer (of compensation for nuisance). And transaction cost can be influenced by legal remedies, such as perfectly specified property rights (when possible) or standard forms of compensation etc. As you can see from these preliminary remarks, transaction cost are tremendously important for an economic understanding of legal norms!

Whereas transaction costs must not be confused with transportation costs this is not so clear with the notion of information costs! With respect to the latter, recall the introductory remarks about intellectual property rights and their relation to information. To bring a person to give away (valuable) information may incur a lot of time and trouble. Moreover, additional time and trouble must be incurred to verify the correctness of the information received. Clearly, information can itself be viewed as a valuable commodity, by which the neat distinction between the resource costs contained in things and the notion of (subjectively perceived) transaction costs tends to be blurred. However, a strict application of property rights will help us here, since in that sense information always pertains to peculiarities of property rights, not property rights themselves. Thus the costs arising from the provision or transmission of information definitely fall into the realm of transaction costs.

Despite their subjective nature, transaction costs are opportunity costs: when disturbed by a stubborn neighbour you sacrifice the pleasures of a sunny Sunday afternoon.

And, moreover, transaction costs are not recoverable. The sacrifice of pleasure may be compensated, but the time spent cannot be regained!

Let us conclude this paragraph with a few additional observations.

As we shall see in the section on contracts, the presence of transaction costs is not restricted to cases of nuisance or negative externalities and attempts to come to grips with the originators of costs as in our earlier examples. As a matter of fact, the procedure of setting up a contract as well as the trouble caused by failure or breach is another fundamental source of transaction costs.

True, the term has been generalized to include all kinds of friction involving means of coordination. Thus, being in a queue for the release of a new passport creates a transaction cost (consider why this is the case!). Also when the environmental authority gives approval for the operation of a newly built plant, this can be a source of quite substantial transaction costs on behalf of the applicant. (Incidentally, this example poses an interesting question inasmuch as long delays in approval will cause lost profits; whether these are part of the transaction costs or a type of pecuniary externality inflicted by the authority on the applicant deserves further investigation.)

Finally, let us recall the essential difference between being disturbed by your neighbour and being disturbed by aircraft. It is not only that after you have identified the neighbour as originator of nuisance you have a fair chance of negotiations with her whereas this is very unlikely in the case of an aircraft disturbing you, there is also a difference in how easily the originators of the disturbance can anticipate whom it might affect. In the case of the neighbour, it is easy to anticipate who could be a potential victim of a potentially disruptive activity. This is definitely not the case when a company operates an air carrier. Certainly, they know that there will probably be a disturbing amount of noise at takeoff or landing, but they can hardly anticipate who will be the victims. Thus the probability if anticipating negotiations about nuisance ex ante in the two cases is entirely different. It turns out that it is difficult if not impossible to specify property rights ex ante so that incentives are created to perform in a way that withholds the disruptive negative externalities. Prohibitive transaction cost on behalf of the victims (and – if they want to secure their interests beforehand – also the creators) require specific legal norms in order to accomplish the goal of social efficiency. As I have already mentioned one way out is to replace property rights by liability rules under certain circumstances.

Costly purchases, failed negotiations and breached contracts

We will now concentrate on activities in markets. Here, property rights are exchanged via trade. A trade in turn is based on a contract. Contracts sometimes evolve tacitly, for example when you take a can of *Fresh* out of the fridge at your grocer's and hand the money in to the salesperson without one word and she accepts it with a smile and a nod of her head. Where the object of the business is less obvious, the contract will most likely be stated explicitly even in written form. It depends how 'complicated' the transaction tends to be.

One indicator for complications is how much time is spent on bargaining and other substantial efforts of making contracts or (as you may have guessed already) transaction costs!

Another indicator for complications are so-called contingencies, which are more or less likely events and conditions that could influence performance in a negative way (delays in delivery, say, or damages from shipping).

I deal with both sources of obstacle or complication later in this chapter.

To begin, a contract specifies the intended and favoured reallocation of property rights. Such a reallocation places property rights where they are most beneficial. If that task is accomplished, the contract is efficient, since no further improvement will then be possible for either party to the contract (remember Pareto optimality?).

The task of an economic analysis of law is the accomplishment of efficient contracts.

Unfortunately, sometimes it turns out that there are substantial complications (in the sense just mentioned) to the accomplishment of that goal. Let us see why.

First, contracts are frequently conducted step by step. To illustrate: delivery follows prepayment where prepayment requires the receipt of an invoice etc. That ought to be clarified beforehand. While some complications could be foreseen and thus be taken into account, others are not. Thus, it need not be obvious at delivery that the commodity at hand does not have the stipulated properties. As an example, when British Rail purchased the high-speed multiple diesel units, they were fitted with diesel engines that were adapted from shipbuilding. Only after thousands of kilometres did it become evident that the engines did not withstand the sometimes hard shocks from rails and points, which were much harder than the vibrancies vessels are exposed to. Nobody foresaw this – an illuminating example of a so-called contingency.

A contract can be called complete when it contains all perceptible contingencies for an exchange of property rights. In that case the contract is perfect, since it should be brought to an (efficient) conclusion under all circumstances.

Where contingencies have been overlooked the contract is incomplete, but as our example has demonstrated, it can sometimes be very hard to foresee a specific contingency. Incomplete contracts may cause conflict and conflict calls for means of conflict resolution. We will deal with this issue in Chapter 4.

Unfortunately, contingencies might not be overlooked incidentally. Sometimes they are simply ignored, because the incorporation of adequate provisions would be costly and the probability of the contingency to materialize is assumed to be very low.

Before we look at some more details we must also be aware that contracts are more valuable the more likely they are to be fulfilled. To see this, consider someone who orders a special showcase for her collectibles (teddy bears, for example). The showcase must be made to measure and a carpenter is engaged to construct it. For the carpenter, fulfilment of the contract becomes crucial because a made-to-measure showcase could hardly be sold otherwise if the customer for some reason does not pay for it.

Labour and materials put into the showcase are thus 'sunk costs', which cannot be recovered. However, even a delay in the settlement of the account reduces the value of the contract. This can be overcome by stipulating a deposit at the time when the contract is written. Thus the value of the contract can be substantially increased ex ante.

We will now return to the difficulties of establishing a contract and the emerging sources of transaction costs.

A typical sales contract entails several steps:

- a suitable partner to the deal must be found
- the conditions for the contract and for the processing must be negotiated
- the contract ought to be fulfilled.

For details of this procedure, we can rely on a list of transaction costs provided by one of the pioneers of transaction cost analysis – Armen Alchian (1979).

The first step will comprise inquiries of who holds what property rights. With respect to the transaction costs involved, we can observe that this step can be considerably facilitated by consultation of the Yellow Pages or even a special agent such as a broker.

The next step is the verification of the property rights of a potential partner. To illustrate, we would probably be very concerned if we established that the beautiful diamond jewellery we discovered at a garage sale had been stolen and was being offered by a fence!

Next, the properties or attributes of commodities are checked. This is typically done by employing merchants as middlemen. Relevant information is communicated via brand names, trademarks, warranties, test drives; it may even be enforced by government regulation. All these means have in common the aim of reducing the cost of information, although they may also be abused, thus revealing opportunistic behaviour on behalf of sellers. Such possibilities notwithstanding, warranties or even insurance contracts serve as signals for appropriate quality. They demonstrate that even the dispersion of risk with exogenously given knowledge can be a source of costs and that this fact enters contracts by means of warranties, liabilities as well as sales or returns.

An essential step is the determination of the price. Note that this is somewhat at variance with established practice of theoretical models in which it is assumed that under conditions of competition prices are exogenous to the parties. Here, in the broad sphere of institutional economics (which was pointed out to you in Chapter 2, remember?), we rely on low transaction cost instead, maintained by some predictability of prices, which in turn implies a certain rigidity. Still, the overall situation is facilitated by brokers and other agents, whose presence in turn indicates the possibility of an almost prohibitively high transaction cost. If this were not the case the (opportunity) cost of employing special agents would hardly be justifiable.

Next, the terms of the contract must be drawn up. This might turn out to be a considerable task given the possibility of aforementioned contingencies. One of the crucial questions here is the issue of allocating the cost emerging from the various risks to the partners in the contract. This becomes trickier the longer the contract is to endure (you can probably guess why!).

Finally, the conditions for trade processing ought to be settled. A lack of care or even opportunistic behaviour on behalf of either side can become a source of trouble, loss of time and other surprises thus calling for appropriate steps. These may include monitoring as the transaction proceeds and other measures, which, in turn, are sources of transaction costs.

The listing is impressive enough but it gives rise to two substantial observations:
1   It demonstrates the degree of simplification present in the traditional textbook models of (competitive) markets, which most elegantly do away with the complications of the still stylized procedure of contracting, thus ignoring the

substantial amount of resources absorbed. Still we may take comfort in the saying that 'simplification is the price of analysis'.

2   The second observation is even more substantial. There are not only many sources of costs in the course of contracting, but also these costs emerge from millions and millions of transactions conducted every day. Thus the question of cost reduction or avoidance is quite pressing. This in turn has already been indicated by offering some hints of how to come to grips with the various entries in the course of their description.

At this point of our discussion it is also noteworthy to point out other means of the reduction of transactions costs such as mutual 'trust'. Trust is especially important when repeated and regular commercial relations are maintained. By the same token, the role of morals or ethical conduct as a source of low transaction costs comes to mind.

Still another possibility – which should not be surprising given the subject of this book – is the emergence or establishment of norms, broadly understood. There are customs and practices that are often not even codified; there are legal restrictions and obligations, such as liability and insurance, compensation schemes for damages and even sanctions for misconduct.

While we will further discuss at least some of these issues, we might first of all ask ourselves whether there is some ideal state which can serve as a benchmark for our further investigations. Such a benchmark exists, and is a universal prerequisite for human interaction under ideal conditions, thus covering tort and contract and other fields, as we will see eventually. We now turn to the Coase theorem.

Coase theorem: a key to an economic analysis of law

The Coase theorem and extensions

Imagine the following everyday situation: there is a sawmill situated in a remote forest. Within earshot of the sawmill, a hunting lodge is available to let. This lodge has long been vacant but now a celebrated novelist considers it as an ideal place for his work. However, he quickly realizes that during working hours the sawmill does not allow him to enjoy the expected quietness of the place. On the contrary, the loud noise of the band saw causes severe disturbance. Our celebrity estimates the damage caused by the noise at €100,000.

There seems at least one way out of that mess: to reconstruct the hunting lodge by moving the study from one side of the building to the other, more remote side. That can be done at a cost of €50,000.

Another alternative is to build a noise protection wall in front of the mill at a cost of €100,000. The revenue of the sawmill amounts to €200,000.

How to proceed? Well, at the outset that depends on the actual property rights at the time when the negative externality becomes effective. Let us assume that initially the operator of the sawmill is entitled to run the mill. That is to say, she has obtained all necessary approvals from the trade authority, the environmental

Table 3.1 Negative externality: advantage sawmill

Option	Net gain (welfare)
The writer moves to another place	100,000 – 100,000 + 200,000 = **200,000**
The writer rebuilds the hunting lodge at his own expense	100,000 – 50,000 + 200,000 = **250,000**
The writer rebuilds the sawmill at his own expense	100,000 – 100,000 + 200,000 = **200,000**
The writer compensates the operator of the mill for closing it down	100,000 – 200,000 = – **100,000**

authority and so on. So the operator is entitled to act even if the novelist feels disturbed. What can be done if the probability that a court will award damages is literally zero, given the allocation of property rights? Table 3.1 lists the available options.

Evidently the best option under prevailing circumstances is to rebuild the hunting lodge at the owner's expense.

Let us now investigate the situation if the writer is entitled to tranquillity; that is to say, the operator of the sawmill has to bear the cost of overcoming the externality. Table 3.2 lists the options available now.

The obvious result of our little exercise is that the best solution in economic terms is the same irrespective of the initial allocation of property rights! The hunting lodge will be rebuilt. The resulting allocation of resources is thus independent of the initial endowment with property rights. Needless to say this was a very crude calculation, which obviously contains several simplifying assumptions and, moreover, we must be aware of the difference in charges between the two cases. I will deal with both points shortly.

First, however, I would like to turn your attention to an additional perspective. Consider the situation in which the mill owner is obliged to take steps. She will first consider rebuilding the plant. But having information about the much lower cost of rebuilding the hunting lodge, she will make an offer to the writer. The writer,

Table 3.2 Negative externality: advantage author

Option	Net gain (welfare)
The owner pays for the writer to move to another place	200,000 – 100,000 + 100,000 = **200,000**
The owner rebuilds the hunting lodge at her own expense	200,000 – 50,000 + 100,000 = **250,000**
The owner bears the cost for the installation of protection devices	200,000 – 100,000 + 100,000 = **200,000**
The owner compensates the writer for his loss	200,000 – 100,000 = **100,000**

in turn, is also well informed and – being a *homo oeconomicus* – will argue that while he accepts the offer of the operator, he proposes that she pays an additional €25,000, which is half the cost resulting from rebuilding the lodge instead of the plant. Note that even in this case the solution of rebuilding the lodge remains the best thing that can be done!

Before entering a more thorough discussion of the issues at hand we can generalize the content of this example, as shown in Figure 3.1.

Here the marginal revenue of a polluter is assumed to change smoothly as output increases, while the marginal cost of the nuisance (damage) to the person affected (the 'pollutee') also steadily increases. In case of unrestricted property rights (laissez faire) for the polluter, she will expand production to the point where MR becomes 0, to X_1. If, by the same token, the pollutee were entitled to stay perfectly undisturbed, the firm would have to close down. The optimum level of production from the point of view of social welfare is at X^*, where the two schedules intersect. This is because at this point marginal revenue equals marginal cost of nuisance.

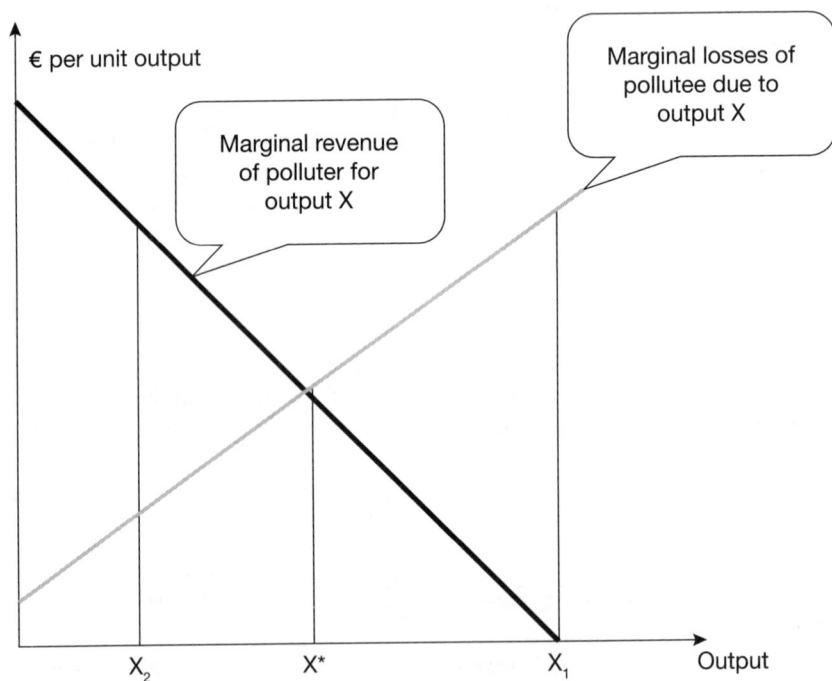

Figure 3.1 Graphical representation of the Coase theorem

Under the conditions discussed in the text, a bargaining equilibrium will be achieved at X^* irrespective of the regime (laissez faire or liability rule). From X_2 or X_1 as initial conditions, bargaining will tend towards X^* when the underpinnings of the theorem are met.

Now let us see what happens if the polluter produces at a level of X_1 and first she is entitled to do so, but then subsequently the pollutee is entitled to go undisturbed.

In the first case, the pollutee can improve her situation by offering compensation for lost revenues up to the point where marginal damage suffered becomes equal to marginal revenue. Beyond that point (to the left) marginal damage is below marginal revenue so that it does not pay to offer additional compensation. So the utmost offer will be at X^*, which leads to the socially optimal allocation.

In the second case, the polluter might be interested in expanding production despite the legal position. Thus she can make an offer for compensation of the marginal damage up to the point where this compensation just equals the marginal revenue. So again they will settle at X^*.

Now consider for some reason an initial situation such as X_2, where the polluter is still interested in expanding output. As long as her gain is above the damage schedule, she could offer compensation, whereas the pollutee could bribe the polluter to curtail output up to point X^*. Again we end up at the socially optimal allocation. As an exercise, try to verify this proposition!

With these findings, we are now in a position to state the **Coase theorem**: given some externality and, provided that there are no transaction costs, the outcome of bargaining will be a social optimum irrespective of the initial legal position.

Stated slightly differently, we may summarize the theorem as follows: if property rights are clearly specified, then the internalization of externalities is possible without the need to effectuate legal damages.

The two wordings of the theorem do, in fact, convey two important implications. Recall first that the perfect specification of property rights will in fact forestall the occurrence of transaction costs. Under such conditions the initial legal position is irrelevant for the resulting allocation. And this in turn has far-reaching consequences both for the economic analysis of law and for theory about the functions of the state.

We must be aware, however, that the theorem holds only under very restrictive conditions. Let us summarize them:

- there are only two (or at least very few) parties involved
- they are perfectly independent from each other, which boils down to the assumption that with respect to purchases perfect competition prevails
- they do not act strategically, which means that they are inclined to cooperate
- this is facilitated by mutual knowledge of schedules of gains and damages, which, in turn, points to the importance of the absence of transaction costs.

So, the theorem is based on 'voluntarism'. The affected parties voluntarily engage in conflict resolution. They neither care for prestige nor do they want to defend their viewpoint! While this can be criticized from both the theoretical point of view (incompatibility with the assumptions underlying the *homo oeconomicus*) as well as empirical observations, the basic virtue of the theorem is that of a benchmark or starting point for economic investigations of legal norms very much like the competitive equilibrium of a perfect market.

Thus, the discussion of the theorem's validity is open.

In that discussion, I proceed as follows:

1   the peculiar difficulty of wealth effects is addressed
2   empirical relevance is questioned
3   the consequences of an increase in the number of people involved are investigated
4   long-term aspects and more fundamental doubts are discussed.

The following problem can best be demonstrated when the affected persons are assumed to be consumers. We are concerned about something called 'wealth effect'. To illustrate: consider our writer in the introductory example. If the hunting lodge had been successfully rebuilt this would have an impact on our writer's appreciation of quietness.

Since, after the renovation, the conditions for quiet work are better than before, our writer might demand even more quiescence! But such a change must be ruled out if the theorem is to hold. While empirically the wealth effect can be expected to be so small that it can be readily neglected, in theoretical analysis one ought to take hold of a specific assumption. Such an assumption is contained in 'quasi-linear' utility functions, as demonstrated by Varian and also addressed by Posner and Dnes. The idea behind such functions can be illustrated by the following example: consider the independent variables of some utility function to be noise (in decibels) and money. Then, in a quasi-linear utility function, the marginal rate of substitution between noise and money is the same (see Varian, 1996: 545–7, especially Figure 31.2).

A problem closely related to the wealth effect is that of the 'endowment effect', which gives rise to the phenomenon that for a distinct loss in utility one sometimes can ask for compensation and sometimes offer compensation (depending on the initial legal conditions). In the first case, one is entitled to ask for compensation for damage sustained. In the second case, one can make an offer in order to deflect damage. In microeconomic theory, these two options are well known as 'equivalent variation' and 'compensatory variation' respectively (for a quick revision you might like to consult Varian again, at 250–4). The upshot is that a person who is asked how much she must receive as compensation for damage suffered will give a higher amount than if she has to make an offer so as to avoid damage, although the decrease in utility is the same in both cases. The reason for this seeming contradiction is that in the first case no budgetary constraint is effective whereas in the second situation it is! If there were no wealth effect, the problem at hand would not obtain. Its relevance for the economic analysis of law is twofold: first, it points to a difficulty in the application of the Kaldor-Hicks test as mentioned earlier. If a crosscheck of the test is made by reversing the process of compensation, the endowment effect would apply, thus probably leading to an outcome different from the original situation. A problem may also turn up in case a court establishes the value of an interdiction, since according to the preceding discussion, this value will not be independent of the initial assignment of property rights!

Let us now turn to the empirical relevance. This can be assessed in two different ways:

- first, one can search for appropriate situations of conflict in history and see whether the theorem applies in conflict resolution
- second, one can undertake experiments, where the outcomes are cooperative solutions in accordance with the Coase theorem.

The historical evidence shows that there are a few investigations drawing on an example given by Coase himself. Cattle from a ranch are roaming into a cornfield on an adjacent farm, thus causing damage to the crops. The profit of the rancher as well as the amount of damage depends on the size of the flock. Under the preconditions of the theorem the farmer and the rancher could accomplish a socially optimal solution of their conflict.

An investigation into lawmaking in nineteenth-century California concerning the prevention of crop damage caused by roaming cattle carried out by economic historian Kenneth Vogel in 1987 does not provide evidence for the Coase theorem. Nevertheless Vogel's findings demonstrate the importance of transaction cost for the accomplishment of the outcome.

Similarly, Robert Ellickson cannot find evidence for the theorem in his 1986 research concerning the impact of different legal norms on conflicts over crop damages caused by roaming cattle, again in California. His findings rather indicate the importance of customs and a sense of justice as guidance to human action!

And now for the experiments: interestingly enough, the results are more encouraging than those in history. The most prominent researchers in the field, Hoffman and Spitzer, ran three experiments in 1982, 1985 and 1986 respectively. Their findings are that cooperative solutions emerged in 90 to 94 per cent of cases, where at the outset the participants found themselves in a situation of conflict. It is noteworthy that these results were obtained even when one of the main assumptions underlying the theorem was relaxed and the number of participants increased to 19 on one side – the other being kept at one to two participants.

The findings of Hoffman and Spitzer trigger curiosity as to what extent they are in accordance with predictions from a theoretical perspective. Before we start our exploration in this regard, it is worth pointing out that the question is of general interest in excess of the consequences of a variation of numbers of participants. Recall that we have already mentioned that the Coase theorem has implications for the role of the state or, more generally speaking, for institutional arrangements that become necessary as the circumstances no longer allow for an autonomous efficient settlement of conflict. To illustrate: consider a conflict between residents and the railway company over the route of a new high-speed train. One such institutional arrangement could be to establish a grassroots organization, which elects a spokesperson, who then bargains with the company's representative, thus effectuating conditions for Coase-like bargaining.

At the outset, the situations are as listed in Table 3.3.

Table 3.3 Situations in which Coase-like bargaining occurs

Participants are cooperative	Participants are non-cooperative
Transaction costs are low Entitlement with the tortfeasor/claimant: • What is the predicted allocation? • What is the economically preferable allocation?	Entitlement with the tortfeasor/claimant: • What is the predicted allocation? • What is the economically preferable allocation?
Transaction costs are high Entitlement with the tortfeasor/claimant: • What is the predicted allocation? • What is the economically preferable allocation?	Entitlement with the tortfeasor/claimant: • What is the predicted allocation? • What is the economically preferable allocation?

In order to give you an idea about the various options contained in Table 3.3, we will return to our writer in the hunting lodge once more. For the sake of argument, let us assume that the opportunity cost of time for the writer amounts to a very high €60,000 when he sets out to convince the management of the sawmill to rebuild the lodge at their expense. Now, if the mill is entitled to continue operation unhampered this would make no difference. But if the writer is entitled to go undisturbed the transaction cost would be an obstacle to bring to bear that right.

Consequently, under such circumstances the accomplishment of the efficient solution depends on the initial conditions! In this case, the suggestions from the Coase theorem are the following:

*   establishing the initial legal conditions by means of assignment of appropriate property rights, which give rise to an efficient solution even in cases where the participants do not cooperate (due to obstacles)
*   at best, the creation of institutions such as a court or alternative means of conflict resolution (which must be operated at relatively lower cost of course, if they are to be considered economic alternatives)
*   in the latter case, the theorem will provide hints to the corrective measures for the accomplishment of an efficient solution.

Needless to say, these are ambitious claims! However, they clearly show why for the scholarly community the Coase theorem is considered both core and starting point for an economic theory of the law.

Our reasoning gives rise to further considerations, however. One is the important issue of the distribution of wealth. Evidently even the efficient outcome of bargaining is by no means neutral with respect to the distribution of wealth – even at a zero transaction cost. Much less so in cases where a reassignment of transaction costs by the legislature is necessary in order to accomplish an efficient solution – as in the case of entitlement of our writer to be undisturbed in the presence of prohibitively high transaction costs.

However, experts might tell us not to worry too much. They assure us that the managers who decide on the location of a new plant will be perfectly aware of expected liabilities or damages according to prevailing legal conditions. They can infer such claims from the low price at which a plot of land is available. In contrast, a location with favourable conditions is usually indicated by a higher price.

Well, that was a little detour. We originally wanted to continue our investigation into an increase of participants and the consequences for the Coase theorem. So let us look at the following example.

Imagine a new site for housing in a residential area. There are nine lots of land according to Figure 3.2. Letters in the nine boxes indicate the owners.

Imagine further that all owners except E are planning to live in single-occupancy houses. E wants to build a high-rise apartment building. The expected gain for E is €65,000. The owners of the other lots are afraid of the traffic and noise they expect will exist once the building is completed, so they are each willing to pay €10,000 in compensation to E if he renounces his plans.

Note that the sum of intended payments exceeds the expected gain for E, so that it should be possible to fully compensate him for the renunciation.

Now, the problem is that only a joint offer of all the residents surrounding E can bring about the intended result. But even if there are no other obstacles to the bargain

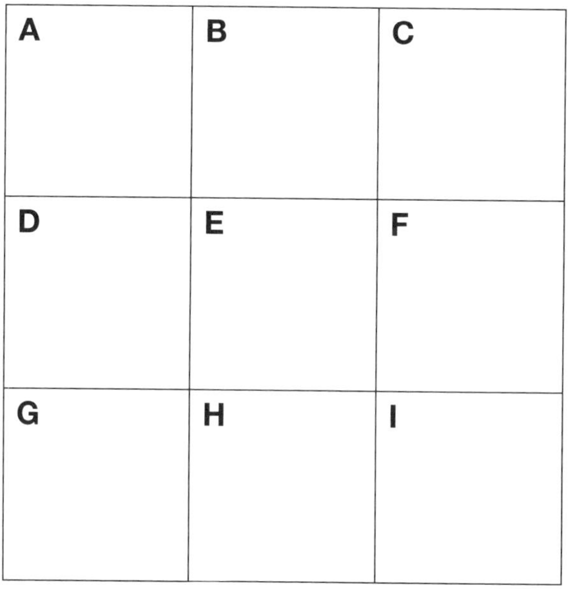

A	B	C
D	E	F
G	H	I

Figure 3.2 The Coase theorem with several parties

The owner of plot E wants to build a high-rise apartment building; on the other plots are family dwellings, facing an externality concerning unhampered view, covered sunlight etc. The families can either be entitled to undisturbed use or the owner of the plot E is entitled to carry out her plans.

such as transaction costs, we can predict that some of the individual residents will try to get a 'free ride'; that is to say, each of them is unable (or unwilling) to solve the problem individually but no one takes the lead to make a joint effort to solve the problem.

The situation does not change if it is up to E to pay off the neighbours in order to allow him to build the apartment block. First of all the gain for E must be well above €80,000 to make compensation of each of the neighbours possible. In addition, E would have to negotiate with each of his neighbours individually. This in turn shifts power to them, since the apartment block can only be built if all conflicts are settled. By performing 'holdout' each of them can delay the settlement or even use this tactic to raise the claim against E.

You will note the similarity between free riding and holdout, which are both individually advantageous courses of action in a situation requiring unanimous joint performance. If such situations can be overcome at all, this implies certain institutional or legal provisions.

We can go one step further and summarize by including situations that have not yet been considered. While the number of affected people varies the common feature is that there are (almost) no transaction costs (see Table 3.4).

Again it is obvious that some of the cases can only be resolved towards an efficient solution if collective action takes place (cells (3), (4), (7) and (8)). The formation of action groups who subsequently nominate a spokesperson is one example of such kind of resolution. It has been observed that this is the way in which many conflicts between enterprises or even public agencies and citizens are handled. However, it is not standard that conflict resolution is accomplished via Coase-like bargaining; an increasing number of cases are handled by 'mediation' instead. This is one of the alternative means to **dispute resolution** where an impartial third party is called in. We will learn more about that in Chapter 4.

There are two additional aspects worth mentioning. First, an attempt has been made (Veljanovski 1982) to understand the outcome according to Coase as a 'competitive market theorem', where – by assumption – because of perfect competition the private and social costs coincide. The way in which this is accomplished is to look at externalities as 'contingent commodities' to which prices are assigned, so that they can be integrated into the process of *tatonnement* (the

Table 3.4 Almost no transaction costs

Number of affected/ legal condition	Entitlement with the polluter (laissez faire)	Polluter liable
One polluter/one pollutee	(1) Efficiency	(2) Efficiency
One polluter/many pollutees	(3) Inefficiency due to free riding	(4) Inefficiency due to holdout
Many polluters/one pollutee	(5) Efficiency, if competition with low bargaining costs	(6) Same as with laissez faire
Many polluters/many pollutees	(7) Inefficiency as in case (3)	(8) Inefficiency as in case (4)

procedure by which the market equilibrium is established). Unfortunately, this idea appears to contradict one of the basic ideas by Coase: the point is that in a perfect market the (imaginary) auctioneer sets prices as parameters for the parties according to excess supply and demand respectively.

However, in the original framework constructed by Coase the 'prices' for externalities are by no means parameters, but rather strategic variables, which are chosen by the conflicting parties themselves.

The final aspect here is that of the 'solution concept' (a term I borrow from game theory here) in the presence of some (negative) externality, which was standard when Coase published his groundbreaking article in 1960. Let us summarize it and thus illustrate the extraordinary shift of viewpoint then advocated by Ronald Coase.

The solution was that developed by Arthur Pigou. The essential presumption is that there is a distinct institutional setting before the externality comes into play, whereas Coase wanted to demonstrate that such a presumption might be premature.

Figure 3.3 summarizes the internalization of a negative externality by means of a pollution tax according to Pigou.

With a given demand schedule and marginal social cost that exceeds private marginal cost (supply schedule) the intersection of demand and supply leave social costs uncovered and thus lead to oversupply as compared to the socially optimal solution. A tax on output leads to the socially optimal market solution. Here, the

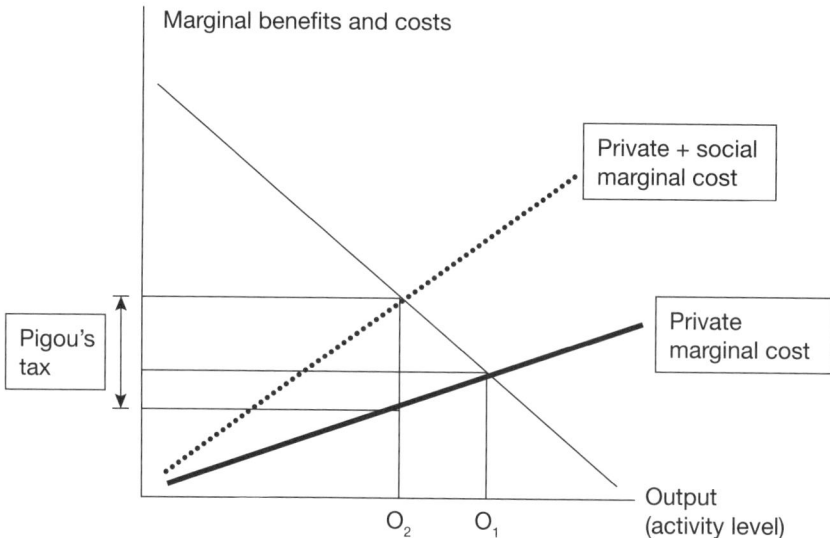

Figure 3.3 Problem of externality solved by a Pigouvian tax

A stylized picture of Pigou's tax: the tax would shift the equilibrium from O_1 to O_2, thus taking internalizing the external cost imposed on society by production of output O.

private property rights are attenuated and an authority makes use of its rights by imposing the tax. Thus Pigou presupposes that no voluntary solution to the situation is possible, probably due to transaction costs or the violation of one of the other conditions under which the 'benchmark' solution by Coase is possible.

The Pigouvian solution is less straightforward than it may appear, by the way: in order to implement the tax one must know the socially correct point of equilibrium, which in turn can only be accomplished when the tax rate is known beforehand – that being an obvious contradiction.

Our next step is far more than a digression: so far we have considered variations in the initial assignment of rights. However, there is an alternative to the full specification and assignment of rights, which is to concede utmost liberty accompanied by a liability rule for wrongdoing. That is to say, people who are potential victims of some negative externality are entitled to damages under certain circumstances ex ante. But the question is whether we can say something about the expediency of either regime – property rights and liability rules – from an economic perspective. Stated differently, the question now is under what circumstances a property right or a liability rule creates better incentives to induce people to act in a desirable way.

When are property rights desirable and when does liability rule?

Let me start with the following useful distinction:

- Conflicts arise from all kinds of nuisance: noise, smell, smoke and other types of negative externality. They typically detract from a sense of good neighbourhood. In legal terminology, they are intrusions or trespasses with possession.
- Conflicts also arise when a person suffers damage from an accident. Being essentially another case of a negative externality, the accident features remarkable differences to the first notion of nuisance given.

How could we handle these two cases? At the outset, there are two possibilities which we have seen already in the course of the presentation of the Coase theorem: the originator (polluter) of the nuisance can go unhampered or the victim (pollutee) can be entitled to privacy. While I am working on this typescript I have the experience of both situations at the same time: the cars outside are quite noisy without violating prevailing norms, but inside the office I am entitled to be protected from smoking.

Now, what about enforcement?

Here we can make the following distinction: indemnities or an entitlement to interdiction.

Note that an indemnity is a compensation for rigour suffered in the past, whereas the interdiction becomes effective for the future. But when is it advisable to apply the principle of compensation and when is an interdiction (by way of an 'injunction') preferable? The answer to this depends on the question of whether transaction costs are present or not.

In case there are no transaction costs, however, we need not undertake further investigations. As we have discussed at length in the absence of transaction costs the initial assignment of rights is irrelevant for the accessibility of an efficient solution. Parties will bargain over the internalization of externalities irrespective of whether entitlement is with the polluter or the victim is entitled to indemnity. (You may like to try your skills by applying this hypothesis to our case of the sawmill and the writer's hunting lodge.)

So we turn to the case where transaction costs are present. At the outset, recall that it is desirable to bring the parties into a position where they can bargain over an efficient solution. But this, in turn, requires the unambiguous specification of property rights. A comparison of indemnities and interdiction evidently is in favour of the interdiction. First, it is always hard to assess the claims in cases of compensation (imagine the problem faced by a court in valuing the loss of inspiration caused by the mill for the writer in our earlier example!) and, second, in the very same situation the injunction – to observe an upper limit of nuisance, say – makes it perfectly clear to what extent a claim to privacy is ruled by the court. Such ruling will, above all, bring the parties into a bargaining position in case the threshold is exceeded.

When there are (prohibitively high) transaction costs, however, the imposition of compensation is more appropriate. Note that this typically is the case for accidents, where the victim cannot be known in advance and hence no negotiations are possible and an injunction (not to start driving) does not make sense. The only way to induce a person to an appropriate level of care is to make her liable for wrongdoing, and to sanction her ex post. These recommendations are rooted in the findings of Calabresi and Melamed (1972).

Two words of caution are appropriate: first of all we must be aware that recommendations such as those by Calabresi and Melamed are directed towards judges (or courts) in a system of common law. Under this legal system, the jurisdiction is given a fairly wide range of discretion. The orientation is towards precedent as long as a judge does not see reason to deviate from the prevalent interpretation of the law (the issue of 'judge-made law', which will be addressed in Chapter 4 in more detail). Now there is no doubt that even in civil law countries with their typically fairly detailed codified norms judges may occasionally deviate from standard interpretations. But contrary to established procedures in the common law the main addressees of recommendations such as the one at hand are legislators, not courts!

Second, we must be aware of the issue of distributional justice, which comes up when the problem of diverse initial endowments with property rights is at stake. To see this, let us turn to the case where an injunction is appropriate. If it is possible for the pollutee to effectuate an injunction, the polluter must pay compensation if she does not comply. She will not comply and compensate instead if this was more profitable for her. Note, however, that the financial status of the pollutee cannot worsen, whereas that of the polluter depends on the value of the initial condition.

The opposite holds when the polluter is entitled to act in a particular way. If the victim now raises an objection, she must inevitably bear the reduction in wealth depending on the compensation for the incommoding activity of the polluter.

Thus the legal position influences wealth and we are back to the familiar problem among lawyers and economists: justice versus efficiency. Fortunately, this time they are not incompatible, since under either distribution of wealth an efficient outcome is feasible.

One final remark: inasmuch as strategic action on behalf of one or all parties in a conflict is present this will be an obstacle to a cooperative solution. Consequently, it can be treated as a case of prohibitive transaction costs. Still a court or an authority could impose an injunction on the polluter, where that level of activity will be just tolerated at which overall welfare will be maximized. Production in excess of the tolerated level will entail the payment of compensation. Under the assumption that polluters are profit maximizers it will thus make no differences whether they intend to act strategically or not. The best thing the polluter can do is to select a level of production that leaves her at her optimal position, inclusive of compensation for victims, of course. Consequently, and provided the measures can be enforced, there is no more room for strategic actions.

Objections

The discussion about the Coase theorem is almost unmanageable. To illustrate, the entry 'externalities and the Coase theorem' in the Bibliography of Law and Economics contains 140 contributions. Therefore, an exhaustive appreciation is an impossible task. While there was (and still is) much praise for Ronald Coase culminating in the opinion that he initiated the emergence of a new paradigm there has always also been fierce criticism. Let us conclude the presentation with three examples of objections.

First, does the theorem neglect important insights from microeconomic theory? The argument runs as follows: according to the theorem, the allocation emerging from bargaining is independent of the initial assignment of property rights. However, in the case of a negative externality between neighbouring households the negotiation cannot be independent of purchasing power. Thus the preferences of either side can be effectuated better the higher the initial endowment with purchasing power, which will be reflected in the willingness to pay or the claim for compensation. Consequently, it is true that the results of bargaining are efficient, but the results will vary according to difference in initial conditions!

Second, the theorem is logically flawed! This argument runs as follows. The logic of the theorem is the following: in a case transaction costs are zero (A), it follows that the initial assignment of property rights does not affect the efficiency in resource allocation (B). So the logic is 'B follows from A'. But B can have two different meanings here, that is to say (1) every assignment of property rights gives rise to an efficient allocation of resources, where efficiency requires some initial assignment of property rights and (2) resources are admitted to efficient use independently of some assignment of property rights. But only either (1) or (2) can hold, so there is an inherent logical contradiction contained in Coase's analysis. Although his findings contain much truth, they cannot obtain as a 'theorem'.

Finally, it was questioned whether the Coase 'theorem' can hold up in the long run. The argument can best be illustrated by an example. I will pick up Coase's favourite case here, that of the farmer and the neighbouring rancher. By assumption, they both act in competitive markets. Therefore their profits must be zero in long-run equilibrium. However, there is a relationship between the two via a negative externality (roaming cattle destroying crops). Despite these circumstances, they are producing at minimal average cost (a condition for the equilibrium to hold). Evidently the average cost is lower under a property rule (laissez faire) than under a liability rule ('polluter pays'). Consequently prices under a property rule must be lower in equilibrium than under the liability rule – given the usual demand schedule. Thus, the levels of internalized damages must be different under different conditions, which is a contradiction to the essence of the theorem.

The Coase theorem has left deep marks and like all innovative ideas has caused much discussion. Despite this it can be truly called a landmark. *And* we are now fit to proceed to a more careful investigation of liability rules!

Liability rules as incentives for care and deterrents to detrimental actions

Preliminaries

There are many reasons for damages. They can be the consequence of an accident, a consequence of sales of a defective commodity or simply recklessness (as in the case of setting fire to the neighbour's fence while burning leaves). Moreover, damages can be caused by faulty settlement of a transaction or breach of contract. Law and economics requires that these reasons should be brought into some order.

Moreover, damages can take various forms. We must distinguish substantial from imaginary damages. Substantial damages may be differentiated into damages suffered and foregone losses. The former is characterized by reduction in wealth due to vandalism, the latter occurs when a contract is broken due to unexpected interruption of delivery. Next, let us have a look at differences and similarities in the treatment of liability rules by lawyers and economists.

We start with a similarity: lawyers and economists alike look at human action as the ultimate source of damages. The focus of lawyers then is to examine to what extent some action or refusal to act that caused damage is a probable consequence of the violation of command, interdiction, the law or morals.

Once damage has resulted the vital question is who ought to bear the loss (at this point we do not yet take insurance into account!).

There is a basic principle in jurisprudence that applies here. The principle is that everyone must be accountable for responsibilities which can be assigned to her (unless she is insane). The essential idea behind this principle is that of 'redress' or, similarly, the 'compensation for loss'. However, lawyers do not deny the preventive measure of liability rules. As the Austrian Professor of civil law Bydlinski has put it (2002, 201): 'the menace of indemnification . . . ultimately should be . . . thorough action'. However, punishment is not the primary concern of tort law. It is noteworthy that even lawyers hold that there should be a certain proportionality between fault and the size of liability. Interestingly, this is in contrast to the civil code, which basically applies to the compensation of harm according to accountability; that is to say, the recovery of such a state as if no harm had taken place (recovery being possible as a monetary equivalent of damage or restitution in kind!).

The economists' viewpoint is slightly different. First, an economist's concern is the valuation of damage in money terms (pounds, dollars, euros). This seems to be straightforward but is not always easily accomplished, especially when it is not material damages that are at stake but less tangible damages, such as pain and suffering. One of the most delicate and controversial issues is the valuation of human life in cases of bodily harm with fatal consequences. As has been pointed out, valuations are needed in the investigations and recommendations concerning effective deterrents. In fact, economists are most concerned with the question of whether tort law contains incentives which can effectively influence attitudes towards risk. Moreover it is not short-term effectiveness that is the primary aim but rather efficiency in the long run.

So, when and to what extent are legal norms desirable?

The answer starts once more from the notion of 'externality'. An externality effectuates when a welfare-enhancing activity by one person affects the utility of someone else. So, no steps towards internalization are necessary as long as no third parties are affected. The reason for this is that in the situation at hand all risks remain with the acting person. However, if a third party is affected – that is to say, suffers harm – then the effectuating person will still enjoy the entire utility but will bear only those risks that accrue to her. Consequently, she has an incentive to take a higher risk than she is willing to bear. Given our basic model of human actions, from this we may infer that the (potentially) affected person may be willing to pay a certain sum of money in order to be less exposed to risks. However, there is no market for this kind of deal ex ante. For example, consider the risks associated with fast driving. In other words, there is no room for Coase-like bargaining, and because of this, an effective legal norm is the appropriate means here. The purpose is to influence action in such a way that the probability of damage is minimized.

This applies to the originator as well as to the victim (as we will call the affected person from now on). Potential originators should be required to observe an appropriate level of care. The victims in turn must not have blind trust in their safety. They must take precautions instead. For our next step, however, we will assume that harm is solely attributed to the originator. Thus it is her level of care that is at stake now. This case is labelled 'unilateral' damage (to illustrate, imagine the situation in which a pedestrian patiently waits for a chance to cross the road but is hit by a car because the driver loses control due to excessive speed).

For such singular events we are now in search for the 'optimal' level of care. The originator must be induced to perform this optimal level of care. This task is accomplished by liability for harm as stated in the legal norm (according to our tasks we abstract from ethical or humanitarian aspects of harmful activities here).

Negligence rule versus strict liability

Essentially a liability rule can follow the two lines indicated in the title. However, there is a third possibility, some kind of market solution, where property rights are exchanged. We will first investigate the first two and then briefly summarize the third. Some simplifying assumptions will be retained, especially those concerning the absence of insurance for risk. Let me explain strict liability first.

The essence of this liability rule is that the cost of potential damage (risk) is allotted to the presumed originator irrespective of the level of care she performs in her actions.

The intentions and consequences of such a rule are as follows. First, marketed commodities can cause harm to the purchaser (user) even with appropriate use; harm can take on the form of a decrease in utility or loss of wealth. The reason for the risk of harm is that there is some residual probability of a faulty product being brought to the market even in case of rigorous quality controls. The risk remains with the producer (or the seller) irrespective of her claim to have observed the utmost possible care. However, will such a rule give rise to efficient action on behalf of the potential originator of damage and harm? The answer to this question is that this depends on what is held to be a reasonable compensation for damage or harm. One can show that the establishment of the personal state which would have been accomplished had there not been damage could bring about the optimal (efficient) incentive to the (potential) originator of damage. However, it strongly depends on the possibility of calculating the exact amount of compensation (typically in the case of a defective product or potential harm caused by an accident, not so much in cases of nuisance, in which the compensation can be complemented by inhibition *pro futuro*)!

The caveat concerning the exact valuation of compensation points to a flaw in the effectuation of strict liability since intervening variables may ultimately cause calculations to be too high or too low as compared to the optimum. In such instances also the incentives are suboptimal. We leave it at that for the moment and shall return to strict liability rule later on.

The negligence rule naturally comes from the same underlying idea as the strict liability rule, and more specifically from the accomplishment of a certain conduct in the presence of potentially harmful negative externalities. The basic difference is that of the specification of a certain code of conduct together with a liability rule as an incentive for compliance. Let us look at an illustrative example. Consider a skating rink, where all the skaters except one are exercising with an appropriate level of care. If the one reckless skater speeds such that she endangers all the others she alone will be made liable for any harm since she did not observe an appropriate level of care that would have made skating safe for all other people on the skating rink.

Even if the basic idea sounds plausible it is tricky to realize. To see this we must be aware of the difficulty in defining the cause of liability. This, in turn, depends on whether we accept a standard of care which excludes a person from becoming liable for negligent action. Only when an appropriate standard of care is defined can we try to shape the incentives in terms of those sanctions that can help us accomplish our desired goal.

Scholars of law and economics have established standards of care as well as schemes for compensation which contain a fairly radical renunciation from those as laid down in legal norms by lawyers; the Austrian Civil Code (section 30, §1293 passim) may serve as an illustrative example here.

Surprisingly, at the beginning of the analytical foundation for standards of care there is an opinion following the judicial decision by judge Learned Hand of the 2nd circuit in a case of 1947 (*United States vs Carroll Towing Co.*, 159, F2d 169). (Incidentally, Learned Hand is extremely popular, so popular in fact that when he published his autobiography in 1973, it immediately became a bestseller!)

Finding out what negligence is using the 'formula of Learned Hand'

In order to understand the **Learned Hand formula**, let us first briefly go through the events that underlie that remarkable judicial decision. To do this we need to imagine the busy harbour of New York, where several barges were secured by one single mooring line, all of them carrying cargo. Now, a tugboat (whose skipper was later a defendant in the court case) approaches in order to pull out one of the barges. The crew wanted the skipper of the barge to assist with releasing the barge at hand, since all of them were tied to the identical mooring line, but they could not find anyone on board. So they did it themselves, but somehow they did not properly secure the remaining barges after having removed the one they towed away. One of the remaining barges broke loose, hit another and because of the collision the latter sank with all its cargo on board.

Consequently, the owner of the sunken vessel sued the owner of the tugboat for negligence causing loss of the barge and cargo. Clearly the skipper of the tugboat argued that the barge owner was at least a contributory to the negligence since he was not on board when there was a request.

How did Learned Hand judge in this suit?

Well, in his decision he explained that the obligation of a skipper is the same as that in other comparable situations where steps in order to avoid damage ought to be taken. Such a situation hinges on the interplay of three variables:

1 the probability that a barge breaks free
2 the severity of damage in case she breaks free
3 the burden of appropriate precautionary steps.

Let P stand for probability of breaking free, V for damage and B for provisions: so we have to find out if $B < PV$.

What does this mean? Let us pursue the judge's explanation. Of course one cannot expect a skipper or barge owner to be present on her vessel all the time. However, if she went ashore for her own entertainment it can be expected that she will have an eye on the barge or at least leave an assistant in charge, given the immense traffic in the harbour at that time. Generalizing this reasoning boils down to the argument that a person becomes liable if the reasonable level of care was lower than the **expected damage** (the loss times the probability of occurrence). The maximum reasonable care is given by B = PV. Given the low opportunity cost of entertainment the owner of the barge that broke loose definitely could have avoided the incident by increasing B, since she easily would still have met the condition as just stated in algebraic form.

This was a good start but not yet satisfactory for the economist. Economists would have asked for the change in expected damage due to a change of precautions or, more technically, what the marginal conditions are. Let us follow the economists' request. To do this, we first specify that both the amount of damage and the probability of occurrence can be influenced by the variation in the level of care. We get:

$$V = V(B) \text{ and } P = P(B)$$

The requirement is the minimization of total costs K (from precautions and expected damage), that is:

$$K = p(B) * V(B) + B$$

We find the optimality condition of the first derivative with respect to our instrumental variable B, and setting it equal to zero:

$$\delta K/\delta B = 0 = (\delta p/\delta B)* V + (\delta V/\delta B)*p + 1$$

In words, the marginal version of Learned Hand's formula requires the sum of marginal changes to equal −1.

It must not be denied that the quantification of each of the three figures in our formula is a tricky undertaking. But still the message contained in the result is that a judge might proceed by asking whether a little more care could have substantially lowered the risk. The Learned Hand formula is a good starting point for such procedure. With respect to the original setting, where the defendant blamed the plaintiff for having neglected her duties, so that in fact the court had to find out which of the two parties involved was to be blamed for wrongdoing, the result (the opinion) contains something which we will pick up on again later: the idea that an economically sound solution to problems of nuisance is to identify the 'cheapest cost avoider' – which is exactly what has been done in the case at hand.

Before we conclude our presentation of Hand's formula we ought to take up the economists' idea about preventive effect of indemnities once more. Recall that we have claimed that the provisions in tort law in this regard are rather weak. Are there suggestions for improvements that follow from Hand's formula? To see this let us assume that a liability rule allows for full monetary compensation of material damages. But can such regulation have a deterrent effect on potential wrongdoers? The answer is no! Even if the damage is evident the suspect must be identified and convicted, which will happen only with a certain probability. This is a well-known weakness in law enforcement. And the immediate consequence is that the compensation must be substantially higher than just the damage. We can visualize this by assuming a so-called zero sum game between the suspect and the victim. Gains for the suspect, ΔB, and losses for the victim, ΔV, will then give the total of $\Delta B - \Delta V = 0$. As long as the probability of enforcement of compensation is below 1 the suspect (the wrongdoer) has no incentive to change her attitudes.

This is what Learned Hand ultimately says: a person becomes liable if she does not observe appropriate precautions when from an action she draws advantages that are smaller than the expected damages due to a negative externality. From this view we get one step further with respect to the compensation necessary to work as a deterrent. Besides the probability that damage P occurs, the compensation needs to be executed, which will be possible with a certain probability Q only. What we get from this reasoning is a formula that gives rise to the possibility of furnishing tort law with a deterrent, taking the form $B \leq P \cdot Q \cdot V$. Stated differently, the amount of compensation must be a multiple of the damage; more specifically, it must be inversely proportional to the probability of enforcement. The lower this probability, the higher the compensation has to be – in order to become effective as deterrent, of course! The problem is that this finding approximates compensation for damage, which is thought to be in the first instance a deterrent to punishment, a measure usually associated with criminal law (on which there is more in Chapter 4)!

Baffling: corresponding incentives of strict liability and negligence rule

Let us dig a little deeper to find out what strict liability and negligence have in common and where they are different. First, we want to find whether and how optimal incentives can be created by each of the liability rules at hand. Second, we will ask if there are typical situations where one or the other is preferable.

We will start with incentives. Incentives are aimed at inducing people to observe an appropriate level of care or diligence. One proxy for care is precautionary steps people take in their activities. In the Austrian civil Code, for example, care is defined as a 'certain degree of industry and alertness'. The code continues by stating that all people are expected to be capable of industry and alertness, if it can be presumed that they are lucid and thus perform a level of care which can be expected of someone with average abilities. Furthermore, someone who acts in such a way that the rights of others are infringed and at the same time does not observe the principles of industry and alertness, is at fault of an oversight. We will use the term 'care' instead, however, and 'precaution' for the performance of care.

The problem here is not just to effectuate an efficient level of care, the tricky issue at hand is to find some objective standard of care. This is what is needed in order to find out which of the two rules is preferable under certain circumstances. If it were a subjective standard of care, the only sensible rule would be strict liability; only strict liability leaves the responsibility entirely with the tortfeasor, which makes it superfluous for a court to find out the actual level of care. It will be obliged to assess the damage instead (we abstract from complications such as the consequences for finding the truth if the presumed tortfeasor presents a proof of her innocence). So the whole exercise at hand makes sense only if we aim towards an objective measure.

Recall that we are starting from the simplistic scenario of **unilateral causation** of harm due to a violation of the law. We ought to establish the conditions for the incentives to act carefully under each of the two rules (or, as they are sometimes termed, 'regimes') at our disposal. The overall goal of our exercise is to accomplish maximum welfare (since we do not only take into account the beneficial effects of an effective incentive scheme but also the costs).

Welfare is calculated from *utility* (or wealth) accruing to the tortfeasor from her action minus the *cost of performance of care* (precaution) minus *expected loss of wealth due to damages*. The cost for performance of care can readily be assumed to increase with precautions. Expected losses of wealth will decrease with precautions (recall the discussion of the Hand formula, where it was assumed that both the probability of occurrence and the severity of loss are affected by precautions). The value of the tortfeasor's actions remains unaffected.

We can now derive the optimal level of care (precautions) by minimizing the total cost for the action at hand. Given our assumptions on costs and benefits and those of a *homo oeconomicus* acting there is a minimum of costs, as shown in Figure 3.4.

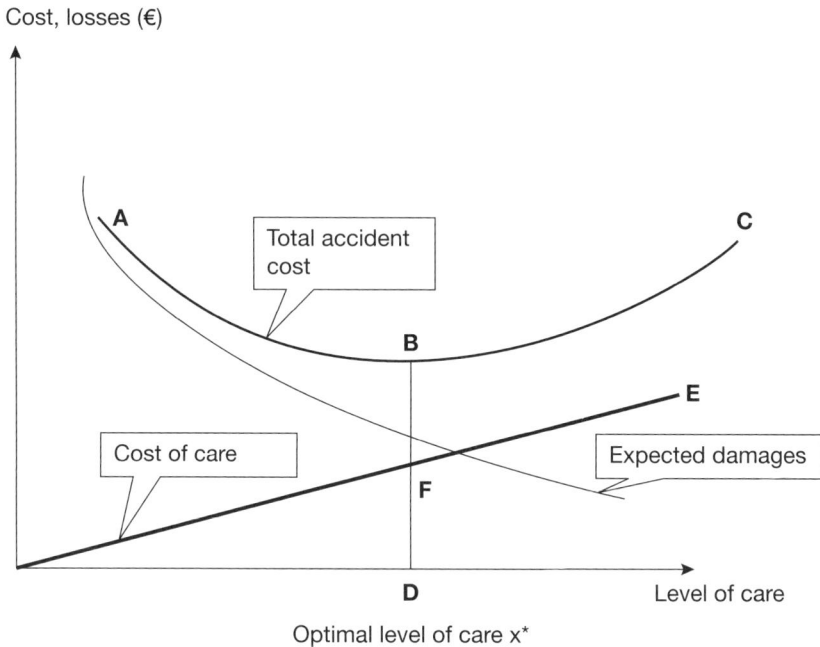

Figure 3.4 Optimal level of care with different liability rules

With the negligence rule, the tortfeasor faces cost along AB, if her level of care is lower than or just optimal, and FE, if observing a suboptimal high level of care. So the best thing to do is to observe the optimal level of care x*. With strict liability the cost for the tortfeasor would be ABC, so she can be expected to observe optimal care, which minimizes her costs.

Source: After Shavell, 1987, 35.

It is exactly this minimum which a tortfeasor will observe. The corresponding level of care is our reference standard!

It is derived as follows. The line OF depicts the (monotonically increasing) cost of precaution x. The downward sloping curve DE indicates that the risk of damage p(x). V(x) decreases as x is increased.

The curve ABC results from the vertical sum of OF and DE, and is the total cost.

The optimal level of precautions is where the cost ABC are minimal, which is at X* and B respectively.

Now let us consider a regime of negligence. With negligence the tortfeasor will have to bear all costs if she misses the due standard of care. But by increasing her efforts she can lower the costs she faces down to point B. To the right of B additional precautions do not pay: even if she is not liable any longer (since she shows good conduct), she would face higher cost due to the now dominating cost of precautions OF. So the best thing to do is to perform the optimal level of precautions X*. What about strict liability? With strict liability the entire curve ABC is the schedule for liability, irrespective of the level of precautions. But under these circumstances the rational tortfeasor can minimize cost by performing optimal precaution at X*.

We get the result that under the conditions and assumptions at hand both regimes contain incentives in the same direction: to exercise optimal care!

However, we must not stop here, since we would not account for some distinctions.

I will deal with one of the important differences in the next paragraph. As things are, it may be the case that in order to minimize the risk of damages both potentially involved parties must see to their precautions. It is the negligence rule that creates the appropriate incentives, whereas the strict liability rule unburdens one side, thus possibly inducing this party to avoid negligence.

Moreover, strict liability as with the product liability of manufacturers puts pressure on them to explore, invest and make use of advanced technologies to lower the risk of damages, whereas with negligence it suffices for them to perform with optimal care under the given circumstances.

Unfortunately, strict liability may become effective only when a victim claims damages in court (by seeking a lawsuit). If victims fail to do so, potential tortfeasors very likely can be expected to lower their efforts to a suboptimal level of care.

This is not the end of the story, however, since we will have to take a closer look on some other circumstances. One typical problem turns up when we drop the assumption that the harmful activity is carried out only once.

What does it mean for liability rules if an activity is carried out more frequently?

Let me start with the illustration of some typical activities that can be exercised with variable frequency: skiing, for example. You may go skiing a couple of days each year or two weeks. Clearly the probability that you fall or – which is more important here – collide with someone else increases with the frequency of the activity. But what about your precautions to avoid collision under the two rules at hand?

Under the negligence rule, given your awareness of liability, it can readily be assumed that you will ski in a way which is non-negligent. However, this refers to the activity performed, not to the frequency of the activity. Thus the risks involved in a lot of skiing are shifted away from you! With strict liability instead, you must face the entire cost of causing a collision with another (less experienced) skier. But that implies that you certainly take into consideration the precautions at each separate occasion and the total amount of the activity as well!

Another perspective becomes apparent when we consider someone who is in the trucking business. If this person thinks of an enlargement of her fleet of trucks then considerations of liability are definitely important. Imagine the enlargement of the fleet of trucks under the negligence rule. The need for precautions will rise with the number of trucks and it may therefore be the case that the optimal level is passed or, in other words, the entrepreneur becomes liable because of negligence just because she operates 'too many' trucks.

Again, a strict liability rule will induce her to consider all costs associated with each of the additional trucks as well as their operation.

While it appears obvious which of the two regimes is to be preferred here there is also a downside, since strict liability means an exoneration from care for potential victims. On the contrary, a negligence rule advises potential victims to observe optimal care as well.

It is also noteworthy that in the course of a trial, strict liability might lead to savings in administrative costs concerning causation and responsibility as compared to the negligence rule, where the proof of causation can be very tricky, time consuming and thus expensive. Clearly, this does not hold in cases where the defendant attempts to bring evidence that the plaintiff acted in a grossly negligent way by ignoring warnings on the product at hand or in instruction manuals. In such cases, high costs are inevitable, but this does not invalidate the overall advantages of strict liability with respect to administrative costs.

Nevertheless, policymakers may be left with a dilemma when they are looking for the 'best' regime and they will be in need of a complimentary measure when they rely on the strict liability rule, which taken by itself is reasonable, but with the drawbacks mentioned earlier.

Whom to charge in cases of contributory negligence and unclear responsibilities?

Contributory negligence

Let us again look at an example in our imaginary skiing resort: an average skier gets to the edge of a slope with an obvious sign warning that it is very steep and recommended for very experienced skiers only. If our average skier proceeds, falls and breaks a leg we could readily assume that she did not observe the appropriate level of precaution. She will hardly recover the costs of hospital treatment and lost earnings from those who maintain the run (usually the operators of the local skilifts).

But assume now that the sign was there but half-covered with snow or even damaged by a recent storm. It may then not be immediately discernible for the skier what danger awaits her. So even if she proceeds at too high a speed given the difficulties ahead, the maintainer of the slope will be blamed for not making sure that the warning was properly visible.

In the latter case, **contributory negligence** will apply, since both sides can be blamed for having acted negligently.

The interesting thing here is that only a negligence rule could give the appropriate incentives (insurance notwithstanding) for both sides (see if you can explain why). A strict liability rule will fail.

However, we must be aware of the conditions under which we have formulated our findings. First of all, we started from a position of neutrality towards risk, and moreover we alleged that we were dealing with fully informed parties and also the parties were assumed to be **solvent**. This is a quite important assumption particularly if firms are involved since with severe damages firms are in danger of becoming insolvent due to high levels of compensation; they could also use alleged insolvency as a threat! Finally, the absence of **litigation** cost is presumed. Further interesting questions remain. For example, what to do (from an economist's point of view), when at the outset it is unclear whom to burden in case of damage. By answering this question we get to the notion of a **least cost avoider**.

The least cost avoider

This concept can be exemplified by stating that the responsibility for damages lies with the person who could have avoided harm at least cost. You will recognize that this principle was already present in the opinion of Learned Hand! By way of illustration, there are two people, Peter and Paul, involved in an accident, which caused harm amounting to €10,000. Peter could have averted the accident at a cost of €200, whereas Paul could have done it at only €100, so Paul is liable – following the prevailing principle of minimizing overall (social) costs. Let us look at an example of a case of failure to follow this principle.

A European importer of crude oil orders a shipload of crude oil from an oil-producing firm in the Middle East. Before the contractor can perform, fighting starts (again), interrupting the supply and thus inhibiting timely delivery. The delay causes substantial losses for the importer. She sues for compensation, but the contractor claims *force majeure*. The court, however, refuses the claim and rules on compensation. The economically correct opinion is that the importer cannot correctly assess the risks involved in production and transportation from a highly unstable region like the Middle East and take appropriate measures. A firm specializing in this kind of business in that area must be familiar with the particular risks of her business and take provisions for performance – such as a secondary supply. So the contractor is the least cost avoider.

Looking for the least cost avoider, in turn, fits into the overall goal of minimizing the (social) costs in the course of handling the legal and economic problems of damage (originating from negative externalities or accidents or whatsoever). Naturally, it is not the only issue in that respect.

A more comprehensive framework would also comprise the following entities besides the least cost avoider:

- the **cheapest insurer**
- the **cheapest briber**.

In the target of minimizing the social costs of optimal prevention of damages or 'deterrence' all three entries ought to be included. Although this concept was first proposed by Guido Calabresi in his seminal book *The Cost of Accidents* (1970), its scope is rather a general one.

To start with, we follow Calabresi in making the distinction between a **general deterrence** and a **specific deterrence**, where general deterrence refers to the fact that each activity generally entails some (opportunity) costs including those for likely consequences of the activity at hand. Our behavioural assumptions imply that the perception of such costs will lead to the attempt to keep them minimal, specifically when adverse effects are involved. This being the case social costs are automatically kept low, thus effectuating the said general deterrence.

Specific deterrence refers to the various negligent actions from which damages originate. It aims at preventing the violation of property rights and disregarding liability rules respectively by establishing appropriate sanctions along with other efficacious means. However, there are several kinds of cost linked to measures of specific deterrence. Therefore, means are sought which help to keep these costs at a minimum. Table 3.5 gives an overview over the sources of costs and likely ways of keeping them low.

Of these three entries the second one has been the most neglected. This is due to the assumption of risk neutrality, which in turn excludes the need to consider insurance! However, what will be the consequences of insurance here? Using the example of the increase of the number of trucks in the hauling firm, we can see that strict liability will lead to a relief for potential victims, which, in turn, must find support from a cost–benefit analysis of the advantages and disadvantages of that regime by government – thus hopefully reflecting the result of a carefully applied Kaldor-Hicks test.

Things may change, when a firm like the hauling firm in our example buys insurance. Insurance may weaken the incentives for optimal care, which would have to be taken into consideration in assessing the cheapest insurer.

Tracing this idea further, it could well be that risk-averse victims also buy insurance since they are afraid of the costs accruing to them in the event of loss. However, by giving up one of the essential assumptions we have made in order to keep the explanation of problems simple, substantial changes in our calculations are very likely, inasmuch as the shape of utility functions changes from linearity to convexity, thus giving rise to quite different optimal solutions of our minimization problem of social cost. So, we ought to come back to the consequences of relaxing our original assumptions eventually.

Table 3.5 Sources of costs and keeping them low

Type of cost	Assignment
Primary cost First of all, they contain the cost depending on the severity and frequency of incidences; moreover the cost of preventive measures are to be included here	Least cost avoider ('who is capable of getting around losses at the minimum cost?')
Secondary cost These are the cost of maintenance for victims as well as compensation. Burdens stemming from these sources can be lowered through appropriate measures such as risk spreading via insurance. Alternatively, governments could step in as frequently is the case with hazards; this is called 'deep pocket'	Cheapest insurer ('what is the most reasonable way of dealing with potential victims and of handling claims to compensation?')
Tertiary cost In the event of loss, various administrative activities are needed such as investigations to the reasons of losses, the identification of responsibilities and so on	Cheapest briber ('how can efforts for the clarification of facts and enforcement be kept to a minimum?')

A third way?

Besides negligence and strict liability there is a third possibility for establishing liability. This possibility consists of a 'market for damage claims'. At that point you might observe that from a certain perspective the Coase theorem has already established a kind of market solution for the internalization of externalities. Following this line of reasoning we could include damage claims as contingencies to a contract. Such contingencies in contracts become effective when the damage occurs. In other words, the probability of damage gives rise to a certain market value of the relevant stipulations in the contract.

Equilibrium prices of such a market inclusive of contingencies will thus reflect the stipulated claims. Note that under this regime the potential tortfeasor could buy the entitlement to compensation from the potential victim and thus become exempt from liability once it is applicable! Under certain circumstances concerning information and the symmetry of initial conditions (including the level of transaction costs accruing to each of the parties involved) prices will reflect precisely the external costs a tortfeasor inflicts on the victim; more precisely the costs will be equal to the damage a court would assess times the probability of occurrence.

Hence, the externalities could be internalized via a market.

Interestingly enough neither law nor court seems to appreciate such a solution. If in a legal transaction exclusion of liability is stipulated (which must necessarily be reflected in the price for that transaction) and the case goes to trial for some reason, a court will not accept the clause! However, there are cases where the preclusion of trade of damage claims – as requested by the courts – has been successfully circumvented. Apparently there are firms that specialize in purchasing patents just in order to avail themselves of damage claims due to violations of the patents – without ever having considered making use of the patent itself.

Contracts

Prologue

Life abounds with situations that entail a contract. Consider the following three illustrations:

- you board a commuter train
- you buy a bottle of mineral water
- you rent a flat.

What do these illustrations have in common and in what respect are they different?

Boarding a commuter train entails acknowledgement of the terms of carriage, but without explicit negotiations. That is to say, by boarding the train you are assumed to accept the stipulated terms. Still a conflict could arise if you were accused of not having met all the terms (because you are not holding a valid ticket) or, likewise, you blame the carrier for not adhering to the conditions stated in the timetable and terms of carriage (cancellation of the selected train, for example). A conflict can thus emerge that may eventually end in litigation. What we should stress here, however, is the way in which such contracts are normally established: they are concluded *tacitly*.

Buying a bottle of mineral water very much follows they same pattern. You may enter the store, take a bottle out of the fridge and move towards the cashier. There is no need to negotiate at all! Still the product may turn out to be unpalatable, with unpleasant consequences on drinking it (as long as you do not consider the transaction costs to be too high to justify replacement).

Renting a flat might be entirely different, inasmuch as you would necessarily pass through several steps from making inquiries about locations, specific properties and conditions, possibly bargaining and finally negotiating the content of the contract. In this case several complications are at stake from the outset. You are at risk of being deceived, the landlord may not believe that you are able to pay and so on. Therefore, to ease negotiations on essential parts of the deal as well as to establish incentives to comply, it appears worthwhile to set up an inventory as well as conditions of relinquishment, which establish the core of the contract (in practice, since the issues are very much alike in every deal of that kind, standard contracts are in use, which we shall address below). Liability rules reflect the risks of misconduct and by the same token state the allocation of costs in case the misconduct occurs.

Other examples pertain to all kinds of consumer durable and more specifically to custom-made products such as a piece of furniture. We will consider such an example in more detail later.

In the meantime, we ought to be aware that there are **long-term contracts** that entail peculiar problems. Consider continuing obligations such as a (open-ended) labour contract. Since there cannot be perfect prediction as to what contingencies may turn up in the course of time, such contracts need to contain fairly robust stipulations in order to provide guidance in case of (yet unexpected) trouble.

It should finally be pointed out that the rapidly expanding body of work on corporate law is to a large extent based on a contractual approach to enterprises (see Chapter 6 for an outline).

To come back to our main concern here we ought to define a contract as a bilateral or multilateral covenant, which establishes binding rules for the partners.

Note in passing that there are also unilateral covenants, such as wills or donations, which would be worth discussing. However, limited space requires them to be sacrificed.

For the purely legal aspects of contracts readers are referred to Bydlinski (2002, Part 3), for a discussion representative for civil law countries, whereas Hay (2005, Chapter 5) is a recommended reference for contracts in common law.

Theoretical foundations for analysis of contractual relations

In the theory of (perfect) markets contracts are somewhat truncated. The coordination between demand and supply is maintained by an equilibrium price. Fully informed participants in that markets have no option to act strategically. Not even bargaining is considered because of the absence of transaction costs and externalities.

A microeconomic theory of contracts only emerges when the assumption is dropped that all parties are fully informed. More specifically, economists have become interested in the possibility of and conditions for (partial) equilibria, when only one side has exclusive information. This is equivalent to a monopoly over the non-informed party. Thus the informed party has the potential to act strategically. Given this initial situation the question emerges whether an optimal solution in the sense of Pareto efficiency is possible at all.

Before we review the framework for the study of this kind of question it is worth pointing out how (orthodox) economists tend look at contracts. First, they would consider every effective institutional constraint as a contract, whether it exists in written form or just as a sort of implicit rule of conduct. Moreover, in the first case the implicit underpinning of the orthodoxy is that the 'contract' can be enforced by courts without difficulty.

And here is the crucial point: economic analysis of law wants to find out whether courts are capable of efficient enforcement.

With respect to methodology, however, we observe a convergence, inasmuch as more and more game theory (the theory of non-cooperative games) comes into use (the leading reference here being Baird, Gertner and Picker, 2003).

Now we will turn to the models in use for the study of contracting under the assumption of asymmetric information. There are three (a more comprehensive treatment is found in Salanié, 2005) which have in common the basic structure of the relationship between a principal (the client of a medical doctor, for example) and the agent (the doctor himself) – and are therefore simply named 'principal–agent models'. The three specifications of the model are the following:

1   *Adverse selection*: under asymmetric information an agent such as an insurer cannot tell what hazard category the principal or insured person belongs to. Consequently the insurer is at risk of losing the customer who prefers to go uninsured because she feels she is cautious enough.
2   *Moral hazard*: people who enjoy coverage from insurance tend to be less cautious than people who are not insured.
3   *Signalling*: here an informed person enjoys an advantage over an uninformed person and may reveal certain characteristics, such as diplomas received, in order to convince her opponent of her qualifications, although the latter has no chance of verification.

So sometimes **hidden information** is present and sometimes **hidden action**. The situation at hand can be classified according to these characteristics.

Armed with these fundamentals we can now ask what the purpose of an economic analysis of contract law might be. This purpose is twofold:

•   Whenever a contract turns out to be faulty, there ought to be rules which will facilitate efficiency. More specifically such rules ought to support a certain assignment as well as the conditions under which it can be accomplished. They should lead to the same result that would have been stipulated in a perfect contract. The said result must match the criterion of Pareto efficiency or, alternatively, its pragmatic counterpart, the Kaldor-Hicks test (which you certainly will remember from Chapter 2?).

    The rationale behind this is that a contractual relation can be brought about among parties who do not know each other beforehand and therefore do not necessarily trust each other. However, the sanctions imposed by the rules are deterrents for misconduct.

•   Moreover, when establishing the contractual rules, legislators should be aware that judges or the courts are also at risk, either of making mistakes when handling a case or of self-interest. Consequently, the regulations need to create incentives so as to preclude all undesirable consequences.

Such advice would hardly be necessary if contracts were perfect. Perfect contracts would bring about Pareto superior allocations automatically, so to speak, but this in turn requires fully informed partners, of a sufficient number not to give rise to mutual dependencies. There must not be any frictions, which are sources of transaction costs. Finally, the contractual relations should not give rise to externalities (thus burdening third parties).

Given these conditions, contracts would:

•   convey all contingencies; that is to say, deal with circumstances that could otherwise hamper performance and thus make contracts suboptimal (examples

are delays, deficiencies, obstacles to delivery, damage in the course of delivery and the like)
- automatically warrant assignment of the risks of contingencies to the least cost avoider or, in case the risk can be somehow insured, to the cheapest insurer (note that we are generalizing the application of Calabresi's categories).

Not unexpectedly, contracts in real life are hardly ever perfect; otherwise this chapter would terminate here, except for one further point: we should be aware of a distinction between the perfect and the complete contract. A complete contract could, in theory, contain every contingency imaginable, so that the outcome meets the conditions for perfection. Interestingly, contracts could be composed in a way which despite the absence of detailed clauses gives rise to completeness. To illustrate: 'Winegrower A by contract delivers 12 bottles of her Chardonnay 2003 tomorrow morning, payable in cash at delivery.'

Despite its briefness this contract leaves no leeway for either side. Chardonnay for cash, that is all! If the winegrower were to have an accident during delivery, she would have to try hard to comply since there is no escape clause . . . that is to say, although no contingencies are listed in the contract, so that it is strictly speaking not complete, it is perfect.

But let us turn to the world of imperfections. Defective contracts are not likely to bring about an allocation which is Pareto superior to the initial state or which does not match the Kaldor–Hicks test.

We are interested in contracts dealing with more complex issues such as renting an apartment or buying a suit. We will leave aside the type of contracts that have been illustrated by the purchase of a cold drink or the use of a commuter train. What we will also not do here is go into details of the law. Readers are referred to Bydlinski (2002) or Hay (2005) for the legal aspects.

However, we will make use of the economic notions mentioned in the introduction to this section, more specifically, the distinction of hidden information and hidden action, that is to say the typical problems that are present, if either side cannot observe what the other side is actually doing, as is the case in principal–agent relationships.

With imperfect contracts, we may find two different situations:

- first, no contract has been accomplished at all (for instance, one party did not have an authorization to negotiate)
- second, a situation where the stipulated contract is not invalid as such, but where processing turns out to be flawed without provisions, thus making the contract an imperfect one (missing rules for contingencies!) and most likely giving rise to a conflict.

As we can see from these two illustrative examples, contracts do not necessarily need to be enforceable. In fact, they can be void for various reasons, not just the two just mentioned. Let us examine them in more detail.

- As far as flaws in the accomplishment of the contract are concerned, besides of the missing authority to negotiate, they may be caused by the exertion of force, (mutual) error or distortion of facts.
- Obstacles to performance are unforeseeable events, not necessarily only *force majeure* (e.g. when a venue is destroyed by fire before an event took place, also the aforementioned missing stipulations for contingencies).

Several questions arise. First of all, we should find why an obstacle developed. It would be even more interesting to find out if someone in particular was responsible for the obstacle and if this originator can be made liable. The spirit of our economic analysis would also call for the question of whether the obstacles could have been avoided ex ante by setting appropriate incentives for originators.

In order to locate responsibilities it is crucial to ask whether in the course of the initiation of the contract either side has made a **promise**. If such a promise has been made any obstacle to performance except *force majeure* must be qualified as breach of contract; breach of contract in turn may give rise to compensation according to the prevailing circumstances.

It appears to be perfectly in line with our model of human action to assume that both sides to a contract that bestows a Pareto improvement must be interested in provisions for performance. On the side of the contractor, such provisions take the form of precautionary steps, which may, of course, be costly. The customer in turn could rely on timely delivery to a greater or lesser extent and could thus incur expenditures that are related to expected performance. We will have a closer look at both of these aspects, precaution and reliance, later. In the more detailed discussion, we must bear in mind that our provisions ought to meet two requests: one refers to flawed but still enforceable contracts and the other to breach of a contract (which makes performance impossible).

Note that meeting these requests could be at variance with hidden information, which could be in the interest of either side for whatever reason. In case of unequal starting conditions due to asymmetries in information the less advantageous party will only be able to enforce relinquishment of the necessary information when she disposes of a credible threat! Use of such a threat can become quite costly.

Hidden action might pose as severe problems as hidden information. Hidden action may emanate from opportunistic behaviour (e.g. foul play or deception). In case one side to the contracts acts opportunistically, detection and surveillance can become very costly for the other!

On top of all these complications, contracts can become more costly the more details are stipulated. Unfortunately, if details are omitted for the sake of thrift, contingencies that will become a source of conflict (and costs) ex post may be missing. This in turn could terminate in the need for mediation, settlement or even trial. These issues are reserved for Chapter 4, in the section on law enforcement.

Breach of contract

We will now deal with situations in which one or both parties do not perform. As has already been mentioned, non-performance can be accidental, negligent or grossly negligent. These cases are associated with different degrees of lack in precaution or inappropriate reliance. The most interesting cases, however, are those where a party consciously (on purpose) withdraws from the contract. This party may have realized that conditions have changed or new opportunities have turned up, which are more promising than the original stipulations. In economic terms: the originally stipulated contract no longer warrants a Pareto improvement. For our *homo oeconomicus*, it is thus rational to breach if unforeseen loss can be avoided or an unexpected and better option pursued. Note that in this case breach may or may not be profitable from the viewpoint of overall welfare. Therefore we must specify:

* Only a breach of contract that meets the Kaldor-Hicks test is termed an **optimal breach of contract**. We must stress here that this is a matter of economics, not of morals!
* Breach, for whatsoever reason, inevitably causes damage for one party. These damages (welfare losses) ought to be either withheld (recall the importance of ex ante considerations in the economic analysis of law) or compensated (something which the defaulting party will not necessarily do voluntarily).

Consequently, we need provisos for both deterrence ex ante and indemnities ex post. We will do this in three steps. First, we will look at the available measures, next we will check their effectiveness and finally we will assess which measures are best suited to certain situations.

The available measures are:

* Compensation of all expected gains from the contract; in this case despite the breach of contract the obligee is put in the same economic position which she would have reached if the contract had been performed.
* Compensation for all expenses the obligee underwent on the expectation that the contract would be performed; thus the obligee is put in the same economic position she would have been in if she had not initiated the contract.
* No compensation, but return of prepayments or comparable outlays, so that economically it is as if the parties to the deal had never been in touch.

Besides these options, forfeits are possible, thus adding a flavour of punishment to the original measures. Moreover, courts could require performance, which boils down to the enforcement of keeping a promise. Finally, the parties to a contract could themselves stipulate warranties or penalties in case of breach.

We may now ask what the incentives and likely outcomes are stemming from the various possibilities just listed. An incentive to shy away from a breach is said to be a 'deterrent'; deterrents are effectuated by the (virtual) costs associated with the willingness to breach a contract. The size of these costs depends on several factors. The most prominent among these factors are the expenditures the obligee (customer) undergoes with respect to expected performance by the liable party. The present value of the expenditure can be viewed as a proxy for reliance on performance. They can be of substantial size: imagine someone who has ordered a garden shed. Expecting early delivery this person has meanwhile ordered the concrete base to be constructed, definitely a costly undertaking. While suboptimal large reliance has induced our obligee to incur a cost, the liable party must be aware of the need to compensate the customer for these outlays in case of non-performance. This in turn might induce her to prefer performance to any kind of breach – unless she unexpectedly receives a superior order, thus being inclined to an (optimal) breach. We will return to this idea later.

Another factor of major importance might be extensive preparations on behalf of the liable party in order to secure performance. Such efforts are a proxy for the precaution on behalf of the liable party (with reference to the order of a garden shed we could think of a carpenter who adjusts the loading space of her lorry to ensure the safe delivery of the garden shed). This example gives the opportunity to point out quite an important point in the problems surrounding performance. Even if the carpenter makes all efforts to deliver in time, there is some risk left that she might not be able to avoid. While an absolutely safe event has a probability of one, this might well be beyond the reach of a liable person ex ante even if she is willing to incur a very high cost in order to perform. There will always be a residual risk of an accident, say, which she cannot circumvent even with a maximum of precautions.

Before we can turn to an assessment of the various incentives, we must be aware of one more essential factor: the attitude towards risk of the parties to the contract, which we ought to address here briefly. Okay, you may object, and say that we have agreed only to consider risk neutrality of our protagonists. Nevertheless, it is quite important to deviate from our general line of reasoning in order to visualize the mode of action of our various measures. More specifically, if we want to prevent breach effectively, it is crucial for the selection of the appropriate measure to know whether either of the parties is risk averse, risk neutral or risk loving.

We start our investigations under the assumption of risk neutrality of both sides. We will relax this assumption slightly in order to examine the consequences.

To facilitate our undertaking, let us imagine the following situation: a contractor intends not to perform. She may intend to do so for several reasons. One could be that the cost of performing turns out to be considerably higher than assumed for the original offer; it could also be that a more rewarding customer turns up, with whom a new contract promises higher profit.

In order to keep our first round of reasoning as simple as possible we make three more assumptions. The first is that **renegotiation** is ruled out. Moreover, breach does not affect **reputation** (or, stated differently, the transactions are taking place totally independently from each other). And finally, the mode of payment is on account.

Now let us look at the likely effects of the three measures regarding liability. First, we look at compensation for all expected gains from the contract. In this case, the money value of the gain in utility by the garden shed under consideration as well as the outlays for the construction of the base – this being the proxy for the degree of reliance the customer places on performance – would have to be compensated for.

Since the money value of the garden shed will be slightly higher than its price and the profit of the carpenter is price minus cost, to which the compensation for reliance cost (the base) must be added, the total sum of damages that the carpenter ought to pay will exceed her profit substantially and thus give a strong incentive to perform. Damages for expected gain can obviously be an efficient means to prevent breach, since the welfare gain from performance is higher than that from breach.

A recommendation concerning legal policy will therefore boil down to the adoption of the measure of full damages for expected gains. The upshot here is that such a rule should ex ante make a trial avoidable and thus establish an economic means to secure performance.

Now let us inspect the second option, compensation for outlays made according to reliance. The cost for the carpenter will amount to the outlays for the pavement of the base. Moreover, in cases of payment on account she will have to give the money back. But now it obviously depends on whether our carpenter has an option for a better deal when she wants to breach the contract. All in all the second option is thus less effective as a deterrent. Our policy recommendation would therefore be not to take compensation for reliance as a means which ex ante can replace enforcement via the courts.

We can be very brief about the effectiveness of the third option now. If it is just return of accounts and minor outlays that are at stake, our carpenter, facing no option for renegotiation about the stipulated price but a more attractive demand by some other customer will hardly be induced to perform. In our policy recommendations we will therefore discourage the adoption of this possibility.

So we might conclude this section by one caveat and one additional observation – caveat first. Imagine a case of breach that goes to court. Imagine further that the law requires full compensation of lost utility plus outlays for reliance. For our judge a very familiar problem turns up: that of valuing the subjective gain in welfare on behalf of the plaintiff. In fact, the plaintiff could attempt to exploit the defendant in a certain sense. For the court this will be reflected in quite a high cost of investigations, a tertiary cost in the sense of Guido Calabresi (recall his three sources of a cost!). It comes as a little surprise that courts therefore shun conceding the money equivalent for lost utility! As an exception – as for the introduction of the Learned Hand formula – we will draw on a case in which the problems were solved by the court ruling that the victim is entitled only to the reasonably foreseeable loss from breach of contract. Only if the plaintiff (victim) had made plain to the later defendant what she intended to spend based on expectations, is the claim to full compensation held justified. If this was not the case the court would concede only compensation for comprehensible costs.

Such practical considerations concerning the qualification of the plaintiff's claims notwithstanding, the former promisee may find herself in a tricky strategic position concerning potential damages for breach. To see this imagine that our carpenter has made additional purchases of €300 since she relies on delivery of the garden shed in time. She expects the value of the entire facility to rise by €500 due to the additional expenses. Unfortunately, there is a 50:50 chance of breach on behalf of the carpenter, which brings the expected return down to €250, but at a cost of €300, which means that breach at this point is not inefficient at all.

Next, we take the little detour announced earlier and drop the assumption of risk neutrality for a moment.

Breach of contract when the parties are not neutral towards risk

At the outset I would like to point out that we will have just a glimpse at the types of problem that evolve from the changed conditions. It is beyond the scope of this introductory text to consider the full range of possibilities here (if you would like to find out more details about the issues in this section you could turn to Miceli, 1997, Chapters 4 and 5).

Let us first consider the following cases (we leave risk loving to a later paragraph) (see Table 3.6 for a summary of the situations).

Case one: in order to illustrate this case let us make use of the earlier example. Our carpenter has already stipulated the contract with the customer named Albert. Shortly afterwards she meets Ben, a customer who is willing to pay a higher price, but takes some time to think it over. Consequently the carpenter has one order from Albert, and a 50:50 chance of another, better order from Ben. To be risk neutral means that her expected gain increases monotonically with increasing profits, marginal utility thus being constant. Customer Albert, however, is now risk averse. That is to say, while he derives a certain utility from the arbour, he now faces as an alternative to enjoying his arbour a 50:50 risk of not being served, but compensated instead. Risk aversion implies that he values delivery more highly than the expected value from either compensation for breach or delivery (his utility function shows positive but decreasing marginal utility).

Applying the Kaldor-Hicks test to this situation requires that Albert is exempt from risk. This is the case when compensation equals the utility Albert would have derived from performance, because only then a customer enjoys compensation independently from the vendor's ultimate decision. The upshot is that all measures except full compensation for the gain fall short of the requirement for the assignment of risk!

Case two: in this case, we can make use of the insights we just gained. More specifically the risk must now be allotted to the customer, Albert. He is now

Table 3.6 Breach of contract where parties are not risk neutral

ARROW Vendor/customer ARROW]	*Risk neutral*	*Risk averse*
Risk neutral	Our standard – case	Case 1
Risk averse	Case 2	Case 3

indifferent as to whether performance and non-performance with compensation occurs. The carpenter in turn must be exempt from risk. Note that alternatively she could be insured, but since we have not yet introduced the institution of insurance, we ought to preclude this option here. There seems to be a strong incentive for a (profitable) breach and this requires a special measure of damages. In fact, our carpenter would have to pass on the entire gain arising from breach (including the higher price she receives from the preferred customer) to the aggrieved Albert. But the usual list of measures does not allow for this kind of damage.

Case three: here both parties are risk averse and this requires risk sharing among them. Who bears what amount of risk depends on the size of deviation in the options of the two parties. The party that has the higher difference in payoff, must bear a larger share of risk. Unfortunately, again neither of the measures for compensation will keep parties from breach.

So, what about risk-loving parties? There are certainly cases of practical importance, where a risk-averse seller meets a risk-loving buyer. Consider a situation where you intend to sell an old teddy bear before it becomes shabby and thus worthless. There are people who love teddies as collectibles and there are also people who specialize in the trade of collectibles, for instance, by buying old teddies because they expect to sell them at a profit. Here you, the seller, are risk averse, since you prefer selling your teddy to the chance of an increase in value or to missing the opportunity to sell it. The buyer in turn is risk loving since she is only purchasing the teddy because she is more confident of selling the teddy at a higher price later than to remain in possession. With respect to collectibles, there are many other examples, such as tin soldiers, dolls or model trains. Given the value of transactions, one prominent example of risk-loving contractors is found in the real estate business. Imagine someone who wants to sell land in a situation of financial distress. It may well be the case that the buyer purchases the property only because she expects to be granted the right to change the use of the land from farm land to residential use, which would be associated with a substantial increase in value.

We have not randomly chosen this example. Rather, the reason is that there are cases of breach (or the prevention of breach, of course) where the law (or the courts respectively) replace the demand for compensation by the demand for completion of the contract. That is to say, in the case of the seller being inclined to breach (for an unexpected better deal) a court would rule for performance rather than compensation. One condition for that type of dispute resolution is the resale value of the matter in dispute. To illustrate, let us look at a brand new average car: once it has been purchased the market value will immediately go down (its value deteriorates, since it is assumed to be a consumer durable). With a lot of land the situation is different. Market value is not dependent on use. If Bruno buys the lot from a seller Adam and then immediately sells it again to Cecily, Bruno is most likely making a profit (why otherwise should he accept the deal?). Since Adam could possibly have sold directly to Cecily himself and thus enjoy the entire welfare gain, the situation is entirely different from one concerning a consumer durable, where the second trade most likely will have incurred a loss by the time of resale. Therefore, if the deal with Cecily was accompanied by a breach, a court can easily forbear from damages by compensation and rule for performance.

Bruno will definitely be happy but Adam would have preferred compensation.

However, there are some implicit assumptions we are making if we leave it at this! First of all, we must be aware of legal costs. While in principle it is possible that the costs of the courts are fully borne by the taxpayers, this does not hold in practice. Moreover, damages by compensation together with just one endorsement mean a saving in transaction costs. The reason is simply that there would have been only one endorsement (Adam to Cecily) instead of two (Adam to Bruno and Bruno to Cecily) and thus only one consignment, one fee for registration and the like; this is a problem the courts are only too familiar with, reservation price of the buyer (the highest price the buyer would be willing to pay) notwithstanding. The court thus faces the problem of how to utilize asymmetric information on behalf of a client and subsequently almost insurmountable transaction costs in getting to a (sound) decision.

Indemnities and warranties

It is taken for granted that at the time of delivery a commodity has neither obvious nor hidden defects. This may still happen, but then the vendor is most probably liable. Note the implicit caveat in the statement: if there is no negligence on behalf of the vendor involved, *vis major* could apply, but it could also very well be the case that it is not the vendor but the manufacturer who is to blame for a deficiency. You will have realized that we are stressing the possibility here that a deal between a vendor and her customer also must concern the manufacturer of the commodity at hand. Both problems accruing to the customer from negligence either on behalf of the vendor or even from the manufacturer are usually covered by legal indemnities. However, it is exactly because of these legal indemnities that the question of why warranties are routinely offered is interesting. By granting a warranty the vendor vouches for certain properties of the material, its quality as expressed by appropriate measures, the assumption of the cost of repair or even replacement in case the item fails to function in the stipulated way.

Let us explore the reasons for such efforts. The literature provides two possible answers. With the first answer we return to the economics of information. It is especially true for durables that investigations into their characteristics are costly. This is the case, because this type of good, 'experience goods' as they are called, usually reveal their properties only after some period of use. While the customer may be able to get an idea of the average properties she can expect after expending effort into an investigation, vendors are likely to anticipate the disutility of such efforts. So in order to seek confidence on behalf of their customers vendors (and manufacturers alike) turn to 'signalling', which I brought to your attention as one of the problems of contracting (remember the meaning of the term and the other two problems of contracting?): this is accomplished in particular by the promise of special warranties. Strangely enough the warranties for different models and brands of a product are frequently the same. This being the case, the whole purpose of warranties appears to be questionable, since the customer is not brought into a position of simplified choice among competing makes.

Let us now turn, therefore, to the second answer. Here, warranties are explained as aiming to split risks between the buyer and the seller. More specifically, in the case of a defective product the seller by assumption of the warranty agrees to bear the cost for those defects, which she can probably control or correct at a lower cost than the buyer. If there are any defects that are a result of inappropriate use on behalf of the buyer and thus, on behalf of the seller, these would be avoidable only at an almost prohibitively high cost and are thus left to the buyer.

Note that warranties are granted for a limited period of time only (which can be quite long, particularly for high-quality fabrics); on the one hand, it depends on the time span within which a defect occurs for which the supplier can be made responsible; on the other hand, the robustness even of high-quality products depends on the intensity of use. Therefore the exclusion of a warranty for intensive use can be efficient inasmuch as it assigns due care to the user, who in this case is the least cost avoider.

For the sake of brevity we ought to stop here, although the topic has not yet been treated exhaustingly. For example, the impact of insurance for malfunction on the granting of warranty is worth further investigation.

Are precautions and reliance mutually exclusive?

This turns out to be a rather tricky question! We will tackle it by means of an example. Imagine an executive board of a large company, which has ordered the design of the annual report by a graphic designer. For the morning following the stipulated date of delivery a press conference is scheduled, where the annual report has to be presented. Press conferences are quite expensive undertakings. Their expected payoffs are also quite high, however, since they add to the reputation of the company and can even have a positive impact on the market value (as reflected in share prices, say).

One can expect the designer to take precautions for timely delivery. To illustrate, she could temporarily draw off staff members from other less urgent work in order to speed up completion of the order at hand. The higher the opportunity cost the designer undergoes the more likely punctual delivery. Unfortunately, the probability of performance cannot reach 100 per cent, for example, the delivery lorry could get caught in an accident by *force majeur*; that is to say, ex ante the probability of performance increases with the amount of precautions but this can only be approximate in the case of unforeseeable risks. What level of precautions will the vendor (our designer) take in absence of any rule of liability? Moreover, can the level of precautions be expected to be efficient? The answer is most likely 'no'. To see this we must be aware that performance gives rise to revenues, but the rent from performance will accrue almost entirely to the customer. If this was not the case, damages would lack a rationale. However, if the designer was liable for the outlays the executive board has made in preparing the press conference with respect to delivery of the report this would be quite a strong incentive to perform.

Now let us change sides and turn to the situation of the executive board. In expectation of the event, it has made preparations such as reservation of a suitable room in a centrally located place and catering. The monetary equivalent of these preparations is a measure of reliance on accurate delivery. Disregarding the damage in reputation for the moment, we can be quite sure that the board will not be extremely cautious in its disposition provided the vendor alone was liable. Stated differently, reliance would be inefficiently high. Bringing reliance down to an efficient level would require that the executive board cannot shift the entire cost of reliance to the designer.

Unfortunately, to the extent the designer is exonerated from cost of precautions she might lessen her efforts! Hence there seems to be a contradiction concerning the appropriate division of due care. This contradiction is not easily resolved. Here is an indication how this could be done.

The efficient solution for the stipulation of the contract requires that the total costs accruing to the parties are minimized. In order to accomplish this task the graphical designer ought to be urged to expand the level of precautions to the point where the expected damages are neither smaller nor larger than those which the executive board could demand at their optimal level of reliance. The damages that the executive board in turn is allowed to claim must be independent of their expenses for reliance since otherwise they would have an incentive to shift their costs to the designer. Obviously the efficient mix of reliance and precautions is tricky, as we noted earlier. Resolving the puzzle requires *compromise*.

Long-term contracts

Contracts that are meant to hold over a longer span of time pose specific peculiarities. Among these there are imperfections that require special precautions. Labour contracts are a well-known example. Where they are open ended, future needs and circumstances are hardly foreseeable. Changing demands may come along with changing functions (from assembly to repairs, say), and also work conditions my change due to technical progress and the like. So, for good reason, terms of contracts are sought that can accommodate such unforeseeable changes. This type of contract is termed a 'contingent contract' because it does not contain specific clauses for all kinds of contingencies but rather rules of understanding in case a certain unexpected situation obtains. Thus, they tend to turn into 'relationships', which are a sort of 'quasi-contract'.

The typical complications of such quasi-contracts are threefold:

- Human beings have only a limited capacity for the selection of the best strategy to get to grips with certain situations; in other words they are characterized by 'bounded rationality'.
- Human beings are opportunistic, that is to say that they will not hesitate to pick the strategy that appears to be the most advantageous for them, even if this strategy is mean or deceptive.
- The conclusion of a contract and performance are heavily dependent on the extent to which the specific skills of the beneficiary can be substituted. This

property of people (and other productive resources of course) is termed 'factor specifity'.

Obviously, less qualified people are easier to replace than those with high factor specifity and, consequently, only for the latter does it pay to adopt special clauses in a contract, such as in case of poaching.

The ideas just presented go back to Oliver E. Williamson, who built a theory of 'relational' contracting on these issues. Note that the absence of each of the three properties would already remove the indeterminateness of a contract!

Here I have deliberately used a labour contract as an illustrative example for a long-term contract. The peculiarities gave rise to what was termed a relational contract.

This is, however, by far not the only kind of long-term contract. In order to get an idea about the large variety of problems that can arise, we will finally have a look at a contract between an assembler and a subcontractor. Such a contractual relation may be seen as a sequence of repeated strategic interactions between the two parties. It can be shown that neither party has an incentive to take advantage of the other as long as the general conditions do not change. In other words, the mutual benefits of cooperation are higher than for opportunistic behaviour (you undoubtedly remember this notion?). However, as the end of the contract approaches this changes the situation substantially. Completion creates a strong incentive to take additional advantage from this step. This is a well-known phenomenon in the last round of a repeated strategic game. And it seems quite natural that the management of the assembler will try to protect them from any attempt at extortion. To protect themselves the management of the assembler could give indemnities on financing the subcontractor's equipment that is necessary for performance. Clever, isn't it? Note that such a proviso boils down to taking the subcontractor **hostage**, something that follows similar lines as the actions among leaders in order to secure peace treaties!

Hard to believe, but it is perfectly rational and thus economical to take hostages – and it the unexpected result of our look at the problems of the last round in long-term contracting.

Standard form contracts

There is an abundance of cases where contracts are not stipulated point by point, but one side to the contract enters a given contractual framework that is preset and unalterable. There are familiar examples like entering a commuter train, using a public library or even usage of the local water supply. In none of these cases will negotiations take place and the conditions are mostly neither checked nor questioned by the customer.

Similarly a buyer and a seller will make use of **standard form contracts** when purchasing a car or renting an apartment. In the majority of cases, the latter type of contracts leaves only some details open to stipulation whereas the bulk of contents are standardized.

Both types have in common one advantage and one disadvantage:

Let us start with the advantage. It would definitely be time consuming if, for example, every would-be-passenger of a commuter train would have to stipulate the conditions of the service individually. It would be both time consuming and still risky if people had to establish what has been termed relational contracts on cars, apartments and the like. So the obvious advantage of the standard term contract is savings in transaction costs!

And the disadvantage? Well, it is claimed by economists in particular that the use of a standard type contract ultimately boils down to monopolizing the (would-be) customer. Neither allocative efficiency nor an improvement of individual and social welfare is automatically warranted; more specifically, the customer may be urged to forego rents. Furthermore, since there are usually no alternatives to the standard type contract, she is left with the option of all or nothing. Note that it is again the saving of transaction cost for substitution that might ultimately leave the customer with a relative gain from accepting the type of contract at hand.

A brief epilogue

This chapter on contractual relations might appear to you to be quite exhaustive. In fact, it only provides a primer in a very fundamental sense. There are two reasons for this. The first is the obvious one that documentation of the entire knowledge about contracts is definitely far beyond the reach of any single book today. If you are curious, you might consult Steven Shavell's *Foundations of Economic Analysis*, Chapter 3 (Cambridge, MA, 2004) or Hans-Bernd Schäfer and Claus Ott, *The Economic Analysis of Civil Law*, Chapters 10–16 (Northampton, MA, 2004) but the full range of research becomes visible only on consulting the journals in our field (listed at the end of this book).

The second reason can best be illustrated by the dynamics of what is termed the public sector: here contracts have traditionally played a role as important as in the private sphere, for example in procurement, tenure tracks for civil servants or treaties among federal entities or states. Moreover, this role is steadily increasing in the course of public sector reform. 'Contracting out' and 'outsourcing' are means of more efficient provision of goods and services that have opened the request for new and complex contracts. Moreover, regulation takes new forms where privatized utilities are to be guided not to abuse their position as natural monopolies and the like (as with railways and telecommunication systems).

That is to say that these changes add weight to the crucial role that contracts have always had in both law and economics. Needless to say, the complexity of some of the emerging contracts poses yet unknown and sometimes unexpected difficulties to lawyers and economic analysts alike. The design, implementation and enforcement of contracts are all around us and you have had just a taster.

4 Lawsuits and law enforcement

Some introductory remarks

The content of this chapter is somewhat mixed, inasmuch as it comprises topics that are in the realms of both private and public affairs.

First, we will deal with litigation in cases such as a claim concerning violated property rights as well as trials before a **jury** because of, say, an accusation that someone has committed a **crime**.

These issues are distinct for the following reasons: while **courts** are in the public domain and thus are provided by the state in either case, prosecution may basically be in the interest of the **plaintiff** in the first case – public concern notwithstanding – but it is definitely in the public interest in the second case, which can be seen from the fact that in this case the public prosecutor takes action.

Second, we will have a look at alternative ways of conflict resolution, such as **arbitration** and **mediation**. Finally we will survey alternative means of **public law enforcement**, such as punishment by **imprisonment** versus **money sanction**.

At this point you might object that it is by no means clear what economics can contribute to these issues. To start with, adjudication strongly influences the distribution of property rights for both material and immaterial commodities. Moreover the infrastructure that includes highly qualified and well paid staff absorbs a substantial amount of public funds.

The costs of the legal system are substantially influenced in turn by the demands of citizens for adjudication via **litigation**. We can go one step further and try to find out the incentives of people for turning to the courts, thus making use of the underlying behavioural model of humans. Insights into the causes of litigation can then help optimize the prevailing system by lowering the costs of running courts, externalizing costs by support for **alternative means of conflict resolution** or even trying to avoid certain kinds of conflict by adoption of more and better standard contracts, more severe liability rules and other preventive measures.

Still another viewpoint of litigation is that of information to potential litigants stemming from outcomes of earlier trials. Thus it is possible to assess future probability of success or failure, which, in turn, will influence the **demand for trials**. **Judges** and legal experts concerned with the design and performance of rules can learn whether existing rules stand the test of time. From the lessons learned both cost-saving measures and/or improvements can be derived. So, in sum, it seems worthwhile to deal with lawsuits and **law enforcement** from an economic perspective.

Before we start our tour, it is worth noting that trials are a special field of application for a specific methodology: *game theory*. Although game theory is certainly not restricted to this area, it allows more than the usual marginal analysis because of its special advantages for the analysis of strategic interaction, which is omnipresent here.

Although I confine myself to the economic aspects, I must also point out that there are some quite important 'meta-economic' perspectives of legal proceedings. It has been observed that justice not only has to be done, but also has to be seen to have been done. Sometimes it is not just the substance of the legal proceedings but rather the fact that they are performed at all which serves as a justification for the legal system in the public.

The economic perspective on trials

Why do trials exist at all?

Let us start our inquiries with a simple but quite important question: what prompts people to take legal action? Moreover: why is it that litigants do not seek **settlement** before they sue, which means leaving it to a judge to decide their case? The answers to these questions shed some light on the demand for litigation.

Once we gain insight into the demand schedule for litigation the question follows whether demand is too high or too low measured against an **optimal amount**. This follows the intentions of our analysis, which is rooted in welfare economics. So what we intend to do is to proceed from explanation (positive analysis) to policy implication (normative analysis). By this token, we also want to find out how the demands for courts can be reduced given the fact that trial is the most costly of all variants of conflict resolution.

Moreover, we are interested in maximizing the number of 'correct' rulings with a given input of resources, as well as minimizing the costs for a given number of rulings. A correct ruling is one that reflects the truth.

Our goals are closely related to the question of which incentives guide potential litigants under prevailing regulations. This in turn will depend on such expenses as the charges and **attorneys' fee** borne by the litigants, since these expenses will definitely curb claims or entitlements. But what are these claims? Usually they are expressed as the money value of the matter in dispute. However, it is not the money value alone but also a certain risk of litigation which has to be kept in mind. It is in the latter that the chance of winning or losing the case is captured.

So let us put these elements together in a more systematic way. As things are, we can look at trials as if they worked by a kind of price mechanism. These prices are the opportunity costs of the litigants. Under the usual behavioural assumptions this implies striving for an efficient outcome of the trial. Consequently, a judicial decision is equivalent to a means of allocation which works as a substitute for a market, since it guides resources so that they yield the highest possible utility (this is by the way the gist of the Chicago School of law and economics). However, mis-interpretations as well as false prices can inhibit efficient solutions. An economist will almost immediately consider whether litigations feature competition – to some extent at least – and whether judges effectuate the 'unseen hand', which (ex post, of course) guides the efficient allocation of commodities (or claims or entitlements respectively). Usually lawyers do not regard the aspect of efficiency as the most important. They prefer to see justice as the most relevant result of adjudication.

At first sight this implies a contradiction, but this is not necessarily the case. Recall our reasoning in connection with the virtues of a Kaldor-Hicks test earlier in Chapter 2! However, we must be aware that we are not talking about the view of the impartial analyst here. We are talking about the role of judges (and lawyers, of course). From this perspective it could well be the case that it is basically the lawyers who keep track of the redistribution of wealth (in the interest of their respective clients), whereas it is the judge who cares for efficiency. The joint efforts of the two determine the final distribution.

Turning to more specific issues, we should first of all observe that it is crucial to know how the **litigation costs** are allocated a priori. The respective burden of costs creates different incentives for the demands for law enforcement via ruling. Several means of allocation are possible (and are also in use):

- First, each litigant must bear her own share (a rule that applies for most of the United States of America and therefore is labelled the **American rule**).
- Second, the underlying rules can foresee that the loser ought to bear the costs accruing to both parties (which applies to continental Europe as well as Great Britain and therefore is either labelled the **European rule** or the **British rule**).
- Third, the cost can essentially be borne by the government. This is especially true if an attorney is provided by government. Moreover, in general the staff and facilities of the courts are paid for by the government and financed via general tax revenues. That is to say, the judicial system is paid for by the taxpayers.

Not surprisingly, the allocation of costs strongly influences efficiency in the discovery of the correct solution (which has not to do with the incentives of the litigants alone but the economy of the trial itself). The point is illustrated by one of the pioneers of law and economics, Gordon Tullock (now at George Mason Law School), when he states that the tradition of the European continent procedural law acts on the maxim of official investigations, whereas in the Anglo-Saxon world the maxims of disposition and of hearings are preferred. The consequences are quite far reaching. To illustrate: if in the USA each of the litigants bears 45 per cent of the cost and 10 per cent is covered by the state, then roughly speaking 55 per cent of the effort is expended on finding out 'the truth', whereas 45 per cent of efforts account to the 'wrong side'.

In Germany, by way of contrast, 90 per cent of the costs are borne by the state and roughly 5 per cent each by the litigants. Hence 95 per cent of efforts are expended to find out the truth.

One of the peculiarities of trials is that the litigants may be guided by strong incentives not to settle their dispute in the forefront of a trial, which renders it difficult to get to an efficient solution. The reason is that courts are then constrained to simulate the correct solution, that is to say, the allocation which matches the highest valuation of the property rights at hand. This makes great demands on judges and moreover procedural law must give them sufficient discretion.

So, to summarize: traditional reasoning would see a case finally settled in an efficient manner, when the alleged rights and entitlements are assigned to the party which values them best.

Responsibilities or liability must be assigned to that party who can bear them at lowest costs (cheapest insurer!). Finally, transaction costs ought to be minimized.

So far we have reviewed some of the fundamental ideas underlying court decisions from an economic perspective. Further elaboration is beyond the scope of this small book and the reader is referred to more comprehensive volumes for details (see Recommended reading both at the end of this chapter and at the end of the book). We shall dig a little deeper, however, by looking at the consequences of applying the two rules of cost bearing to examples. Let us start with the American rule (of course you remember the term?).

Imagine two litigants, Billy and Blunt, seek legal action. Billy considers suing Blunt. Being the plaintiff he values his claim at €100,000 and the probability of winning at 80 per cent or $p = 0.8$. According to the American rule he would have to bear costs of, say, €20,000 irrespective of the outcome. So the value of legal action for Billy is $0.8*100,000 - 20,000 > 0$.

What about Blunt, the **defendant**? He expects to lose the case with a probability of 40 per cent or $p = 0.4$, which boils down to paying the €100,000 to Billy. In addition to that, the cost of the trial to him is €30,000. So his calculation looks like this: he faces a loss of $0.4*100,000 + 30,000$.

Now, assume that before the trial someone suggests that Blunt makes an offer to Billy of €60,000 with the idea of settlement out of court. Will they accept and therefore avoid trial?

For Billy, the calculation is: $0.8*100,000 - 20,000 = 60,000$; he could get exactly what he can expect to gain.

For Blunt, the calculation is: $0.4*100,000 + 30,000 > 60,000$; that is to say, he would also gain compared to what he would face if he lost the trial.

So we can see the possibility of settlement out of court. The necessary condition is that the costs of litigation are greater or at least equal to the difference accruing from expected payments based on the value of the claim. The condition is clearly met in our example: $0.4*100,000 + 30,000 \geq 0.8*100,000 - 20,000$, or, stated differently, $20,000 + 30,000 \geq (0.8 - 0.4)*100,000$!

Therefore, a fairly easy calculation should precede litigation in every case in order to see whether it can be avoided, provided that the value of the claim can be calculated, of course!

However, let us see what happens if the probabilities change, for Billy (the plaintiff) to $p_P = 0.9$ and for Blunt (the defendant) $p_D = 0.2$. In this case, the earlier inequality turns around and a lawsuit becomes inevitable. Obviously, it is the subjective perception of success or failure that influences the decision to sue. In our example the plaintiff is very optimistic about his case ($p_P = 0.9$), whereas the defendant is rather pessimistic. You may like to carry out further experiments by assuming different states of information for the litigants to see what the likely outcome will be. What you have to bear in mind, however, is the role of cost sharing.

This is a good starting point for an investigation into the effects of the British or continental rule. In order to demonstrate the impact of this rule we have to change the setting a little. Billy may still expect to gain €100,000 with the probability p_P =0.8. Blunt in turn gives himself a 50:50 chance of losing, his probability thus amounting to $p_D = 0.5$. The total costs (court fees) amount to €20,000.

The expected value for the plaintiff is now: 0.8*100,000 – (1– 0.8)* 20,000, that is +76,000.

For the defendant, Blunt, the following applies: in case of a win: 0.5*0, but in case of defeat 0.5*0 – (1 – 0.5)*(100,000 + 20,000), which amounts to an expected value of – €60,000.

Billy will sue since his minimal claim is substantially higher than the maximum offer Blunt can make in order to avoid the trial. It is noteworthy that the sum of the probabilities is larger than 1 (which is possible only because they are subjective probabilities).

What does this seeming sidestep mean? To see this we will modify the assumptions underlying our example, so let the cost of trial rise to €40,000. The expected value of plaintiff Billy's claim will go down to €72,000 (can you verify this?) and that of defendant Blunt becomes – €70,000. That is to say, with the cost of trial going up the expected value of the claim becomes lower and lower for the plaintiff. By the same token, the defendant would have to make ever greater concessions if he wanted to avoid trial.

The cost of trial (as given through the fees) takes the nature of a commodity tax on the claims of the plaintiff – even if they are justified! From this the following points can be inferred: the schedule for fees must take into account that access to adjudication must not be curbed in an undue way. To accomplish this, the cost of running the courts should be borne by the taxpayers. Unfortunately, the latter suggestion is flawed inasmuch as it boils down to subsidizing of disputatious citizens by the more peaceable ones! This in turn highlights the importance of alternative means of conflict resolution such as arbitration, mediation or even 'rent-a-judge' (where the parties agree to bring their case to a former and now retired professional judge, who is selected by mutual agreement and paid accordingly).

Influence of attorneys' fees

Until now, we have neglected what is held to be one of the most important elements of litigation and, by the same token, crucial in determining the costs of trials: lawyers (barristers, solicitors or attorneys) and their fees. Fees may be contingent fees depending on the value of the claim or performance-related fees based, for example, on time. We have omitted the consideration of attorneys' fees so far but from our earlier discussion it should be clear that additional costs will bring about changes in the assessments of success or failure on behalf of the litigants, but no entirely new aspects. What is interesting here is that attorneys' fees become part of the cost of litigation so that the rules of cost bearing can be extended to this additional element. Before we have a closer look at this issue it is necessary to have a look at the motivation of lawyers. So, to paraphrase the title of a well-known essay by Posner (1993): 'What do lawyers maximize?' – well, in their own words: the same as anyone else does. In other words, by assumption they are *homini oeconomici*, who are interested in maximizing revenues from conducting cases. Depending on the type of fee they will thus try to protract litigation or to spend additional effort on winning the more rewarding cases. I hurry to add that this can be done neither excessively nor to the disadvantage of clients. There are constraints such as the standing orders of the profession, as well as codes of conduct enforced by **professional associations** (the 'chamber of lawyers' in Austria for instance and the well known 'bar associations' in Anglo-Saxon countries). Moreover, reputation is such a valuable asset for self-employed people in general and lawyers in particular that – to the benefit of their clients – practising lawyers will hardly maximize their revenues excessively.

This was almost a detour into a theory of lawyer behaviour! Besides, it reminded us quite nicely of one of the fundamental presuppositions of law and economics – methodological individualism.

Let us start our investigations into the effects of different rules of cost sharing all over again. We begin with the American rule. Recall that it demands that each party bears her share of the litigation costs. But what are the consequences for the litigants? Starting with the plaintiff: even if she calculates a high probability of winning a case she can never enjoy the full value of the claim. Even fully justified claims are thus attenuated through the rule of cost bearing.

For the defendant it is true that she would have to bear costs even if it turned out that she was innocent! From this it can be seen that the American rule can be criticized for the following reasons. Even if a suit was filed unjustified the defendant might be induced to offer an amount of money out of court just in order to prevent even bigger losses! This would be one way of avoiding the probable higher cost of facing the trial.

This raises the question of whether, under such circumstances, settlement is a likely option at all. The answer is that it depends on the subjective probabilities that are attached to the outcome by the litigants and whether when added together they are bigger than 1. The numerical examples given earlier fully apply. However, let us assume that there is an impartial observer who is perfectly aware that the total probability of victory or defeat must be 1. We can show that in the case where an impartial observer decides for the litigants whether to bring law suit or not, the observer will always propose settlement!

Let us see why. Our plaintiff, Billy, is still optimistic and his expected value E_p is: $0.8*100,000 - (1 - 0.8)*20,000 = +76,000$.

For the defendant, it is true that the expected value E_D is: $0.2*0 - (1 - 0.2)*(100,000 + 20,000) = -96,000$.

So they are well advised to seek settlement!

But even if there is a chance of 50:50 of winning (where Billy is much less optimistic), settlement is still to be preferred, since now

$E_P = 46,000 > E_D = -60,000$ (certainly you can easily prove this by yourself?); it may be noted in passing that this illustrates the potential of mediators or other types of arbitration!

The calculations so far were quite simple and can easily be expended. At the same time we should not overlook that even these simple examples are flawed:

- They do not show how parties get to their differing appraisals of success or failure; thus, they are of limited explanatory value.
- Also, they cannot cover if and how settlements are accomplished in the course of bargaining.

There are other models that do better in that respect. Consider the assumption of asymmetric information as a starting point. Its characteristics are that (1) a defendant has information concerning the probability for the plaintiff to win that the latter does not have and (2) that there is rudimentary bargaining, in which the plaintiff makes just one offer for settlement of the 'take-it-or-leave-it' type. A plaintiff may presume that the defendant with a low p will refuse the offer and a defendant with a high p will accept it. For the plaintiff it can be a fairly tricky question to find out the optimal offer: while the overall gain will be the higher the higher the offer, the risk that the offer will be refused also increases, which will compel him to bear his part of the cost of litigation. So even after a change of the methodological approach to the issue the costs of litigation remain crucial.

Is there an optimal number of trials?

For the economist the quest for efficiency is a primary goal. Therefore, the socially efficient number of trials is a topic of major concern. Unfortunately, our earlier examples do not give a hint as to whether the emerging number of trials is too large or too small. The only thing we can say is that the European rule tends to deter potential plaintiffs with a low probability of winning their case.

However, for the socially efficient number of trials not only the wishes of litigants should be observed. Various social costs and benefits are associated with trials and these are only partially covered by the fees the litigants are willing to take on.

Let us look at some of the social costs, which a litigant is unlikely to consider in her calculation. First of all, there is the remuneration of judges and a fee for the court. Moreover, the opportunity costs of lay judges have to be taken into account as well as the utilization of infrastructure. There are social benefits as well, of course. The proof and prosecution of misconduct are held to have a deterrent effect on future potential lawbreakers. However, these effects cannot be expected to work automatically since court decisions need publicity in order to be effective. For the sake of completeness, it should also be pointed out that the form of liabilities, as well as the rigour with which they are executed, do add to the deterrent effect.

Another benefit is that of the information about future cases which is contained in single court decisions. Thus transaction costs can be saved and the expectations towards the judiciary stabilized. Traditionally, these effects are held to be particularly important in common law but this holds for civil law countries as well!

The advantages, such social benefits notwithstanding, are hard to quantify. In the terminology of cost–benefit analysis they are 'intangibles'; even if there are no figures for these effects they should be described carefully and thus form important complementary information.

Nevertheless, there must be a belief that the overall impact of these benefits is of notable size: the enormous amount of resources that is absorbed by the judicial system can hardly be justified by the accomplishment of fair allocations of claims and entitlements among litigants alone.

As you might correctly state at this stage of the discussion, there are no further hints regarding the question of whether the number of trials is too high or too low apart from a clear definition of the optimal number of cases. This is correct, but, unfortunately, the issue has not yet been resolved satisfactorily. There is only a presumption that the number of cases tends to be higher than optimal, which is supported by occasional observations.

Queues and bottlenecks

It is generally held that courts in general and trial courts in particular are overstrained. That is to say, in many European countries there are at least bottlenecks in capacity. More formally this means that the number of new cases exceeds the number of processed cases and queuing emerges. Delays in processing sometimes amount to several years! Consequently, the opportunity costs of time as well as of foregone compensations accumulate. One side-effect of such findings is that alternative means of conflict resolution become more attractive, such as arbitration boards or the private judges mentioned earlier. Unfortunately, there are cases where the initial beliefs of the litigants about their prospect of success keeps them from seeking relief in alternatives of conflict resolution.

There are, however, other reasons for queuing:

- One reason is said to be the private interest of solicitors to unduly stretch trials in order to increase their revenues.
- Moreover, it is not just a misperception of the prospect of success that tempts litigants to stick to trials. It has been observed that there are cases where lawsuits are filed although the value of the claim is definitely lower than the likely costs of litigation or, alternatively, the probability of success is very low, so that overall the net gain is almost certainly negative. The upshot here is that a plaintiff would rather stop filing shortly before the trial is due because she just wants to put to test her credibility from the defendant's point of view!

If the latter offers a certain amount of money for settlement, this is a gain for the plaintiff and in case the defendant refuses payment there will be no trial. However, as long as such issues are pending, some capacities of courts are blocked.

- Another source of bottlenecks is a misperception of chance, which leads to an increase in the expenditure of effort and money in order to push the case, although this is in sharp contrast to the objective facts. While capacities are thus blocked the consequence of such risk-loving attitudes are both losses for the litigant as well as sunk costs, which are borne by the public.

- By way of a little detour it is worth pointing out that sometimes a person's threat may even lead to relief for the court or some authority. Imagine the procedure of approval of sites for the construction of new buildings. According to the legal procedure, neighbours to such a site can claim they will be subjected to nuisance and hence demand precautionary measures on behalf of the applicant. It has been reported, however, that neighbours offered to waive their rights for an appropriate payment – in advance, of course! Note that in both cases the applicant and the potential defendant in litigation face 'credible threats' on behalf of their opponents. But unlike the lawsuit, where courts must be involved in order for the threat to be effective, the actions of neighbours incur a relief for the authority although it is questionable whether the request for compensation payments is lawful at all.

- Interestingly enough, although it is widely held that the courts are the least responsible for bottlenecks judges can be assumed to seek idiosyncratic goals as well. This point is taken up later in a digression.

Legal assistance

When a person demands **legal assistance**, once again a principal–agent problem emerges. The problem was already addressed when we introduced contractual relations (see pp. 75–90). A solicitor is the agent of her client. Consequently all the familiar problems between principals and agents might turn up, since the agent may have interests that are at variance with those of her client (recall the problem of protraction of trials!). However, the principal can most likely not observe the actions of the agent and can exert control over her only at fairly high cost.

One of the peculiarities that are present in the relation between a client and her solicitor stems from the incentives brought about by prevailing regulations. The most prominent among these regulations is that of solicitors' remuneration. As has been mentioned earlier, we can basically distinguish between two systems. Fees may be contingent fees depending on the value of the claim or performance-related fees based, for instance, on time spent. Each of the two systems will have a distinct impact on the solicitors' actions. Thus, the predictions concerning the solicitor's advice to seek trial or settlement will vary, given the expected values for success or defeat. To illustrate, if the fee was dependent on specific services (per diem allowances for instance) it is more likely that the solicitor will favour additional court hearings.

As we have seen before there are some constraints on solicitors' actions. One stems from the present value of standing (or reputation). This will be curbed by self-interest as well as failure. A lawyer who is known for her all too obvious pursuit of self-interest and/or failure will not be in great demand on the market. Moreover, such misconduct will have spillover effects on the profession (i.e. generate negative externalities). This in turn points to an explanation for the existence of professional associations and the enforcement of a disciplinary order.

Admittedly there is an ambiguity in professional associations inasmuch as they also exist in order to defend or pursue the interests of their members. This is done by lobbying, or in more economy-prone parlance, by '**rent seeking**'. As the term indicates, effort is spent not on the generation of additional services but rather on influencing the legislature and government for the sake of additional benefits – thus rent seeking is a means of redistribution rather than allocation (we will meet this concept once more in Chapter 5 on public law).

It is worth pointing out that it is not always the agency of the lawyer that is at stake. The problem is that the relationship between the client and the solicitor is sometimes characterized by mutual asymmetric information. To illustrate, it is far from trivial why and how a person chooses a certain lawyer. Imagine a defendant who indicates that she wants a solicitor who is willing to take on a case that, at the outset, has a very high probability of failure. In this case, the lawyer may be at risk of not receiving all the necessary information from her would-be client. Another example of a strategic problem for the lawyer would be a litigant who is risk-loving, but for this reason is not willing to reveal all the necessary information to her solicitor. Such strategic action grows out of the fact that the risk loving person prefers a trial with high variance in the probability of success to settlement, even if the payoff is the same. The lawyer may even face a client who remains in a state of 'rational ignorance' inasmuch as she draws no additional benefits from expending effort for additional knowledge of the legal procedure and hence stays uninformed.

Given such circumstances, it is up to the lawyer whether she is willing to bear the additional costs of collecting information about her clients. Moreover, she is protected by the lack of a limiting contract.

Judges

Despite their essential role in adjudication judges are not among the excessively analysed stakeholders in the field of jurisdiction. This holds for councils and juries as well. However, let us briefly take stock.

To start with, I will once more refer to the (1993) article by Richard Posner, which I have already mentioned when talking about lawyers. This time, however, I use the full and correct title: 'What do judges and justices maximize? The same thing everybody else does'. Even if there are some distinctions concerning rank and affiliation to civil law courts or criminal law courts, it is widely held that besides arguments following the utility function, several other socioeconomic variables do influence a judge's sentence and **opinion**. The most relevant of these variables are education, income, employment and prior conviction (the last being an issue that leads beyond economics proper although it can substantially influence a judge's behaviour). The alleged influence of experts on judges follows the same line of reasoning.

But let us go back to the utility function and constraints of the judge. We will keep our exposition simple, however, and mention only the most important variables. Here the time a judge spends working compared to her leisure time, which can be dedicated to other activities, is held to be most important. Salary, reputation, career opportunities and – particularly for judges in higher ranks – popularity all ought to be taken into account. A proxy for career opportunities is the number of sentences that are revised by appellate courts, although this proxy has ultimately been found to be problematic, since dissenting and innovative interpretations may increase the risk of being brought to an appellate court, but at the same time may prove the courage and skills of the judge. As far as popularity is concerned, you remember the autobiography of Judge Learned Hand? This would hardly have become the bestseller it did had popularity not played a role in his career!

You might wonder why I have not mentioned the independence of judges among the beneficial variables. This is because independence is a peculiar type of constraint rather than an argument in the utility function. More specifically, it is one of the institutional conditions that are meant to foreclose the dependence of the judge's reputation from undue preference for one of the litigants or even the attorney.

Another virtue that has come to light is a characteristic of a judge's personality, the desire to serve justice. This may reflect a disposition for altruism. Certainly this is an important issue. However, we will not apply it here explicitly, since we can readily assume that altruism is a likely consequence of socialization. This in turn would lead us beyond the scope of the simple economic approach, although altruism has been incorporated into modes of utility maximization. Moreover, altruism could be introduced in a more indirect way – despite the fact that the argument by which this is accomplished appears to be counterintuitive at first sight. The argument runs as follows: an increase in leisure time can definitely be expected to increase utility. However, it has been observed that judges who are passionate lawyers are quite frequently preoccupied with legal matters. They like to study earlier cases or questions of general interest. Thus, they derive additional utility from activities pertinent to their profession. This, in turn, will improve their knowledge and understanding and thus add to the quality of the professional work (what judges are actually doing is amalgamating a professional interest with a hobby). Clearly, this can be expected to apply to judges in different ranks to a different extent. To illustrate, the young judge probably has different aspirations from those of the renowned justice at the end of her career.

A word on salary is also due. In the European continental tradition at least, salaries are not subject to negotiations but follow a fixed scheme (in Austria, judges in this respect constitute a special group within the relevant legal norms for civil servants). So it might rather be the aspiration to promotion that influences utility; at best, salary will affect it only indirectly. This does not mean, however, that salary is altogether unimportant. The opposite is true inasmuch as pay is quite important in assessing the opportunity cost of the choice of profession. Consider a lawyer, who has the choice between becoming an attorney at law or a judge. If the initial salary is too low, the lawyer might prefer to become an attorney, other variables being equal, of course (*ceteris paribus*). If the initial salary is high, competition for the limited number of posts would become tougher and the career prospects for the individual weaker.

Let me draw your attention to another feature of the profession (which is closely related to the issues of achievement as well as reputation). To start with, imagine that an amendment to traffic law has been enacted, which has been pushed by the retail business association. The subject of the amendment is a privilege concerning parking in short-term parking zones. Now, a consumer violates the regulation by using a parking lot without a permit. One of the shopkeepers sues the customer (who, obviously, was not one of his own customers). When the judge who goes into the merits of the case finds that the evidence perfectly matches the facts of the case, she implicitly supports the successful lobbying of the association. If she tries to interpret the newly enacted rule more leniently, thus implicitly weakening the strength of the lobby, she may act in a corrective way towards gaining equal opportunity to utilize a scarce resource (parking lots). Even this innocuous example demonstrates how the willingness to use discretionary power can shape the enactment of the law.

We may go one step further in order to put into perspective an apparent peculiarity of common law systems. What we are talking about is 'judge-made law', which boils down to taking a certain sentence and opinion as exemplary for subsequent cases that bear a sufficient level of similarity. Recall that we have stated that the emphasis on procedural rules together with the orientation towards 'precedent' is a distinct feature of common law.

Back in a civil law country we may find the following. Imagine a court of first instance which has just handled the case of a creditor who sued a commercial bank after she suffered a loss because the bank where she held her deposits went bankrupt. Just like every other bank in Austria, the bank is subject to supervision by an authority. Now it has fairly recently been audited, but the auditors did not find any severe irregularities. In the course of her investigations, the judge finds that, in a certain sense, the auditors not only act as agents of the board of governors but that they also represent the supervisory authority. The upshot is that having drawn this conclusion, the judge rules that the state was partly liable since its representatives did not spot the flaws in the auditors' report. This is a typical example of an innovative view that demonstrates the possibility of judge-made law in civil law countries. While this chapter was being written, it was not clear what the appellate court would decide. Nevertheless it can be inferred from the situation just described that, in principle, even in civil law countries judges can bring about changes in the perception and interpretation of existing legal rules. This, in turn, underlines the importance of the understanding of the driving forces underlying judges' actions.

Exemption from legal charges, legal aid and insurance for legal costs

As we have seen the cost of litigation can influence both the access to the law and the outcomes. Thus, court costs and attorneys fees have allocative and distributive effects. In cases where these effects are obstacles to access to adjudication, governments might interfere by granting exemptions from legal charges and/or **legal aid**. I ought to point out here that the allocative and distributional distortions might appear to be innocuous as long as the simplifying assumption of risk neutrality holds. However the change for the worse can be quite large if large inequalities of income of the litigants arise jointly with pronounced risk aversion!

Where people have experienced the burden of litigation costs or where legal action appears to be inevitable they will consider insurance for legal costs.

For several reasons insurance for legal costs (legal expenses insurance, **legal protection insurance**) poses some problems from the perspective of welfare economics. To illustrate, imagine the European (or British) rule for legal charges. With insurance it becomes much less likely that settlement is preferred to trial. For disputatious people this means that they can shift the burden of charges in case of defeat. Thus their cost of litigation is reduced to the opportunity cost of time and other efforts. These ought to be balanced against the insurance premium, of course. Insurance premiums are not just calculated to cover the insurance company's expenses for administration; they ought to cover the average cost of all litigants. Inasmuch as litigants can thus shift the burden for law suits, they will most likely act recklessly, because their inclination to sue will be higher than if they had to bear the full share of the costs. Above all, they may even act negligently, thus causing harm which eventually leads to the exertion of a law suit. Thus insurance can cause allocative inefficiencies. Still there is another viewpoint of interest here. Imagine an insured party that is uncertain about the outcome of suit. However, if the defendant does not have insurance, for the potential plaintiff this opens the option of a credible threat, which in turn might induce the defendant to agree to a detrimental settlement! Note that this conjecture can explain why despite the widely used insurance for legal costs the number of trials does not increase substantially.

Although we will stop here, this does not mean that the topic has been treated exhaustively. Again, this caveat is meant to encourage further investigation.

Alternative conflict resolution

Lawsuits are by no means the only form of conflict resolution. There are at least two other means, dependent on whether and how actively a court is involved. In Austria, for example, there is a special act, regulating a variety of issues which are classified as non-trial or voluntary. Interestingly enough, we find foreclosure, inheritance as well as divorce as the most interesting examples. Despite the name it is a court which handles the issues at stake!

A very well-known means of conflict resolution outside a court, but still adjudicatory in nature, is arbitration. This is a binding procedure, where following an arbitration hearing an arbitrator (a retired judge or an attorney) renders a decision.

If parties agree to arbitration they usually waive their right to a trial. That is to say, arbitration flows out of a sort of pre-dispute contract, in which the parties agree that in case a dispute should arise they will not turn to the court system.

Besides the contractual subjugation under the procedure, parties ought to agree on an arbitrator, an impartial person whom both sides trust. This arbitrator in turn reads and examines evidence, hears testimony and renders an opinion on liability and damages.

More recently most attention has been given to one means of conflict resolution that is, in fact, entirely voluntary – mediation. It is characterized by the in-depth investigation into the reasons for a conflict and the search for a consensual solution. A peculiar property is the employment of an impartial agent, who acts as a broker but is not entitled to take any decisions. By its very nature the consensual solution must be Pareto optimal and is thus frequently described as a 'win–win' situation for the parties. Most frequently mediation is applied in cases of disputes within families or among couples, for settlements of associates in businesses and in cases of controversial projects with respect to environmental issues (a case of public affairs). While the results of mediations are assumed to be binding they are nevertheless voluntary and thus lack any provision for enforcement.

Non-trial conflict resolution, arbitration and mediation are by no means all the possible alternatives: where members of close-knit groups pursue long-term commercial or interpersonal relationships they frequently anticipate the potential for conflict in future interactions. As a consequence they create ways to resolve their disputes by internal norms rather than legal rules maintained by courts and enforced by the state. Such internal norms are held to work less expensively and more quickly than formal law.

To see what the virtues of these types on conflict resolution are and to throw some light on likely problems, we will go back to the rationale for trial.

As we have seen trials occur when there is a misperception of the possibility of victory or defeat. Such misperceptions are reflected in the fact that the sum of subjective probabilities assigned to likely outcomes is higher than one and they tend to be costly, as the length and outcomes of trials are not so clear ex ante. In fact, trials are only a fairly small fraction of all the ways in which conflicts can be handled. But at the same time, without the option of trials the option of pre-trial settlement would be used much less. In other words, the option to initiate legal action, which is both risky and costly, can be seen as a threat to seek settlement.

However, one obstacle to settlement is obviously misinterpretation of the facts or, stated differently, a lack of information. This in turn can lead to distrust, which leads to an explanation for why both court-induced settlements and settlements out of court are worked under the auspices of an impartial third party: the arbitrator, the mediator and the like: 'These devices work principally by increasing the information that parties have about each other and thus tend to reduce the possibility of bargaining impasses' (Shavell, 2004, 414).

What we have just described are examples of what has been labelled **bargaining in the shadow of the law**. In other words, without the existence of legal and enforceable rules the means of bargaining and settlement would hardly be effective.

This is by no means an exhaustive treatment of the issues at hand but rather an appetizer for more comprehensive studies.

On law enforcement

Public and private enforcement

To start with, strictly speaking the heading should read 'additional perspectives of law enforcement', since liability rules as well as the option of trial and settlement are all means of enforcing legal regulations. One peculiarity of the following discussion is its focus on public enforcement. Of course, there is also **private enforcement**. As a matter of fact the processes by which violations of the law are investigated and the violator prosecuted are found in the fields of property, tort and contract, and more specifically marriage law, environmental law or trade law.

Enforcement is pursued by litigants, attorneys and detectives, as well as by boards of arbitration. Still, for good reasons these acting entities are sometimes complemented or even substituted by public institutions such as authorities and courts, by the appearance of prosecutors and judges, police detectives and tax inspectors.

There are four strands of reasoning for the explanation of these forms of appearance. One draws on the distinction between private interests in prosecution and enforcement, on the one hand, and a public interest, on the other hand. This can be illustrated by the desire of private parties to seek damages and the need to prevent the constitutional state from sustaining damages. The latter goal is accomplished by both the threat of punishment ex ante and the actual imposition of sanctions ex post.

Since each of these means of enforcement is resource absorbing, the question of what might be efficient levels of enforcement arises, both in the private and the public sphere and also whether the prevailing activities tend to overenforce or underenforce. To illustrate, it is plausible that in private enforcement a tendency towards overenforcement is likely as long as the expected gain from prosecution exceeds the cost incurred by the activity. With public enforcement, in turn, the decisive constraint is the share of budget (or taxpayers' money, respectively) that is dedicated to the task. If the strong assumption holds that violations are detected with a probability of one then the allocation of budgets could be optimal. However, the uncertainty of identification and conviction of criminals sometimes make it most likely that the efforts fall short of the optimum. As probabilities are low the punishment must be substantially increased in order to accomplish the task of **deterrence** ex ante and credibility ex post.

Prosecution and enforcement organized by the public may also have the advantage of economies of scale, such as in dragnet investigation; and it may be necessary to rely on the coercive monopoly of the state in order to gather otherwise hidden information or to effectively enforce compliance with a ruling.

Let us now look at the issues at hand in a more systematic way:

- Enforcement covers such issues as: how to prevent a (potential) tortfeasor from harmful activity; note that at the outset no distinction is made with respect to the intent of a harmful activity. That is to say that at this state of the discussion cases of criminal intent are covered as well as cases of rough negligence.

- Enforcement also deals with the issue of how justice can be done to a claimant.
- Moreover, the issue of how many resources ought to be dedicated to the prosecution and to the sanctioning of a lawbreaker is at stake.
- Last, the question of what the most effective instruments of deterrence and punishment are arises. The sanctions can be in monetary terms or can be imprisonment.

It is important to point out that the considerations concerning enforcement by no means need to be confined to individuals. Nowadays gangs, mafia-like organizations and other collectives may pose peculiar problems, not to forget legal entities such as corporations. Since this is just an introductory text, we will basically focus on individuals, however.

I shall proceed as follows: first, I will present a distinction between actions that have the potential for harmful consequences and those that have already caused harm. We then turn to the well known issue of 'crime and punishment' followed by a discussion of monetary sanctions versus imprisonment.

A fundamental problem of (public) enforcement

You will recall that we are talking about both the prevention of and sanctions for **illicit actions**. By the term illicit actions, I mean those that are likely to cause damage in such a way that its occurrence can be predicted with a distinct probability.

Our basic concern is to *deter illicit action*. In accomplishing this task we may well face the problem that a certain potentially dangerous act has been carried out, but without having caused harm. To illustrate: someone throws a stone from a ridge but, fortunately, does not hit the hiker walking underneath. Such an act has the *potential* to cause harm. If we want to deter a person from carrying out such act, then the sanction times the probability that the sanction will be effectuated must be larger than the gain in utility from that act (where utility may be just the *titillation* associated with throwing the stone).

Let the titillation be equivalent to 50 and let the sanction be 100. The probability that it can be effectuated is p and $p = 0.3$. The deterring effect amounts to $100 * 0.3 = 30$ which is definitely smaller than 50. So in order to neutralize the titillating effect, the sanction (fine) would have to be $50:0.3 = 166.67$!

Unfortunately, we have to bear in mind that the potentially harmful act might lead to effective harm only with a certain probability. Let this probability be h and $h = 0.2$. Other things being equal we get a deterring effect of $0.3 * 0.2 * 100 = 6$; and 6 definitely is much smaller than 30 and thus falls even shorter of the desired effect. However, if the fine were raised to $50:0.06 = 833.33$, a deterring effect would be obtained.

The promulgation of fines of this size may pose severe problems. For example, the fine may exceed the liquidity of a person. It has also been observed that politicians avoid the stipulation of such high fines. Besides, we must be aware that in our example we assumed that the potentially harmful act has actually been carried out. Still the probability that the sanction can be effectuated is quite small. Now assume that we wanted to deter people from carrying out such dangerous acts at all! We must readily assume that the effectiveness of our measures will be even less likely than in the case where an illicit act could be observed. This points towards a fundamental dilemma of deterrence inasmuch as preventive measures will be less effective than sanctions for dangerous acts, since in the latter case we can draw on better information than in the former. Stated differently, from the economic perspective sanctions for harmful acts are preferable to preventive measures.

For the sake of completeness, let us restate the full **objective function** for the relevant law-enforcing measures. It comprises the potential gains (titillation) of an act minus damage minus outlays for enforcement, which consists of identifying of the wrongdoer, executing a law and imposing the sanction. The identification of the wrongdoer deserves special attention for the following reason: frequently the identification is possible only through witnesses who can give testimony about the wanted person. For the prosecutor this poses a problem of asymmetric information, which is reinforced by the fact that the witness might hesitate to give testimony because she is afraid of an act of revenge on behalf of the wrongdoer. This can be overcome by an incentive to the witness in terms of a **bounty**. The bounty in turn is (part of) the cost of identifying the wrongdoer. Clearly the latter could try to prevent testimony by offering hush money. The maximum amount she can offer will be the maximum expected sanction.

At that state of affairs we are, however, about to leave the domain of economics inasmuch as the wrongdoer could threaten a potential witness with reprisals, which would most likely keep her from cooperation with authorities. Such familiar problems are apt to raise the cost of law enforcement substantially.

An 'equilibrium' number of crimes?

Your intuition here most probably is that problems of the kind just addressed are unlikely to occur in cases of petty negligence, but rather in cases where harm has been done to a person deliberately. This is quite correct! We have thus quietly arrived in the domain of crime. Theft, robbery and murder are typical acts with criminal intent. But we must also bear in mind tax evasion and corruption as well as so-called **victimless crimes**, such as carrying illegal weapons, smuggling, drugs trafficking and pornography. What has economics to say about all this?

Before we set out to offer some answers we ought to stop and think about the following: the economics of crime and law enforcement rests on the assumption that criminal intent reflects rational decision making. Individuals carrying out crimes are thus treated as if they acted rationally. Crimes driven by emotions are thus beyond the scope of economic reasoning. It is at this point that an oppositional point of view comes in sight: crimes are not just the result of intentional acts. They are an outcome determined by biological and socioeconomic factors. The importance of this view must not be denied. Longlasting unemployment as well as large disparities in income and wealth, to name just two influential variables, do push up the crime rate. Still, intent or deliberateness is crucial for the classification of a harmful act as a crime. And we follow good economic practice if we assume that intent can be modelled as the rational pursuit of utility, even if we thus risk that the reminder of this chapter does not cover crime as a whole.

Still there is a large range of crimes that can essentially be explained by means of a cost–benefit calculus in which the (in)effectiveness of measures for prevention or prosecution is cast in economic terms. By the same token the minimization of the social cost of law enforcement is sought.

Whether sanctions such as a penalty or imprisonment are a deterrent against crime at all depends on:

- the probability that it can be effectuated
- the severity of the sanction.

But what tempts a person to commit the crime? It is the utility derived from an illicit act. To illustrate, consider embezzlement. Utility will increase with the amount of embezzled money. Applying standard theory the marginal utility increases with an increase of embezzled money at a decreasing rate. However, committing a crime incurs costs. Preparations have to be made, equipment purchased (such as picklocks), to which the opportunity cost of foregone activities must be added. In short, the gains from crimes are available only at a price. We can thus establish a 'demand schedule' for the crime at hand, which reflects the willingness to pay of the criminal for embezzlement of a certain size, which can readily be measured in monetary terms.

Now let us turn to prevention, prosecution and sanctions again. The joint impact of all three gives the deterrent effect on the criminal. More specifically deterrence is effectuated by:

- the amount and type of expected punishment
- the size of public measures for the prevention and prosecution of crimes which society is willing to bear in terms of taxes
- and, finally, private measures such as special locks and so on, which potential victims are willing to finance.

Disregarding the last point for the moment we find an interesting interdependence of the other two variables. Note that the probability of enactment of the sanction depends on the willingness to expend additional costs for prevention and prosecution. However, if this is true then it suggests that a very high level of punishment can compensate for low spending on deterrence. However, practice tells us that the opposite is more likely: a high probability of conviction and punishment is the more appropriate means. This is shown in the Figure 4.1, where only certain conviction can effectively deter a crime.

Figure 4.1 depicts the cost–benefit calculus of a criminal (an embezzler, say) when the punishment is given. The probabilities of its being effectuated, however, vary. They are assumed to be 1 or definitely well below 1. Embezzlement is chosen

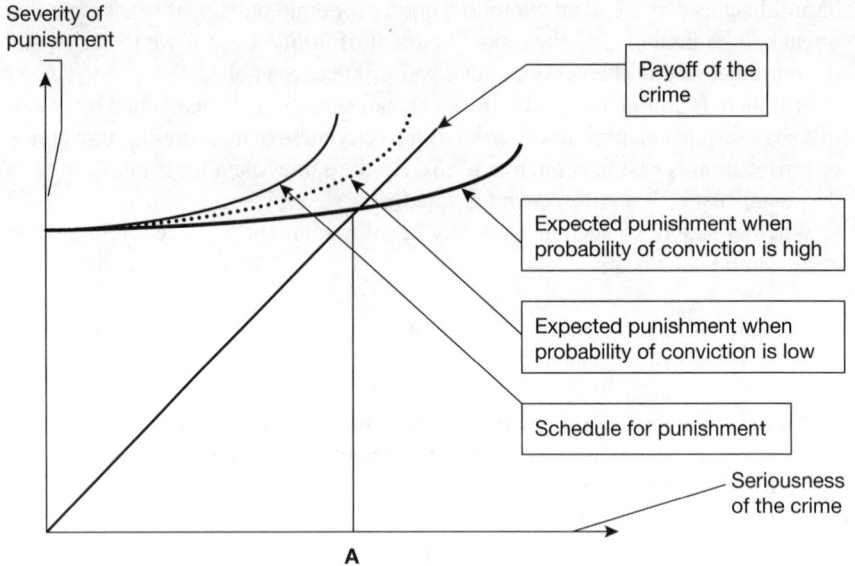

Figure 4.1 Individual cost–benefit calculus of a criminal

Payoff is assumed to increase with the seriousness of the crime. Whether deterrence is effective or not depends on the probability with which the punishment effectuates. With high probability of conviction crimes right of A are deterred.

as the crime, since in this case the severity of the act can (as already has been said) readily be measured in monetary terms.

According to our earlier reasoning we can link the inclination to commit crimes (or the demand schedule for crimes) to the cost which are incurred by police and taxpayers at large to prevent and prosecute crimes.

Assuming that these costs increase with the number of crimes that ought to be prevented or prosecuted (thus making potential wrongdoers aware of their risks), we can derive Figure 4.2 which gives rise to the prediction of the number of inevitable crimes under the prevailing circumstances.

Now, let us assume that the law enforcement efforts are increased. What will be the consequence for the number of predictable crimes? Exactly: since the cost curve shifts up and to the left, the number of crimes 'in equilibrium' must drop. (You could now try to show the consequences for the demand for as well as the number of criminal acts when the prosecution of crimes for some reason becomes less rigorous.)

Recall that at the beginning of this section, I mentioned measures that can be taken by private individuals. These comprise the installation of special locks, video surveillance and so on. Clearly, they are complementary to public efforts of enforcement. However, it may be the case that private parties or households feel uneasy because in their perception public enforcement is insufficient or just not

Marginal utility and
marginal cost of
committing crimes

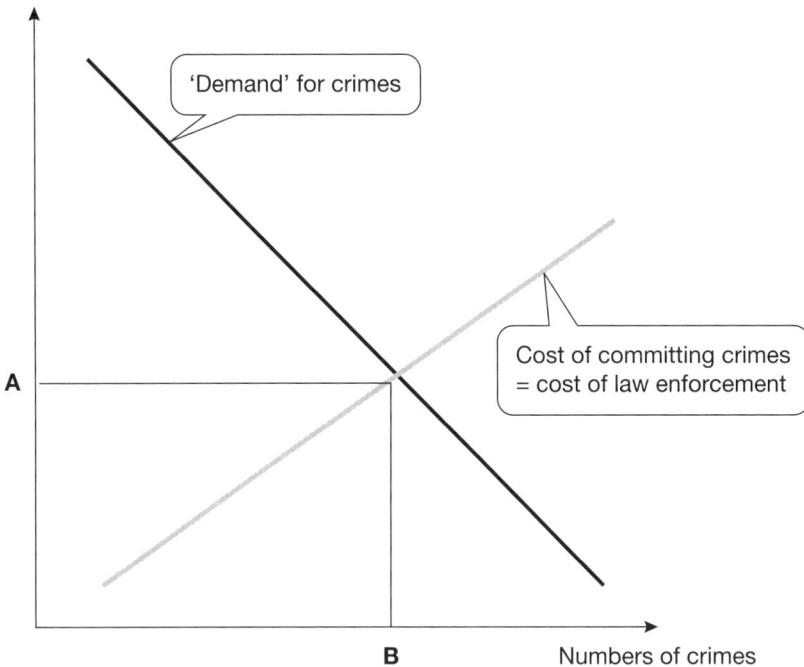

Figure 4.2 Equilibrium crime rate

When the law of demand applies to criminals (marginal utility being positive but
decreasing with the number of criminal acts) and a given marginal cost function for
commitment of crimes, there is an equilibrium level of crimes (well above zero!) at B,
where marginal gains equal marginal costs at A.

effective enough. Under such circumstances, the costs private parties are willing
to incur are borne because substitutes to public measures are sought.

The more money is spent on appropriate devices, the more crimes can be deterred
(*ceteris paribus*). The effect of private measures can again be depicted in a graph
that resembles demand for crimes and the increase in cost with the efforts to deter
crimes.

Having reviewed the principal conditions for the willingness to commit crimes
and appropriate economic conditions for law enforcement we may finally summarize all costs which ought to be considered when the social **cost of crime** is to
be minimized (in the spirit of a welfare analysis). First, there are the costs that
accrue to criminals: learning skills, purchasing equipment, spotting opportunities
and other activities that cause an opportunity cost. Second, there are the costs of
protection and prosecution, borne by the public. Third, there are private costs of

protection from becoming a victim. Finally, the welfare losses caused by bodily and mental harm, as well as those of moving to safer residential areas ought to be included.

Ways of punishment

In the final section of this chapter, we turn to one particular aspect of law enforcement, which proves important for both intended deterrence and the (social) cost of punishment. It is about **prevention versus sanctions** and money fines versus imprisonment as measures of punishment.

Let us look at the issue of deterrence first. Its effectiveness will depend on the income and wealth of a wrongdoer. Fines intentionally create a disutility for their recipient, even if there is only a certain probability that they will be effectuated. In order to be an effective deterrent, the size of the fine times the probability of effectuation must marginally exceed all gains from the crime, that is to say material gains as well as whatever intrinsic satisfaction is gained (a component of forfeit notwithstanding, although morally this touches on the issue of socially supported revenge). Moreover, it must be clear at the outset that money fines should increase with the severity of a crime. Given the inherent logic of marginal calculus, lump-sum fines will be cancelled out as the wrongdoer does a cost–benefit calculus of the net benefits of the intended criminal offence. However, in principle, the tool will only work with a solvent offender. We ought to be careful here and take an even closer look: what if her solvency is low? Then the deterrence effect might be blurred by the fact that the fine cannot be fully enforced (i.e. the opportunity cost for the punished person drops to zero, once the boundary of her solvency is reached by the size of a fine). There are actually three options: one is to take hold of future earnings by compulsory retention of a fixed percentage of future income. The second is to impose the obligation to do a certain type of work as a forfeit. The third is to combine a fine and imprisonment.

So, when is imprisonment alone adequate? From what has been said already it follows that it is the only means of punishment in case of insolvency. However, this is not completely true. Imprisonment can create substantial opportunity costs to the wrongdoer and thus the deterrent effect of imprisonment can be higher than that of a money sanction even in cases of a very solvent person. In fact, the opposite is true, namely that being taken to prison creates a higher disutility even than an excessively high fine, depending on the average earnings per unit of time.

We must be aware that imprisonment can serve two more options. By removing a person from society her potential to impair others is brought down for the time of imprisonment. Also, rehabilitation of the criminal can be sought. However, although both aspects have considerable economic components, we cannot go into details here. It must not be overlooked that imprisonment is a costly variant of punishment! In general, it is considerably more costly than monetary sanctions.

This brings us to the question of the preferable policy for the enforcer in terms of cost. Now, from the viewpoint of expenditure of resources imprisonment is (much) more costly than monetary sanctions. However, evidently the intended effect on wrongdoers has to be borne in mind as well. This boils down to the question of the likely optimal solution both in terms of deterrence and public spending. What the solution could look like is summarized in Figure 4.3.

On the axes of Figure 4.3, the severity of punishment by either monetary sanctions or imprisonment are plotted assuming an appropriate scale. The 'isoquant' I^0 represents a certain level for which combinations of monetary fines and imprisonment have the same deterrent effect. The price schedule in turn represents the rate at which fines can be turned into imprisonment. It captures what has been pointed out already: that the imposition of the monetary fine is less costly than that of prison. The optimal solution is given at the point of tangency.

This, however, is not the end of the story, but it should suffice to illustrate the contribution of economics to the issue of punishment. Two remarks must be added:

1   There is an ever growing literature on issues such as **organized crime**, corruption, drug trafficking and related fields, which partly is theoretical in

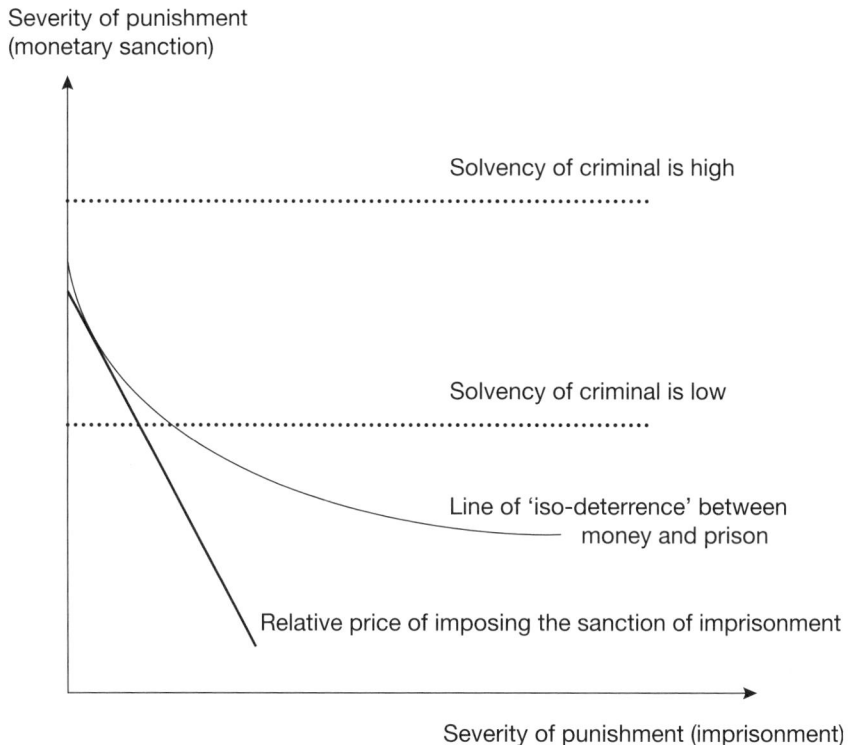

Severity of punishment
(monetary sanction)

Solvency of criminal is high

Solvency of criminal is low

Line of 'iso-deterrence' between
money and prison

Relative price of imposing the sanction of imprisonment

Severity of punishment (imprisonment)

Figure 4.3 Punishment by monetary sanctions or imprisonment

Given the high price for imprisonment relative to monetary sanctions, it is efficient to punish solvent criminals by monetary sanctions; with low solvency, a combination of both is appropriate.

nature but encompasses a growing number of empirical works (which sometimes appears under the label of 'jurimetric' analysis). One area that is much investigated in the United States is that of the relation between possession of firearms, gun control and fatalities.

2   We have not mentioned the existing research on the relationship between crimes and the **death penalty**. As a matter of fact, the existing literature does not contain a conclusive answer to the efficacy of the death penalty. The issue at hand cannot be determined by theory but is a fundamentally empirical matter. What can be said, however, is that it is very costly for society: trials are excessively long and juries are extremely expensive. So from the economic perspective the death penalty is quite problematic – to say the least.

Key terms

alternative means of conflict resolution	legal aid
American rule	legal assistance
arbitration	legal protection insurance
attorney's fee	litigation
bargaining in the shadow of the law	litigation costs
bounty	mediation
British (European) rule	money sanction
cost of crime	objective function
courts	opinion
crime	optimal amount
death penalty	organized crime
defendant	plaintiff
demand for trials	prevention vs sanctions
deterrence	private enforcement
illicit action	professional associations (bar)
imprisonment	public law enforcement
judges	rent seeking
jury	settlement
law enforcement	victimless crimes

Recommended reading

Adams, Michael, *Ökonomische Analyse des Zivilprozesses* (Economic Analysis of Civil Action), Meisenheim/Glan, 1981.

Becker, Gary S., Crime and punishment: an economic approach, *Journal of Political Economy*, 76, 1968, 169.

Bundesministerium für Justiz, Lewisch, Peter and Rechberger, Walter H., *100 Jahre ZPO – Ökonomische Analyse des Zivilprozesses* [100 Years Of Civil Action – Code], Vienna 1998.

Cooter, Robert, The objectives of private and public judges, *Public Choice*, 41, 1983, 107.

Cooter, Robert D. and Rubinfeld, Daniel L., Economic analysis of legal disputes and their resolution, *Journal of Economic Literature*, 27, 1989, 1067.

Landes, William and Posner, Richard A., Adjudication as a private good, *Journal of Legal Studies*, 8, 1979, 235.

Polinsky, A. Mitchell and Shavell, Steven, The economic theory of public enforcement of law, *Journal of Economic Literature*, 38, 2000, 45.

Posner, Richard A., What do judges and justices maximize? (The same thing everybody else does), *Supreme Court Economic Review*, 3, 1993, 1–41.

Shavell, Steven, *Foundations of Economic Analysis of Law*, Cambridge, MA, 2004.

Tullock, Gordon, *The Logic of the Law*, New York, 1971.

Tullock, Gordon, *Trials on Trial – The Pure Theory of Legal Procedure*, New York, 1980.

5 The law and economics of the public sector

Legislative and executive

Constitutional law and administrative law: neglected fields?

Where the economic approach to the fields of **constitutional law** and **administrative law** is at stake, the situation in the United States is slightly different from that in the German-speaking sphere (and Europe in general): this is particularly striking with respect to ongoing research in these fields, where the USA is well ahead of the continent. This is surprising inasmuch as the joint consideration of legal and economic aspects of states has a very long tradition, in particular in the German-speaking sphere. In fact, the importance of (theoretical) economic analysis for the solution of legal problems was emphasized by outstanding scholars such as Joseph von Sonnenfels as early as the eighteenth century. Sonnenfels was the first professor of political economy at the law faculty of Vienna University and his two-volume textbook *Police, Action and Finance* (*Administration, Markets and Financing*) marks a first high point in the combination of economic and legal approaches to issues of society. This concern can be traced back to *Kameralismus* (**cameralism**, the specific German version of mercantilism) and continued in the provision of studies of *Staatswissenschaft* or political economics in most law schools, which strangely enough were abandoned only in the 1970s – at the time when the economic analysis of law gained momentum in the leading American law schools and the most prominent schools such as Yale Law School established such programmes as, for instance, that on 'Law, economics and public policy'! This is not to say that in Europe there were no scholars at all, but a book such as the volume *Öffentliches Recht als ein Gegenstand ökonomischer Forschung* (Public Law as a subject of economic research) (Engel and Morlok, 1998) then really formed a landmark and clearly marked a turn in the perception of that field of research.

The recognition of the need for more interdisciplinary research was triggered by familiar movements such as public sector reform along with downsizing, outsourcing and the adoption of new public management, at least at the beginning of the 1980s. Interestingly enough, a good deal of this boost came from the broad support for regulatory impact analysis by the OECD and subsequently by the European Union (see Chapter 6 for a brief review).

Note that I am not claiming that there was no relevant research at all throughout most of the 20th century. Of course there were occasional studies and some pioneering publications; frequently these were undertaken by lawyers or entered the literature in terms of cost–benefit analysis by advisors to the government, concerning specific issues in lawmaking. But there was then – with the exception of a couple of research centres – no systematic activity. This holds specifically for administration, although the problems posed by the underlying principle of statutory law are somewhat different to those in common law. It applies less to constitutional law, which is the main focus of the first part of this chapter.

So turning to lawmaking and more specifically to issues pertinent to constitutional law, we can clearly build on well-established bodies of knowledge. First of all, there is the field of **public choice**, both in the explanatory as well as the normative specification. Dennis Mueller's textbook on public choice (2005) is the first reference here. The application to and the commonality with the law is discussed in Farber and Frickey (1991). One other major source is the new institutional economics, which you have already heard about in Chapter 1. A comprehensive reference here is Furubotn and Richter (1991, Chapter 9 in particular). For readers, who are familiar with the German language it should be pointed out that the textbook by Blankart (2001) is, to a large extent, written in the spirit of public choice.

Before we can set out for a survey of issues of constitutional law, two introductory remarks are in order, the first relating to terminology and the second to methodology.

As you know, this textbook was originally written for the German-speaking world. It is interesting but also sometimes confusing that the three main countries in which German is spoken, namely, Germany, Switzerland and Austria, differ in the use of technical terms; and this peculiarity is shared with Great Britain and the USA. The following will make use of a somewhat streamlined terminology, but readers must be aware that consultation of sources and materials might require the consultation of a special dictionary for legal terminology.

Second, one can approach the subject issue from two different perspectives, one being the **public interest perspective** and the other (not surprising) the **private interest perspective**:

- *Public interest*. This view signifies that both the legislative and the executive branches consider the improvement of general welfare in both the design as well as the implementation of legal norms. Therefore they will follow advice by impartial experts on how to meet the standards of Pareto optimality, where private activities fail to accomplish this task. Thus the public interest reflects the need for norms concerning collective goods, externalities, the containment of market power, norms and standardization, where these are not brought about by private initiative. Moreover, the causation and safeguarding of just (fair) distribution of equal opportunities, income and wealth are at stake. Note that performance of a public interest on behalf of legislators and the executive branch possibly entails a correction of subjectively driven individual actions. It is for this reason that the public interest is associated with **paternalism** (see also the notion of the 'benevolent dictator' in the theoretical literature about public goods!). Where the explicit correction of individual demands is at stake for the same reasons the corresponding actions are labelled **merit goods**,

large-scale privatizations – without any provisions concerning the responsibility of a minister – would definitely violate the constitution.

Conventional theory of the functions of the state: a revision course

The typical starting point for a theory of the functions of the state is found in the insight that the market mechanism fails as a means of **coordination**. It is generally agreed that this holds for matters of allocation and (re-)distribution, but there is disagreement on how well it holds for the stabilization of the economy.

We will go through a list of conditions for government activities later. It must be stressed, however, that the purpose of this section is to present some of the underpinnings for an economic discussion of **constitutional acts** and administrative law, broadly defined, but that this does not imply that there can be no alternatives to the state in handling these issues. Nowadays, besides states, there are an ever increasing number of international organizations such as the UN or the **WTO**, which handle what are essentially 'public goods' (this type of organization has eventually been labelled a **QUANGO**, i.e. quasi-non-governmental organization). Moreover, there are officially recognized but wholly voluntary **NGOs**, which should be mentioned here, from Greenpeace to the Red Cross and Red Crescent and charitable organizations on the level of local parishes.

This multiplicity would justify a broader discussion on the needs and limits of state interference where coordination is otherwise lacking. This could be done along the lines of the principle of **subsidiarity** (as laid down in the treaty of Rome, Article Va, but going back to the Roman Catholic Encyclica *Quadragesimo Anno* of 1931 by Pope Pius XI): this principle states that problem solving should be left to the smallest subunit of society which is just capable of managing the issue at hand (which could be a family, a private club or a community, but at times ought to be the EU council in Brussels). From an economic perspective, the theory of (**fiscal**) **federalism** jointly with the theory of clubs provides the tools for analysing this type of problem.

In a nutshell, then, the theory of market failure alone cannot serve as an exhaustive justification for shaping the functions of the state. In fact, it even appears inappropriate to shape what has been termed 'core functions' in the course of the discussion about a 'constitution for the European Union' as well as a similar discussion about a substantial revision of the constitution for the republic of Austria. In that respect, Box 5.1, which lists characteristic issues for state activity, is just a rough scheme intended to facilitate the further discussion in the present chapter of the book.

Self-restraint through cooperation and coordination

Remember the question we raised at the very beginning of this book, namely, why should rational self-interested people observe constraints in the form of legal norms? One reason was that it can be in the mutual interest to establish a responsibility for harm, such as betraying or stealing. Although such restraint could in principle be

Box 5.1 Issues for state activity

Here are some characteristic issues that go under the label either of market failure or 'public goods'.

Pure collective goods: beneficiaries or users of such goods are never in one another's way (unless there are some limits in capacity, of course); in more technical terms there is no rivalry among users and, moreover, exclusion is impossible or at least extremely costly – examples are security, defence and the merits of diplomacy.

Negative externalities: the burden imposed on third parties in the course of an activity that is beneficial or gainful for its originator is neither voluntarily borne nor compensated (due to violations of the conditions for the Coase theorem to apply), with the consequence that the activity level at hand is inefficiently high – typical examples are found in environment pollution.

Positive externalities: third parties benefit from beneficial or gainful activity of the originator without taking their share of cost or price for the benefits received, with the consequence that the activity level is suboptimally low – as in the case of vaccinations against epidemic illnesses or the impact of individual education on welfare-enhancing economic growth.

Merit goods: because of a misperception of the impact on well-being, demand is either too high (e.g. alcohol addiction) or too low (e.g. continuing education).

Option goods: there is no stable demand function due to stochastic shifts caused by weather or risks of accidents, so that users cannot readily be charged efficient prices – which typically is the case for casualty hospitals, preserved natural areas or even railway lines in areas where air transportation dominates.

Variants of option goods are the following:

Sites with 'prestige value': even if people do not intend to visit a site they want the historical importance of their residential area to be documented.

'Bequest value': residents are proud to be able to leave something to future generations who cannot yet reveal their preferences and hence cannot yet value the assets themselves.

The site allows for an '*existence value*', inasmuch as removal for the sake of a more profitable use of the parcel would cause the site to be irretrievably lost.

Sites with '*educational value*', which, in turn, can foster cultural identity, raise awareness about traditions and create aesthetic perceptions.

Natural monopolies: these occur due to the fact that with decreasing average and marginal costs, it does not pay to operate more than one plant; in such cases, marginal cost pricing requires that the fixed costs are, for example, borne by the state and monopoly power made subject to regulation. Note, however, that there are instances where installation of a certain capacity entails exceeding minimal costs, provided that demand is also at a sufficiently high level. (In this case there is room for a second or third provider.)

Misperception of risks: people tend to be short sighted and tend to make mistakes, which can be met by compulsory old age pension schemes, for example (making this issue closely resemble merit goods).

the result of spontaneous agreement (a view held by economist Friedrich August von Hayek), it could also be the outcome of collective decision making. This, in turn, is characteristic of laws that are (abuses aside) typical results of democratic procedures in the legislature.

So before we proceed to legislation on the constitutional level, let us look at two illustrations of the way in which a need for cooperation for the sake of coordination can emerge. We shall start with

1   a rationale for a right of way

2   **'prisoner's dilemma'**.

Imagine two motorists, A and B, approaching an intersection. In what follows, we look at the various ways in which each could try to pass the intersection, given that the other vehicle is approaching. We will make the choice of action dependent on the gain associated with the actions. In doing this, we can depict the situation in a matrix typically used for the normal form of a game (see Table 5.1).

The two options for passing the intersection are 'wait' or 'do not wait', which is equivalent to leaving the right of way to either motorist. Which action ('strategy' in terms of game theory) is chosen depends on the valuation of a loss of time, which is captured in the 'payoffs'.

In [1], both face a loss of time, while in [2], A suffers the loss while B enjoys the benefit of a run through; exactly the opposite is true for [3], whereas in [4], they will collide, with dire (if not fatal) consequences. Now, let us for expository reasons apply the alleged virtues of the market as a means of coordination. In this case the motorists jump out of their cars, in order to bid for the right of way, which obviously will go to B, following the Kaldor-Hicks test. Two objections can be raised against this procedure: first, given the loss associated with waiting just to let the other driver pass (cell [1]), the transaction cost of bidding are likely prohibitive and, second, it could be that in future situations the probability of approaching the intersection from the right side or the left side is 0.5 for both.

It is not hard to see the virtues of an approved rule that the right of way goes to the motorist approaching from the right side. It will minimize the social cost for both – unless they are not risk loving, of course.

Our second example, the 'prisoner's dilemma', has been widely used for the exploration of problems in the provision of public goods in the presence of 'free riding'. It also served as the starting point for the introduction of a security service (police) in a state of transition from **anarchy** to the acknowledgement of property rights, thus illustrating the origin of a 'protective state'. This underlines the relevance of the problem for an analytic approach to issues of the constitutional state.

Table 5.1 Matrix of normal form of game

	B waits	*B does not wait*
A waits	[1] −3, −3	[2] −3, 7
A does not wait	[3] 5, −3	[4] −8, −8

The background is as follows. In the state of anarchy, two neighbours, who by assumption survive by collecting fruits, will spend effort on collection, but being not yet bound by any property rule they also spend effort on stealing each other's stocks, which, in turn, requires additional efforts to protect themselves from loss. The efforts to steal and to protect cause a disutility. The mutual acknowledgement of private property is a welfare-enhancing improvement in this situation, to which both can agree – but clearly the rational, self-interested peasant is tempted to violate the right of her neighbour when she expects him to be so naive as to believe in compliance. Only the presence of a security service can produce a solution here. The police officer, as we will call her in short, will create security as a publicly provided service. Her presence will deter both peasants at a time. However, the service has to be paid for. The advantage accrued to the service is expressed by the willingness to pay. According to the conditions for the efficient provision of a collective good or service, the aggregated willingness to pay must cover the marginal cost of provision. Let us simply assume for now that the gains and the willingness to pay are symmetric. Now, it is well known that there is no rivalry in use so that once established each peasant will feel free not to pay her share of the cost. If the cost were €160 and the willingness to pay concurrently €120, then the payoffs for the two strategies of our peasants A and B can again be denoted in matrix form (see Table 5.2).

It is easy to see that cooperation would be profitable for both (cell [1]), but this is dominated by [2] on behalf of B, which, in turn, makes [3] preferable for A, who then realizes that [4] would be even better . . . , so A and B find the best situation for them in [2] and [4] respectively. This contradiction in turn inhibits the introduction of the service.

For the solution to the dilemma we could follow several lines: one is found in the theory of repeated games, in which it is demonstrated that as the repetition of the situation goes to infinity a cooperative outcome emerges. This has been demonstrated most impressively in a mathematical model by Schotter (1981). One could also ask whether there are changes in strategy on behalf of the participants which could lead to a quicker convergence: a seminal result is **tit for tat** (Axelrod, 1984). Here the solution is brought about if the players cooperate on the first move (which cannot lead to convergence if the opponent started with defection) and then do whatever the other player does on the previous move.

These aspects notwithstanding, we must be aware that a prisoner's dilemma can also be overcome when a third party has the legitimate power to implement a solution. With respect to the constitutional state that could be brought about by assigning to the third party the power to tax. Such an approach is traced by Nozick (1974).

Table 5.2 Matrix of peasants' strategies

	B agrees	*B does not agree*
A agrees	[1] 40, 40	[2] –40, 120
A does not agree	[4] 120, –40	[3] 0, 0

Although we have reached the starting point for a most fascinating tour of the state of the art in the understanding of conflict and cooperation, which is essential for the understanding of the origin and the objective of the law we must stop here, but not without encouraging you to indulge in the vast literature.

Legislation on a constitutional level

Distinction between form and substance of constitutional acts

For a better understanding of the problems that are sometimes associated with constitutional acts it proves useful to adopt the distinction between a constitutional act in a formal sense in contrast to substantial sense (where the distinction is part of current doctrine; see Mayer-Maly, 1999, 139).

When constitutional acts in a formal sense are at stake, then naturally this entails a demanding guarantee of duration. This in turn explains why such norms need to materialize under special conditions: one condition is a qualified majority decision (up to **unanimity**); the other minimum requirement concerns the turnout (half or two thirds of the legislative body).

As far as the substance of an act is concerned, whether it qualifies as constitutional obviously depends on the content. Usually there is little controversy about the following issues: the rules of lawmaking, entitlements and obligations of the top governmental bodies, possible federalism, legal protection and fundamental rights. However, there is an ongoing debate about likely other contents, as is readily demonstrated in recent processes of constitutional reform (see the European Union and, even more incisively, the debate in Austria). The quest for the reasonable substance of laws to be considered as a matter of constitution is linked to economics, of course, inasmuch as one would readily assume alignment with the theory of **pure collective goods** as well as the need for unanimity. Only when both the properties of the issue at hand and the way in which it is decided fulfil certain minimal requirements can one expect the basic framework of the state to exhibit a stable equilibrium.

At this point, a critical view of real-life lawmaking can serve as a good example for the use of economics to this end. We must thank those scholars of public choice who established and partly tested models in which the conditions under which a motion can be established are demonstrated, not just as an ordinary act but as an act on the constitutional level. While the formal requirements are thus perfectly met, the substantial content of such acts can be questionable. They do not necessarily reflect a broad consensus of the voters but rather the interests of lobbies who were able to accomplish the support of a sufficient number of members of parliament. Thus for example regulations are fostered which are profitable for special groups only and not for the sake of distributive justice but rather for the sake of economic advantages over other groups.

The somewhat disturbing lesson from such possibilities is that the formal prerequisite for a substantial constitutional act is a necessary but not a sufficient condition for that act really to be constitutional in substance. You will definitely agree that this exhibits a challenge for the analyst: to conceive rules for rules that contain the necessary incentives to prohibit abuse of the legislature. This is part of the economic analysis of constitutions as well as of constitutional economics.

The difference between the two seemingly identical fields is the following. As stated earlier, the constitution is essentially a set of rules designed to facilitate rule making. Its purpose is the stabilisation of social interaction; it specifies rights and obligations that are (and must be) observable and enforceable. In other words a constitution is essentially a contract intended to secure the mutual gains from social cooperation. These gains are a public good; therefore the maintenance of the constitutional contract gives rise to a problem that will not resolve itself naturally. In the presence of opportunism the agreement achieved through the contract must be enforceable.

Constitutional economics is concerned with actions taken within the constitutional rules. In German, this is quite evocatively labelled *Ordnungspolitik*. In the remainder of this section we will concentrate on constitutional acts. To this end we can make use of theories of collective decision making, the theory of **voter turnout** as well as theories of **campaign funding**, the theory of public goods and fiscal federalism.

Also of interest here are theories of political competition and **logrolling** (mutual support for motions which would not find a sufficient majority from one party alone). Moreover, rent seeking ought to be mentioned, i.e. the use of resources not for productive ends but for the influence on decision makers (one example has been given already, when the possibility of establishing the requirements of formal constitutional acts was at stake). (In a later section, we will get to know an amazing practical example of rent seeking.) Finally the role of the judiciary must not be overlooked! Clearly, this list of approaches is by no means exhaustive. To illustrate, the **Leviathan** approach to the power of the state has much to do with the quest for constitutional retrenchments of the power of the state. This idea goes back to Thomas Hobbes, who postulated that the abstention of ruling power by the individual causes a type of state that is no longer obliged to give account of its actions. Challenging as it is, closer examination of this theory would definitely exceed the limits of an introduction to the subject matter. However, if your curiosity has been stirred by these remarks, you may find it interesting to have a look at James Buchanan (1978).

We shall conclude this section with a look at the division of powers in the constitutional state. The division of powers can take two forms, one focusing on a horizontal division and the other on the vertical division. With reference to a horizontal division of powers, the question is whether there is a rationale for the separation of legislature, executive branch and the judiciary.

As far as the vertical restraint on power is concerned, the question arises of what the rationale for fiscal federalism is (the assignment of the power to tax and the obligation for the provision of public goods to different governmental units). Let us keep to the horizontal restraints. The standard argument is that rational and self-seeking rulers would abuse their monopoly power: Consequently there is a tradeoff between the likely efficiency of a single ruling entity and all kinds of externality at prohibitively high transaction costs for the public: hence the separation of powers.

While this is widely accepted for democracies, it is interesting to note that both communist and fascist political philosophers denied the need for the **division of powers** by arguing that there is harmony between the will of the people and the actions of their leaders.

Of course, the separation of powers could lead to a loss in efficiency in how the state's agenda is handled. In fact this could benefit from a large-scale cost–benefit analysis, where the losses due to the power of exploitation are held against the gains from restricting that very power to exploit.

One view which was eventually brought forward in research on the administrative state and **bureaucracy** is that citizens in their well-understood self-interest prefer to see the performance of the public agenda in the hands of expert **civil servants** rather than in the hands of elected politicians! Public sector reformers claim that this view is valid only for the so-called core functions of the state nowadays, whereas many former public services can be left to private enterprises, thus replacing the machinery of combined democratic and bureaucratic modes of coordination by that of markets.

The separation of powers was to some extent practised in Greek municipal republics! The pioneering book on the issue is Montesquieu's *The Spirit of Laws* of 1748. John Locke is also concerned about the separation of powers in his *Two Treatises on Government*. The separation of powers is a topic for scholarly reasoning, as can be illustrated by the conference on the occasion of the 300th birthday of Montesquieu entitled *Separation of Powers in the Constitutional State*; the conference volume was edited by Detlef Merten in 1997. Another monograph of interest is Marshaw (1997).

Economic aspects of lawmaking

Why constitutional acts are decided on by qualified majority decision

Before we can deal with the question in the title we need to answer another, preliminary question: what is the intended purpose of voting? The stylized answer is that it serves as a means for the coordination among people when other means of coordination (are likely to) fail.

Consider a **voting rule**: it is hardly imaginable that it could be the result of a competitive auction; the same is true for a paternalistic command, if the participants are conceded a certain degree of autonomy. Note, however, that such an account must be rooted in an ontological justification (i.e. it is presumed as existing, either from experience (Aristotle) or from reasoning (Kant); it cannot by itself be derived by economics).

Votes (democratic procedures) can serve the following purposes:

- A decision about a subject (recent examples of straightforward issues in Austria were, first, the reduction of the number of pupils in class for high schools in order to improve the quality of education and, second, the establishment of a basic income for needy Austrian citizens – both were subjects of **petitions** for referendum (!), which is a means of **direct democracy** in the republic of Austria).

• The decision about procedural issues such as voting rules, for example the minimum number of signatories required for a petition for referendum to make it an agenda item for parliament.

• The decision to delegate the entitlement of decision making to other (groups of) people (delegates, congress members, parties). This process we can call an 'election'.

What is the economic problem here? Actually, there are two. The first is the issue of the formation of collective preferences, which is dealt with on a theoretical basis by collective choice theory and subsequently by social choice, a branch of applied economics. But to find out the preferences of the electorate entails costs thus leading to the quest for efficiency.

The issue at hand is further complicated by the following consideration: for decisions to be taken democratically, two preliminary questions ought to be answered. First, who has a right to participate and, second, what majority should be decisive. Now, in principle, the answers to these questions implies that the same two questions have to be answered beforehand, which leads to something called **infinite regress**. This is a well-known problem with voting rules. Kenneth Arrow, in his seminal analysis of voting rules, solved this puzzling problem by postulating a couple of preconditions that ought to be met in collective decision making. Arrow's result, the **impossibility theorem**, will be summarized shortly! The problem of who ought to have a vote can also be analyzed on theoretical grounds using economics. One illustrative example is the issue of 'citizenship'. Dennis Mueller has derived the conditions under which immigrants achieve citizenship, which entails the right to take part in the democratic process of a state (see 'Rights and citizenship in the European Union' in Blankart and Mueller, 2004, 61).

It is almost a matter of intuition to see that the question of a 'right to vote', which expresses an inalienable right of a citizen, affects the entire citizenry and thus establishes one example of an (almost) unanimous decision. This in turn suggests a constitutional matter. But given the problem illustrated by the prisoner's dilemma together with the problem of establishing the rules for collective decision making we must be aware that such constitutional matters contain legal, political, philosophical and moral questions and a challenge for the economist at the same time. The general question is why *homini oeconomici* in their own interest should agree to common rules, which define limitations to their range of actions. To illustrate: how has the agreement been accomplished that in democratic decisions in principle each vote has the same weight irrespective of initial wealth (violations notwithstanding)? The relevance of these issues for jurisprudence should be obvious: while the need for a formal procedure of the creation of constitutional acts is obvious, one cannot be sure that the observation of procedure alone can secure the stability of the intended task. To this end, an analytical approach such as that of social choice is indispensable.

But what about the criterion for feasible solutions in constitutional matters? Here the answer of the economist is straightforward: Pareto efficiency! But Pareto efficiency requires unanimity. Despite the fact that some quite uncomfortable consequences are associated with this requirement we must also be aware of its virtues. One such virtue is that if all citizens have voted deliberately and freely and the result is unanimous, this implies a politically stable solution is possible for the problem at hand.

However, a few observations result from this:

- The accomplishment of unanimity is facilitated considerably when the preferences in the electorate are similar, that is to say the electorate is fairly homogenous.
- In cases where preferences are dispersed, a vote is reasonably prepared for by **bargaining** about the possibilities of an agreeable compromise.
- Bargaining is time consuming and thus incurs a cost. This indicates that unanimity can be a costly objective.
- A peculiar problem with unanimity is that it gives individual voters who have a dissenting opinion on the subject matter tremendous power. They can block the required unanimity by a veto, which, in turn, is hardly in the interest of the other voters.

From these considerations, it is obvious that the requirement of unanimity for an act to pass the legislature must be carefully contemplated, not only because of the underlying principles of democracy but also as a result of the problems which are disclosed by application of economic reasoning.

Economics suggests that even with an electorate with fairly homogenous preferences – following a recommendation of the celebrated Swedish economist Knut Wicksell in 1896 – unanimity is replaced by some rule of **near unanimity**. An even weaker demand is met by the qualified majority decision, as practised by the European parliament. Clearly, such relaxations can entail a loss of stability of a political equilibrium. It is worth noting in passing that this kind of instability is reinforced by low turnouts or abstentions from voting. As a response to this kind of risk, voting rules frequently require the presence (participation) of a certain minimum number of voters (quorum) and even compulsory participation in elections.

By way of a little digression we should look at ways in which the consent that is entailed in constitutional acts is accomplished in practice. Interestingly enough, the procedures by which this is achieved are partly themselves subject to legal regulation (to illustrate: in Austria, parties that are present in the national assembly with a certain minimum number of delegates are entitled to form a parliamentary club which, in turn, is a precondition for benefits; we shall see in a minute that these parliamentary clubs have economic meaning in the daily struggle for consent).

Earlier we noticed that democratic decision making can be costly, particularly when the electorate has dispersed preferences. In order to facilitate the struggle for consent, democracies usually rely on some sort of step-by-step procedure. That is to say, both bargaining and voting on motions does not take place entirely in plenary sessions. In fact, the cost of bargaining and compromising would be very high (and increases with the number of participants). So part of the activities are externalized or delegated, both to hearings and preliminary negotiations in official parliamentary subcommittees as well as to the aforementioned parliamentary clubs. These in turn may turn to interest groups and partisan associations.

A good example of such multilevel democratic procedure is provided by the various commissions (or caucuses) that were in charge of the preparation and presentation of the various entries for the envisaged 'European constitution'. Needless to say, the negotiations for the sake of accomplishing votes with qualified majority on the single elements of the constitution in plenary sessions, for example, would have created a prohibitively high cost of consent.

While we note that the externalizing of decision-making costs is not confined to constitutional issues but also applies to less demanding matters, we can make our way to lawmaking under **majority rule**.

Attractions and dangers of majority voting

Simple majority voting appears to be a straightforward way of democratic decision making. Imagine the following stylized situation: there are three motions on alternative ways to solve a problem, on which 100 people have to decide. After voting the votes are counted and the motion that gets more than half of the votes (minimum is 51 out of 100) is accepted. If that were it, there would be no need to talk about dangers. Unfortunately, and not unexpectedly, even this simple illustration entails problems. Votes can be open or by ballot. When they are open, a rule about the sequence of votes appears to be appropriate. Moreover, what if a large number of voters abstain; should the result count anyway? Subsequently, we hope to shed some light on these and related issues.

Before doing this, let us have a quick look on the way in which public choice has adopted majority rule in order to be able to derive hypotheses about the likely outcomes of ballots. Again the intention is to give you an idea about the ways in which economists have approached essential issues in lawmaking.

So let us again assume that there are 100 people in the electorate. And imagine that these people can be arranged in a row according to their preferences concerning the issue at hand, with the assumption that each person in the electorate has, in fact, one and only one most preferred outcome! For simplicity, let us assume there is a motion on a government subsidy for farmers and the voters are arranged by their best preference for the proposed size of the subsidy, going from very small (€/£/$100, say) to very large (€1,000). Application of the majority rule implies that the motion that is preferred by the 51st person in the row, will determine whether the motion is accepted or not. In this simple setting it is the **median voter**, who is decisive (statistically a median is that element in an ordered multitude that divides the multitude in two equally seized halves). Unfortunately, there are further problems that disrupt the seemingly neat result. Among these problems are the following: what if not all members of the electorate vote? Then the predictive power of the model is definitely gone. What if it were not a single issue but a bunch of options? What if it were not a direct vote but a more complex system where the electorate first elects delegates? What if the vote were not on single issues but on political parties and their platforms? Each of these questions relates to everyday politics and demand regulations for democratic proceedings to be operable.

Investigating this kind of problem from an economic perspective clearly entails the quest for efficiency and effectiveness, issues of justice notwithstanding! Given the huge importance of majority decisions in our society (from the board of directors of private associations to enterprises, professional associations and NGOs such as the United Nations and their security council to our democracies) it is no surprise that it attracts utmost attention.

We will highlight some of the theoretical and practical issues concerning the legislature of democracies later. In doing this, we will have to make some reservations. Thus we will concentrate on issues of **representative democracy**. Problems of direct democracy are addressed only to the extent that they help reach a better understanding of the more complex issues at hand.

Representative democracy entails legislative bodies, which are composed of delegates usually sent in by political parties (in the case of a party list system, which is typical for most European democracies) or which represent electoral constituencies in which they gained the most votes, usually with the strong support of one political party (majority rule, as common in the Anglo-American sphere). Parties and delegates form the 'supply side' in the legislative process whereas citizen voters as well as interest groups (lobbyists) are on the 'demand side'. Since we have in mind the peculiarities of legal norms for democracies, it is necessary to draw on the distinction of suppliers and demanders, since the interests on both sides can be quite different and therefore the constraints ought to accommodate the diverse needs. We will leave it at that, although there are other stakeholders who could be considered, such as the bureaucracy – but they will be considered explicitly in more detailed investigations later on.

However, we will open our excursion with an illuminating digression and briefly address the 'voting paradox' and Kenneth Arrow's seminal 'impossibility theorem'.

A VOTING PARADOX AND A PROPOSAL FOR RESOLUTION

A frequently cited problem in voting runs as follows (and originally is labelled the 'Condorcet paradox', after the French eighteenth-century philosopher, mathematician and politician Marie-Jean-Antoine-Nicolas Caritat, Marquis de Condorcet). There are three alternatives solutions to some problem (such as allocating funds for the purpose of environmental protection, say) and three people are to select one solution by vote. They vote on pairs of alternatives as shown in Figure 5.1 (where > means 'is preferred to' and < the opposite).

One can immediately see that the outcome is indeterminate since each motion beats the other by a majority, but which motion is accepted is dependent on the sequence of votes.

Voter/alternative	A	B	C	A
1		>	>	<
2		<	>	>
3		>	<	>
Aggregate votes		2:1	2:1	2:1

Figure 5.1 Voting on pairs of alternatives

As can easily be seen from the example, one of the reasons for cycling is the fact that one of the voters has very remarkable preferences, to say the least: Voter 3 prefers a small to a medium budget, but at the same time, a large to a medium budget too.

The problem drew the attention of many scholars. One of them was Kenneth Arrow (Nobel laureate), who wanted to get to the bottom of the issue and find out whether there are ways out of this kind of problem. More specifically, he wanted to know whether there was a way of aggregating voting preferences that could map individual preference orderings into a consistent social ordering. His answer is: in principle not! In order to arrive at this seminal result he based his investigations on some plausible assumptions or 'axioms' concerning the standards of democracy. We need to list these in order to highlight one of the proposed ways out of the dilemma (which we will use for our further review later).

The axioms are:

- All preference orderings are permitted (even such strange ones as those of Voter 3 in our example).
- Everybody must have the right that her most preferred solution is adopted.
- Nobody's most preferred solution must dominate that of others.
- Irrelevant alternatives are omitted (meaning roughly that in case one alternative D is added, no ordering of the existing ones is reversed only for the reason of the additional motion).

It can be shown that Arrow's puzzle can only be resolved by dropping at least one of the axioms. The most canonical approach is to drop axiom one and to request that voters have one best alternative in their ordering. This means that the ordering has one single peak. With some qualifications (which for the sake of brevity must not detain us here), this restriction opens the way for the median voter model in its simplest form (which was used earlier to illustrate majority voting). The model is first developed and widely applied to voting in committees and other electorates by Black (1958).

We are now ready to continue our survey.

Efficiency and stability of a majority rule

Efficiency

At the outset, we should recall the general objective of the economic approach to law to maximize welfare or alternatively to minimize social cost. However, a majority rule creates winners as well as losers. Thus starting from an initial state the simple majority cannot lead to a Pareto improvement. Consequently it is not unlikely that the initial state, the **status quo** is preferred over every other alternative, as long as only preferences are counted at least. In the case of valuation matters, however, there is the familiar backdoor to see whether the result of a vote passes the Kaldor-Hicks test.

One obvious question that follows from this finding is under what circumstances the condition will be met. Seeking the answer to this question leads to another well-known but nevertheless delicate problem, which goes under the label of **preference intensity**. I will illustrate this by means of an example. Imagine five colleagues who are trying to decide which restaurant to choose for dinner for their group. This boils down to the vote on a collective good, since only if all five stick together can they enjoy their meal in good company. Let's say that someone suggests Hardy's Beer Keg and that three of the others agree, but the fifth one jumps up and shouts: 'No, I'll never go there!'

In having a closer look on what is happening here we gain an interesting insight into the efficiency of the majority rule. Still, it is appropriate to keep our presentation as simple as possible. That is to say, our measure for welfare maximization is wealth. Alternatively, we could stick to the ordinal scale of utility theory or likewise to a utilitarian approach. Both would require a much deeper discussion of the median voter model, but this definitely would exceed the purpose of this introduction.

Now let us make use of the earlier digression on single-peaked preferences. Thus, by assumption our five colleagues are able to order their preferences in such a way that there is one most preferred solution. In Figure 5.2 the preferences of our small group are centred symmetrically around that of colleague number three.

From Figure 5.2 one can see that the advantages that numbers one and two draw from the selection of the third person's most preferred alternative will exactly offset the disadvantages for four and five. Here then the median, colleague number three, is decisive and this solution of the problem is efficient. Note that in this case the average and the median coincide.

Let us take a look at Figure 5.3. Here by assumption the most preferred solution of five lies far to the right of the other peak preferences. That is to say that five attributes a much higher value to her preferred solution than all the others. Given the 'rule of the game' simple majority voting would again favour the median, colleague three. But contrary to the situation of Figure 5.2 the gains in wealth by the winners will no longer compensate the losses of the losers due to the high valuation by five. Thus we get a 'political equilibrium', which is no longer efficient with respect to our objective of wealth maximization!

The findings have an interesting implication! The familiar principle of **one man one vote** can be interpreted as a constraint on preference intensity. That is to say

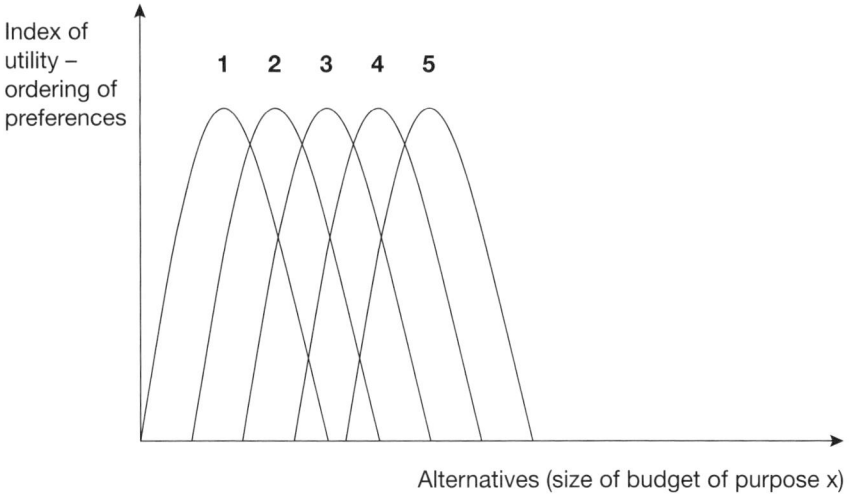

Figure 5.2 When the median voter is decisive

When the ordering of preferences for some issue is not symmetric and the number of people is odd, the median 3 is decisive and the solution will be efficient according to the Kaldor-Hicks test.

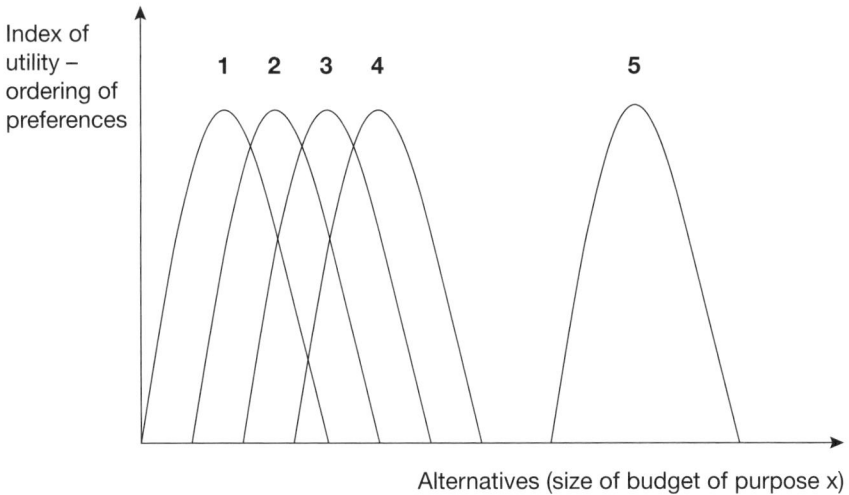

Figure 5.3 Ordering of preferences of the voters is no longer symmetric

When the ordering of preferences for some issue is not symmetric and the number of people is odd, the median 3 is decisive but due to the valuation by 5, the solution might not be efficient, since the Kaldor-Hicks test may fail.

in cases of a skewed distribution of wealth it is certainly an obstacle to an efficient solution, but at the same time it warrants an egalitarian participation. It serves a measure for justice!

Stability

Let us start our inquiries on stability by the observation that in real life people do not necessarily have one most preferred alternative or 'single-peaked preferences' as assumed for the discussion of conditions for an equilibrium outcome. To illustrate: there are people who, in fact, share the opinion that environment protection justifies a high level of public spending. However, if the same people are told that there is a shortage of appropriate funds they prefer to do without spending money on the issue. You will have recognized the preference ordering of our third voter in Condorcet's paradox of voting. So you will also remember the finding that in the presence of such extreme preference orderings the alternative which is supported by a majority depends on the sequence of votes. This turns our attention to a phenomenon that is quite important in democratic settings. An individual who is entitled to decide the sequence of votes on alternative motions is given considerable influence over the outcome (specifically when the preferences of the participating voters are known to her with some probability). Thus **agenda setting** becomes an important issue in voting procedures. More specifically, it opens strategic opportunities to those who are in charge of carrying out a vote. This in turn gives rise to the demand for bylaws or standing orders. Unfortunately, it is not so easy to come to grips with the objectionable consequences of strategic agenda setting. One option would be to leave agenda setting to an outsider, although this is unsatisfactory inasmuch as one has to observe the interests and incentives of such an agent.

With agenda setting another problem arises, which is that in principle motions can be brought over and over again. There are rules that ban repeated voting on the same issue, but there are exceptions. One special case is to reassume a vote under very restrictive conditions. For example it could have been overlooked when bringing the motion that the vote for a certain alternative has unforeseen negative consequences. However, in general, voting rules are structured so as to preclude the enforcement of a preferred solution by repeated voting on the same issue – which could be, by the way, a strategy to enforce a solution for which a number of voters have a strong preference intensity. So again it is not only on grounds of efficiency that we find such regulations but again the accomplishment of a standard of justice.

Voter turnout

We observe that there are countries in which voting in general elections is compulsory. In fact we have left out absenteeism from the ballot in our investigations so far. From what has been said about efficiency and stability of outcomes it can be inferred, however, that large scale absenteeism can give great power to **passionate minorities**, thus shifting the outcomes of elections away from the truly representative group of voters. As a consequence, such elections can never be efficient in the sense of wealth maximization (recall our reasoning of earlier? pp. 132–4).

Why is it that voter turnout can be so low and why is it that people go to the ballot at all? To see this, let us set up a cost–benefit calculus for a single voter. To cast one's vote, S, depends on the existence of a most preferred alternative, B, and the opportunity cost of participation in the election, K. Now, evidently, the chance of influencing the outcome of an election depends on the (expected) number of participants. Although this is obvious we should have a closer look at the problem. Imagine a town council of ten people. Each of them faces a probability b of 1:10 that the most preferred motion wins. By contrast, in a referendum of 5 million people that one of them sees the most favourite alternative winning, the probability is 1:5 million. Under such circumstances, $b \times B$, the expected gain from voting hardly covers the bus ticket for going to the polling station or some other sacrifice that can be cast as an opportunity cost. This gives rise to the disturbing conjecture that in referendum and general elections the turnout will converge to zero. However, specifically those with high intensity of preference may expect the low turnout and thus find it profitable to go to the ballot. This in turn suggests that the turnout (*ceteris paribus*, of course) will hardly ever reach zero. This warrants two more observations.

First, leaving a decision to others by abstaining depends to some extent on the expectations concerning the rate of participation of the others. Those who go to the ballot irrespective of such considerations may have a high intensity of preference for the issues at hand (the support for a political party, a certain candidate) and thus they count as 'passionate minority'.

Second, applying a plain model of the cost–benefit calculus, economists failed to make empirically appropriate predictions about turnout. As a matter of fact turnout is regularly considerably higher than predicted. Therefore, a variable D was brought into play. D covers such phenomena as 'sense of duty', a certain way of socialization to bourgeois habits and standards as well as ideological party affiliation.

We find many legal remedies for overcoming such difficulties and they are quite often in line with an economic rationale. One obvious example is a high *quorum* (presence of a minimum share of voters of the constituency), which can reduce the skewedness of an outcome. Another example is the duty to vote, already mentioned. Unfortunately, the efficacy of obligatory voting is questionable (to see this recall what has been said about the deterrent effect of sanctions in Chapters 3 and 4, respectively).

But we must not forget that so far we concentrated on the 'demand side' of democratic procedures: voter preferences, turnout and the like. Let us cast an eye over the supply side and the options initiators of votes and elections have at their disposal. Campaigns are meant to influence voting behaviour in two ways: they can inform and furthermore persuade voters to vote for a certain motion or candidate, but, by the same token, they can increase turnout. Consequently, democracies are wary of likely abuses in campaigns and have implemented a vast number of regulations concerning election campaigns, the sources of money, the contents of slogans and messages and so on.

Political parties and lobbyists alike have eventually turned to the provision of buses or even ambulances to bring people from remote places to the ballot or to help disabled people to vote. Sometimes such policies get close to the 'buying' of votes and are thus becoming topics for regulation as well as for court cases. In any case, they affect the fairness of party competition in democracies. However, this gives rise to political or even ethical aspects of lawmaking and thus is beyond the scope of this book.

Let us return to the interface between economics and the law by shedding some light on the importance of voting rules. Here the Council of the European Union can serve as an excellent example. One can see how the assignment of voting rights influences the likelihood of success in the pursuit of national interests. The reason for this is that each member has a different number of voters according to the size of the member state. A qualified majority decision requires 71 per cent of total votes and a blocking minority of approximately 30 per cent. Given the various assignments of votes, the possible coalitions for the enforcement of a motion and those which will block the motion can be calculated. One result of this exercise is that three large members (Germany, Great Britain and Italy, say) can enforce any motion whereas it needs seven smaller members to block a motion. That is to say the rules for how the votes are assigned together with freedom of association determine the voting power of the member states as represented by the members of the council.

An interesting question remains to be answered here: why and how should council members cooperate in order to push a given motion? Of course, there are instances that give rise to concordant interests among council members. However, it is also frequently observed that cooperation works as follows: in order to ascertain that their own favourite motion be enforced, one member makes a concession to vote for another member's favourite motion in exchange for support for their own favourite. Clearly, the individual preferences for the two motions must not be too far apart. This is one way in which short-term alliances are formed. This strategy is called logrolling. At first glance it facilitates decision making in democracies, but it should not be overlooked that it can lead to an excessively large number of laws enacted by the legislature. However, a restriction on the freedom of association, which would appear advisable here, is also quite problematic, since it definitely entails an opportunity cost for the affected agents. How ballot regulations (can) affect options such a logrolling has not yet been explicitly analysed. Still you may infer some clues from the discussion in our next section, which focuses on ballot regulations. Their importance is underlined by the fact that in representative governments, the elected representatives are the agents who are obliged to explore, collect and realize the preferences of their voters. However, the way in which the agents are selected is highly influential on their performance. So, let us have a look.

Ballot regulations

Majority voting

We are dealing with the basics of representative democracy here. One widely used way of electing representatives is to split the whole country up into a substantial number of constituencies, each of which is represented by one delegate in the legislative body. The candidate elected must receive a simple majority of votes in the constituency. On first sight, this is a case of the median voter model we introduced earlier, so our candidates ought to attract centre ground! However, campaigns are costly and therefore we can be sure that candidates are supported either by wealthy political parties or by wealthy interest groups. This fact can lead to some kind of dilemma: while it can be expected that voters know the person who is their constituency representative, they can at the same time not be sure about her activities during the legislature, since it may very well be the case that she is more preoccupied with pleasing her financiers rather than her constituents. The problem is worsened by the fact that the financiers might not be known to the public (and frequently do not want to become known). This, in turn, is a reason for distrust and a likely source for **corruption**. The immediate legal consequences of these shortcomings of the majority voting system are a call for the disclosure of finances for campaigns and limits to funding. It also opens a very interesting discussion about the advantages of public funding of election campaigns.

While the advantages of the system of majority voting are obvious (simple and transparent rules for election, fairly low cost of administration and identification of the delegate by the electorate), it has been observed that the overall political equilibrium of a democracy is less stable, since in the constituencies where the candidates running for office win by a small margin, majorities can easily switch, thus strongly affecting the overall composition of the legislative bodies.

Our final observation is not only limited to majority voting, but is also of relevance for the other major ballot regulation – the **proportional representation** election system (which we will address next). There are candidates who participate in the campaign although their chance of winning is minimal or even non-existent. To the economist at least it might appear strange to expend a lot of resources without any perceptible payoff. However, such representatives of some passionate minorities can substantially influence outcomes when they successfully fight a candidate whom they oppose. Frequently, such candidates take the opportunity of a higher perception of their messages during the campaign to make their ideas as well as themselves better known to the public. Since this holds for small parties and 'single issue groups' as well we have bridged the gap to the alternative ballot regulation already.

Proportional representation

In its simplest form, in this system political parties running for office present lists of candidates for each constituency. The number of votes is then converted into seats according to some key. Additional so-called 'residual seats' can be awarded from facultative surpluses of votes in the constituencies, which are lumped together provided that at least one seat was achieved in one of the constituencies. Another feature of proportional representation is the requirement of a party to achieve a minimum percentage of all votes (frequently 3 or 5 per cent).

One of the most widely used keys for the calculation of seats to which a party is entitled was proposed by D'Hondt, a Belgian lawyer, who proposed it in 1840.

It is also known as Jefferson's in the USA and sometimes named after Habenbach-Bischoff, a Swiss physicist. (See www.en.wikipedia.org/wiki/Voting_system# The_ballot.)

Again, the rationale for having a closer look at the **D'Hondt rule** is to demonstrate the strong influence of a regulation concerning specific methods of calculation or weighting on the composition of legislative bodies.

The D'Hondt method works as follows. Imagine a legislative body with ten seats and 1,000 voters who had the choice between three parties. The votes cast for each party are written adjacent to each other in descending order. Next, three columns are made by dividing each of the figures subsequently by two, three, four and so on. Since ten seats are to be assigned ten numbers are needed to see what the crucial 'voting number' is. Seats are then assigned accordingly (see Table 5.3).

Some of the virtues of proportional representation are the potential to represent a larger spectrum of political platforms in the legislature and to make the legislative body less susceptible to sudden changes. Moreover, it appears to be more open to new political forces.

But let us study some of the features by reverting to the review of issues of political competition examined earlier.

First, irrespective of the key for turning votes into seats parties can head for the median voter thus presenting platforms matching the centre of the political spectrum. However, parties may depend on two types of voter, namely, partisans who are registered members and frequently contribute by membership fees, on the one hand, and voters who tend to switch between parties, on the other hand. Then the selection of a platform can become a delicate problem, since changes (toward the centre, say), which can attract additional voters (away from competing parties), may at the same time disturb partisans who feel that the essentials of the party's position are being lost. Consequently, the party will try to present the platform that maximizes the number of achievable votes. This is given when a change in the platform's content causes the marginal number of losses to precisely match the marginal number of votes gained.

Now let us look at the assignment of seats according to our example. Even if party A accomplishes the task of maximizing votes, it is not in an enviable position. Given simple majority rule for the legislative body, in order to enforce motions the party with most seats will still need either to form a coalition with one of the

Table 5.3 D'Hondt method of seat allocation

	Party A	*Party B*	*Party C*
1	460	310	230
1/2	230	155	115
1/3	153,33	103,33	76,67
1/4	115	77,5	
1/5	92 (= voting number)		
Seats	5	3	2

competitors or it must try to enforce every single motion by means of logrolling with one of the other parties.

There is an interesting result in the economics of voting that predicts the formation of the 'minimal winning coalition' with the party with the smallest number of seats necessary to secure majority in the legislative body (which is party C, in our case). However, contemplate the consequences for the stability of the legislature if the platforms of the two partners are far apart!

Things could be worse, however! Imagine a distribution of seats so that nine instead of three parties are present. In this case the formation of a coalition most likely becomes extremely time consuming and consequently a political equilibrium becomes very unlikely, and so does effective policymaking.

The lesson learned from such reasoning is that it can be in the interest of the citizens that legal regulations concerning voting procedures put modest restrictions on candidacy and conditions of success. One such restriction is a threshold in terms of the necessary percentage of all votes. But it is important to see that this does not automatically lead to discrimination against smaller parties. Such barriers to entry (into the official political arena) may create an incentive to tie lists together in the run-up to the elections. In economic terms, small parties are prompted to make use of economies of scale by mergers.

There is an interesting example for this kind of impact in Austria: in the 1970s, originally two 'green parties' targeted seats in the Austrian national assembly. They did so during two campaigns and failed. Eventually, they tied their lists together and have increased their number of seats ever since then!

Now, we must be clear about one point here: we have only seen the proverbial tip of the iceberg! The law on campaigns, elections and party representation in the legislature abounds with detailed regulations. You might like to have a look into the Austrian ordinance on federal elections (*Federal Law Gazette* 471 of 1992 with amendments) or the German Federal Election Act of 1975.

For the USA, the principal regulations for elections on the federal level are found in Articles I and II and various amendments to the Constitution. American scholars are well advised to also look at relevant court opinions.

Besides all this, there are many more regulations concerning campaign financing, unfair campaigns and so on, which have not yet been investigated using the economic approach, so there is much still to be done.

Importance of interest groups and economics of lawmaking

For a change, we will start this section with a citation from a major German weekly (*Die Zeit*, 6 of 31 January 2002). What we can read there is this: 'Ein Handel mit *haut gout*' (A business with a peculiar taste). The article reports that the German association of pharmaceutical industries successfully put the German government in their place when they inhibited an amendment of healthcare regulations. More specifically, there was at stake an amendment to the federal regulation on pharmaceuticals with the intent of limiting expenditure for drugs on behalf of health insurance institutions. This should have been accomplished by an upper limit on expenditures, which boils down to a cut in retail prices. The association reacted by offering a subsidy of €200 million for the health fund institutions as a compensation for dropping the appropriate paragraph in the amendment. This offer was submitted to the federal chancellor and – surprise, surprise! – the price cut was not part of the government bill.

Before we turn to an economic investigation of the event, I hasten to make clear that such attempts are not confined to interest groups such as lobbyists. Strictly speaking a very similar thing takes place when an incumbent majority attempts to modify a ballot regulation in a favourable way so as to increase the likeliness of staying in power! However, since 'third time is the charm', we may recall the example that Breton gives (1974). He reports an amendment to the Canadian General Security Act, which passed parliament in Ottawa for the following reason: the union of police forces of Canada was interested in achieving the chair in Canada's federation of unions. Unfortunately, they lacked the appropriate number of members. So they stated a campaign on the urgent need for better security, which could be brought about by employing additional policemen – and they succeeded!

What do the three illustrations have in common? They are all instances of rent seeking. This term describes activities that do not bring about immediate increases in the amounts of goods and services (which would be welfare enhancing), but are ultimately absorbed in unproductive activities – such as lobbying. The notion came into use when the following issue was analysed: imagine a monopoly that extracts a consumer surplus by Cournot pricing or rationing of supplies. Clearly, this curbs economic welfare and one can readily expect that governments will pursue appropriate policies rooted in **consumerism** and enforced by their agencies. Now, the worst thing that could happen to the management and the shareholders of the monopoly is that they are forced by way of an appropriate act to cut back prices to a (near) competitive level. This boils down to the loss of the appropriated consumer surplus and the monopoly profit based thereon. In order to defend its market power, the monopoly could use as much as the total accumulated rents for lobbying activities, seeking out expertise or engaging in trials, since the emerging welfare position would ultimately be the same as if the government were more successful – that is what rent seeking means (in a nutshell). As a matter of fact, rent seeking is omnipresent in lawmaking – and is quite often successful. How this works can by summarized in Figure 5.4.

Let us assume that one interest group wants to defend a favourable regulation (barriers to entry) and that the intensity of the regulation can be measured along the horizontal axis. At point 0, the efforts would have been in vain, but at point B the group would have been utterly successful. Their willingness to expend resources decreases with the level of success. Thus we get a familiar demand schedule 0B for defending prevailing regulation. Now, influencing delegates incurs a cost. For reasons of simplicity, let the marginal cost of lobbying (receptions, nice meals, etc.) be constant at C. Then with the given demand schedule the interest group will be able to 'buy' a level of regulation, A, which is not their favourite level but is much better than complete deregulation.

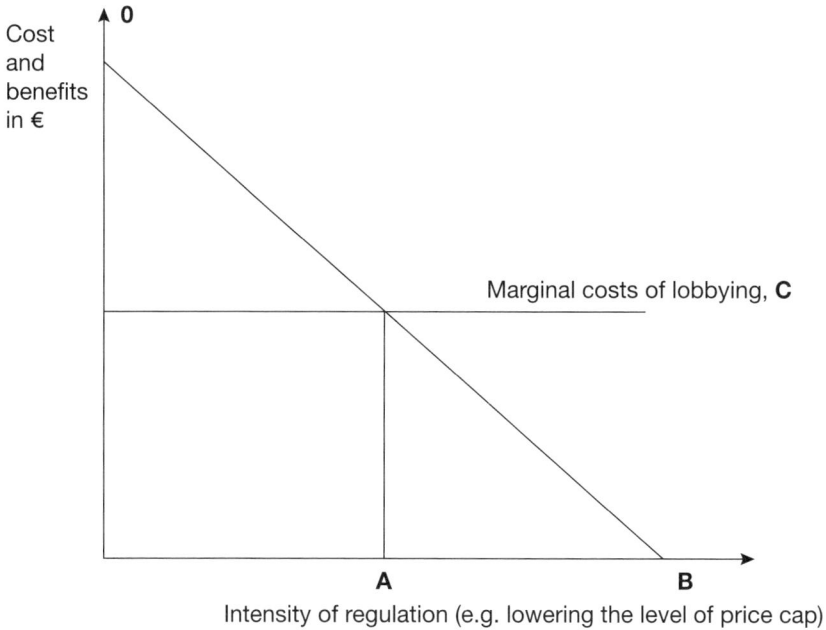

Figure 5.4 A stylized market for influencing legislation on regulation

Demand follows the usual schedule, since the marginal gain of success is positive but decreasing. The marginal costs of lobbying the members of the legislative body are assumed to be constant. A is the equilibrium level of regulation that can be achieved.

We can go one step further by observing that victory under certain circumstances need not be longlasting if the vote in the legislative body were by simple majority. Political majorities are subject to change and thus the amendment is not necessarily longlasting. So what strong interest groups might try to accomplish is a qualified majority vote, as is necessary for amendments on a constitutional level! In fact, there are examples where motions were pushed so as to pass by majorities that make it much more unlikely that they can easily be voted down in future.

Finally, recall what we have noted about courts in the case of laws that are based on effective rent seeking and inevitable inefficiencies or violations of measures of justice. Depending on the discretion conceded to the judge (which will definitely vary according to the legal system) the economic and distributional effects of laws can, of course, be mitigated, but they could also be reinforced!

Looking at laws from the perspective of how they are made or their 'production' can definitely be a thrilling undertaking.

A digression on citizens' rights and the privatization of public utilities

Public sector reform by downsizing, outsourcing and various ways of privatization have been predominant topics in the politics of the 1970s, 1980s and 1990s. These issues are at the core of law and economics, since every step in accomplishing the inherent political and economic goals necessarily requires a legal act. Several relevant problems emerge.

One of these is that quite often the executive branches (governments) were given freedom by parliaments to enact the necessary steps by means of decrees – which, in turn, give rise to debatable practices in the separation of powers.

One objective is to cut back the state to the accomplishment of core functions, which is equivalent to saying that in the future only core functions are held to be coordinated by voting and administration, whereas the other functions are conferred to the market or to NGOs (non-government organizations) – both of which carry the label 'private'. A general observation concerning the still ongoing process is that from the perspective of the demand side a good number of these undertakings are carried out in an authoritative manner. This is particularly true for countries with the rare elements of direct democracy such as referendum. Decision makers seem to presume that citizen-voters will cheer any measure apt to increase efficiency. But this leads to a striking paradox! In a nutshell, on one hand, allocations, which are performed by bureaucratic agencies and authorities, will necessarily suffer from inefficiencies due to the authoritative manner in which they are carried out. On the other hand, the maximum consent required by the criterion of Pareto efficiency can hardly be expected to be accomplished by way of referendum given the diversity of citizens' preferences.

Nevertheless even if an authoritative decision were beneficial in some narrow sense of improvements in allocative and productive efficiency, our generalized objective of social welfare would require us to take into account a couple of delicate issues. Take public utilities, such as the water supply or power supply as examples. Originally, citizens were clients of public agencies, but with privatization they are turned into (ordinary) customers. The point here is that both states differ considerably in terms of risks, rights and likely transaction costs – that is to say that as I have claimed before, a priori, we cannot readily assume that the citizens are indifferent between the two alternatives. The two states may even not be comparable. More specifically, we must ask with respect to the provision of services whether citizens have aspirations which exceed the straightforward goals of productive as well as qualitative efficiency. It has frequently been claimed that the average citizen's main concern is continuity and predictability of services. Let us finish with one more consideration that can highlight the dramatic changes citizens all over the world are facing at present. Where states carry out their functions by means of public agencies, authorities and enterprises, they are public property and thus in a certain sense owned by the people. A good deal of the operating costs and investments are covered by tax revenues. The peculiar property of this ownership is that in comparison to a joint stock company holders of these 'assets' cannot buy and sell shares. There is a way of wealth transfer, however, which works via people voting with their feet. Through leaving and entering countries, migrants indirectly change the composition of their wealth, although the trade values are literally zero.

Of course, they have the option of 'voice', such as grievances, protests and tax evasion. Privatizing public enterprises may lead to a decrease of the **tax burden** (directly or indirectly via the share of taxes absorbed in paying interest for public debt), but in an initial fiscal equilibrium it definitely does not lead to something like a dividend. With provision of services by the market, the claims and options and citizens' rights are substantially changed.

A famous economist once stated that a philosopher is someone who puts more questions than she can answer. So, these observations may leave you in the position of a philosopher for the time being. Scholars of constitutional law have nevertheless scrutinized the procedures we addressed earlier and there is an ongoing discussion bringing in viewpoints of law, economics and politics, on whether the processes always meet the general conditions of the constitutional state and those of overall welfare in particular. The concern about this topic is reflected in conferences (see the Austrian Legal Venue at www.juristentag.at/files/juristentag_2003/verfassungsrecht_15.pdf).

Public administration

Towards a scheme

As one scholar recently observed, administrative law ultimately serves the purpose of securing the rule of law, respecting private rights and protecting the liberty and property of citizens. It does this by ensuring by appropriate means that agencies act within constitutional limitations and within the authority as delegated by the legislature. Of course, one can add a slightly more economic flavour to this view. Since the earlier description implicitly conveys multiple principal–agent relationships, the core thesis on the role of administrative law by William Bishop fits in nicely here. He claims that what it is about is reducing to an optimal level the agency costs that arise when public officials are appointed as agents to carry out tasks for the benefit of their principals, where the principals are, in various contexts, the people, the legislature or the ministry (Bishop, 1990). More specifically, an elected legislative body enacts statutes and delegates their implementation to executive officials; next, an administrative body implements the relevant law through adjudication, rulemaking or other forms of administrative decision, typically official notification, approval and the like.

To this end, it is worth noting that administrative law (in general) defines the structural position of agencies and authorities within the governmental system, specifies the procedure they must follow and determines the availability and scope for reviewing their action. The last typically entails an independent judiciary, although some differences are found here in the German-speaking area and within the boundaries of common law.

However, this masks some very important features, which are subsumed under the label of administrative law on the continent. In turning to these issues, we move toward a scheme that serves as a guideline for a review of some of the key points of **public administration**.

The first distinction we should bear in mind is that of **general** and **specific administrative law**.

General administrative law comprises the whole range of government activities and procedures, procurement or public employees' service regulations in particular.

Specific administrative law applies to particular activities of the state such as police, the school system, construction, trade or civil aeronautics. You may correctly observe that this has something to do with **regulation**, since obviously construction and trade are usually mainly left to the private market. In fact, in the Austrian legal system (which serves as an example here) one distinct field of administration can approximately be translated as 'economic administrative law' (*Wirtschaftsverwaltungsrecht*), which according to prominent writers in the field such as Anthony Ogus is equivalent to the term 'regulation' (see Ogus, 1994, 2).

Another even more customary distinction is that between **sovereign administration** and **administration for private businesses**. The distinction hinges on the application of public law or private law. Where the state exerts legitimate power, as for example in traffic control, it is an issue of public law whereas the provision of public utilities by a government agency entails private law.

It is interesting and highly relevant in the ongoing process of denationalization that both legal forms can apply to the same entity concomitantly! To the scholar of the economic analysis of law, this can eventually pose quite tricky problems (but is also a challenge). This has to do with the broad endeavour to privatize all kinds of services. To illustrate: the former Austrian agency for civil aviation not only handled slots for landing and takeoff and flight routes, it was also in charge of approval for newly launched models of aircraft or permits for airlines in general. These activities typically are acts of state.

Some time ago the agency was privatized and thus turned into a limited liability company, Austro Control. Even those functions that are acts of state are handled by the new company. To that end, it makes use of public law! (It is definitely a good question: whether such issues as approval of new aircraft can be handled in a different legal form than public law . . . but it is almost needless to add that this is at the root of law and economics!)

À propos privatization: we ought to distinguish two basic options here. One is privatization in a formal sense. That is to say, a former agency which was part of the bureaucratic hierarchy is turned into a firm according to company law (preferably a limited liability company, less so a joint stock company). The privatization is formal, because ownership remains with the state.

Privatization in a substantial sense includes a change in ownership as well. Substantial privatization can be partial, of course, when governments want to preserve what can be a controlling influence or just minority rights. Since public utilities are normally subject of the 'rule of law', frequently privatizations do not adopt 'pure' forms of companies according to company law, but rather **hybrid organizations**.

While in practice the discussion about non-standard solutions entails political as well as jurisprudential controversies the essential question of efficiency is rarely put. As a matter of fact, much needs to be done in that field of research.

Before we turn to an overview of selected fields of administration, I should point out that the complex issues associated with privatization of functions of the state are not the only challenges to current research. The legal framework for media and communication ought to be mentioned here, since rapid technical progress entails institutional change, which in turn brings about uncertainties and externalities.

Public sector reform has taken up 'electronic government' (**e-government** for short) and thus opened new and superior possibilities but also new problems. One is data security and privacy. The need for a 'digital signature' is one of the immediate consequences. While e-government can definitely help save substantially on transaction costs, it incurs the cost of appropriate innovations and subsequent investments. And thus we are once more reminded of a saying ascribed to Milton Friedman: 'There's no such thing as a free lunch', meaning that there are always opportunity costs present.

We will continue by reviewing some more and also some less familiar shortcomings and deficiencies of public administration.

Sources of inefficiency in government bureaucracy

Theories

Let us review some of the most influential explanations for the inefficiency of government bureaucracies. We will consider:

- theory of **undersupply**
- theory of **oversupply**
- procedural failures
- failures stemming from the involvement of **bureaucrats in politics**
- corruption.

THEORY OF UNDERSUPPLY

This theory starts from the presumption that insufficient incentives allow chief officers to spend undue time pursuing their private interests. A good illustration is the suggestion of Northcote Parkinson that prestige increases with the number of subordinates, so that chief officers try to maximize their number of subordinates, provided they have sufficient leeway to do so. In more technical terms they exhibit 'discretionary behaviour' (which – by the way – is by no means restricted to the public sector; it can also be observed with managers in private firms or even non-profit organizations). So the results of prestige-maximizing chief officers are offices or authorities that are overstaffed.

Note that alternatively prestige can also be pursued by luxury furnishings or all kinds of 'emoluments' (when the new headquarters of the Austrian association for public health insurance was opened in Vienna, a rumour circulated that in the offices of the chief officers the inspectors of the federal auditing agency found expensive carpets and waste paper baskets made of brass!).

The theory of undersupply is summarized in Figure 5.5. Here the chief officer maximizes a prestige function with staff and output as explanatory variables. The output of the office depends on staff and other inputs and is constrained by a budget, from which the inputs are financed at going market prices. The actual output is where the highest possible indifference curve of the prestige function touches the output possibility frontier and that is definitely at a point below the optimum output.

It can be noted that the model is a variation of the familiar principal–agent model with an implicit superior and the chief officer as the agent. The outcome of the model implies that the cost of monitoring and control for the supposed superior are prohibitively high. So the model is a 'back of the envelope calculation' in order to illustrate the underlying idea. More elaborate models are available.

The model depicts an 'interior relationship' in contrast to the following theory.

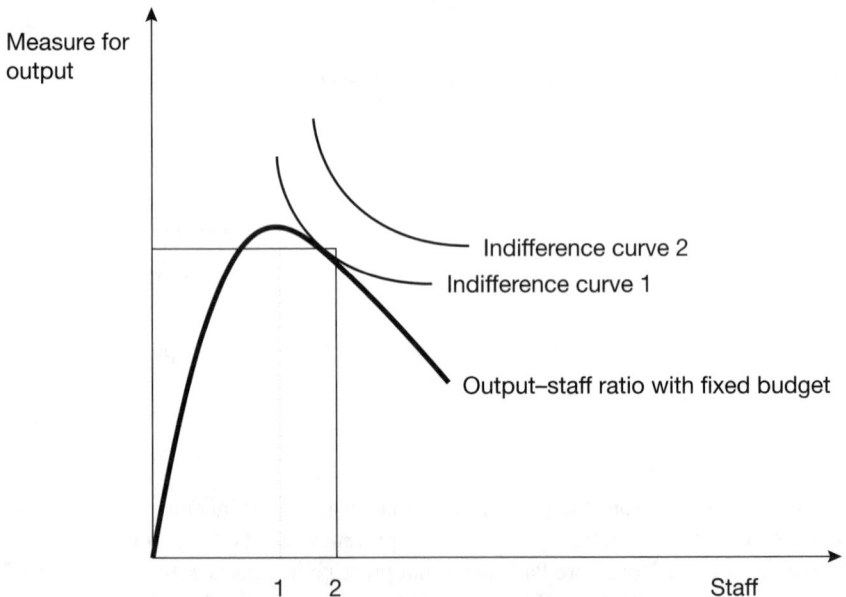

Figure 5.5 When a chief bureaucrat is maximizing prestige

When a chief bureaucrat is maximizing prestige, the output of the agency is suboptimal low and the agency overstaffed. The optimal output would be at 1, the actual output is at 2.

THEORY OF OVERSUPPLY

This theory is essentially based on an 'exterior relationship', although it is at the same time another principal–agent model. The interaction here is between a chief officer and a legislative body, which is in charge of funding, representing the taxpayer voters. The representation is given by willingness to pay schedule A–E for the output of the department. According to this theory, the chief officer seeks to maximize the budget for her department or subunit. The theory in its purest form can be summarized by Figure 5.6. The chief officer determines the output for one fiscal year (number of passports to be issued or the number of patient days and so on). She knows the marginal cost curve for cost-efficient provision B–D! So she can calculate the total cost GK for the intended output (the integral under the marginal cost curve). This is what she now demands as a budget. Alternatively, she could look at the maximum output on the willingness to pay schedule and demand the maximum budget possible (which means that the entire consumer surplus is appropriated by the department). However, as the figure shows in our example the budget B equals total cost GK. By assumption this is possible because the legislative body lacks information about the conditions for supply.

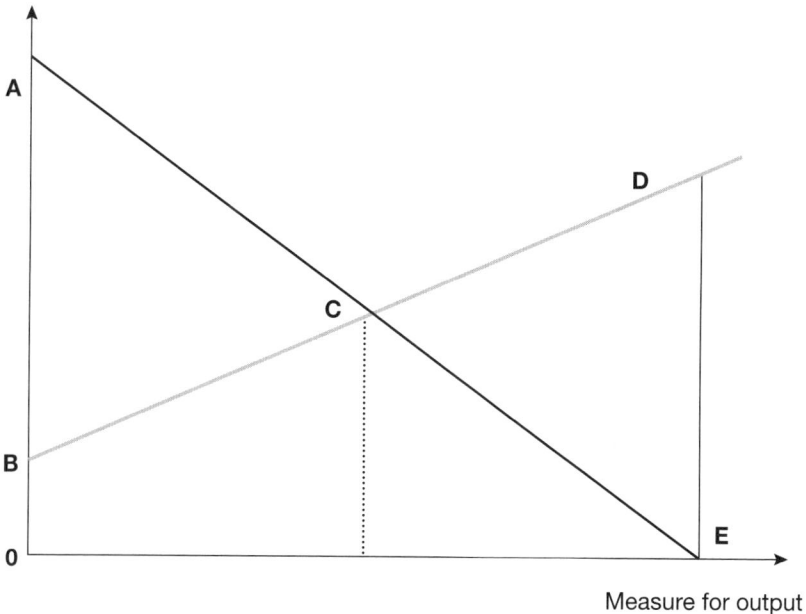

Figure 5.6 A stylized picture of the budget-maximizing agency

AE gives the willingness to pay of citizens as represented by a legislative body; BCD is the (minimal) marginal cost of providing the service at hand by the agency. Exploiting the willingness to pay leads to inefficiently high output E. The optimum would be at C.

Consequently, the output of the department is to the right of the optimal output (the intersection of willingness to pay and the marginal cost curve).

Note that this theory has one interesting implication for auditing. Inasmuch as auditors do not dispose of demand schedules for services but stick rather to the statutory yardsticks of economy, efficiency and efficacy, they will hardly be able to detect the inefficiency at hand, since it is brought about at minimum marginal cost (i.e. no overstaffing, unnecessary luxuries or emoluments etc.). One policy conclusion that follows from such an observation is that auditors should make use of cost–benefit analysis so that they need to look at supply as well as demand conditions, thus considerably improving the effectiveness of their business.

However, let us imagine that the chief officer demands the maximum budget possible, that is B > GK. In this case, over some time the department can set aside considerable reserves. Critics of this theory have pointed out, however, that it is very unlikely that these reserves would not be used for luxuries or voluntary gratifications and the like. Yet another objection that has been raised is that the sort of misallocation of financial means is never restricted to just one sophisticated department – but the consequences of such widely used customs would first be an inevitable rise in the tax burden and subsequently large-scale tax evasion or even a tax revolt.

Moreover, the ignorance of delegates has been called into question. In fact, there are models that assume that the body of delegates is fully aware of the attempts of agencies to get more than they need. This phenomenon is called **incremental budgeting** and it bears some importance for the law inasmuch as budgetary procedures have tried to come to grips with this kind of practice by changing from **bottom-up budgeting** to **top-down budgeting**.

The hypotheses that have been put forward concerning incremental budgeting are as follows: in a certain year, chief officers take the budget that was made available in the previous year and put a markup on it, which consists of the expected rate of inflation plus a real increase (in the spirit of our theory of oversupply). Now the principal (the body of delegates) is aware of such practices, so they cut back the claim by a fixed percentage. However, the department may still enjoy an increase, although part of the achieved rent is lost. The reason for why departments are likely to be more successful than the delegates is seen in the fact that delegates need to handle a large number of claims, so that they are not able to check each claim in detail. Given their limited capacity they prefer to use rules of thumb.

PROCEDURAL FAILURES

Many services provided by bureaucrats are typically administered on a first-come, first-served basis. Where the number of clients in a queue increases more rapidly than the number of slots available to deal with them, demand for the service at hand is controlled by **rationing by waiting**. Waiting time evolves as a kind of pricing and this kind of pricing is a source of welfare losses.

A much debated example is that of procedures for the approval of new buildings, but also sites for new buildings or new streets. While the rationale for such approvals is an ex ante control over nuisance or risk to neighbours, they tend to incur a high cost in terms of profits foregone or explicit out-of-pocket costs because of their duration. While the duration usually has a variety of reasons, one is definitely lacking incentives. Also there may be bottlenecks in the capacity of the authorities. For another area of public administration, the award of social benefits, there is empirical evidence that officers in charge have occasionally abused their discretionary power by detaining some legitimate claims. The emerging welfare losses comprise not only the delayed benefits but also 'time-and-trouble costs' provoked by grievances and the launch of appeals. It is important to point out that there are other sources of welfare losses, that give rise to legal remedies, for which bureaucrats must not be blamed. One such source is the ignorance of applicants concerning formal requirements. Still another source is sociological in nature, since a needy person might shun a visit to the department because she does not want to be seen by her neighbours, because it would make it obvious that she is poor.

Such findings underline the importance not only of appropriate incentives or the menace of sanctions but also of improvements in access to the services. Great expectations are held for e-government, which would allow applications to be handled discreetly to the benefit of anxious citizens.

Another much lauded invention is that of the **one-shop stops**, where the originally dispersed formalities concerning nuisance, safety regulations and other matters are handled by one office. Clearly, electronic processing and streamlining pose new problems such as data security or the secure identification of a person by means of an electronic signature. Such provisions do not just call for previously unknown legal remedies but are at the same time challenges for technology!

BUREAUCRATS IN POLITICS

In European states, civil servants make up 20 per cent of total employees. So apparently they represent substantial voting power. Since it can readily be expected that they share an interest in various issues such as pay, job security and the like, this gives rise to the plausible hypothesis that civil servants will act fairly uniformly at the ballot. There are few empirical studies, which make use of the availability of appropriate data in Switzerland. It is well known that Switzerland is the Shangrila of direct democracy. Bearing this in mind, two findings are worth mentioning here. First, as long as referendum pertains to issues of general interest, bureaucrats are not found to act as a more or less homogenous group at the ballot. However, when it comes to issues such as changes in salaries or amendments to the civil servants' code, civil servants not only show a higher turnout than usual but also – not unexpectedly – a more uniform vote as well.

Such findings can hardly be generalized, but they can provide evidence that under certain circumstances bureaucrats can and will act according to the theory's predictions.

Another important feature of bureaucrats is that they are organized into associations that pursue their interests in politics. There are countries with public employees' unions which definitely convey private interests most effectively. This will be illustrated later in connection with the much debated tenure track for civil servants.

But civil servants are also active on the supply side of politics inasmuch as there are countries where they make themselves available as members of parliament. In the legislative bodies of Austria and Germany, at times they make up for one quarter of all delegates! To this end one must be aware that this is facilitated by the low opportunity costs that civil servants face when they take time off from their posts to take part in politics. In contrast to Great Britain and many other countries, civil service regulations in Germany and Austria permit such time off for the pursuit of political office. This also holds for pay according to seniority, which presently is gradually being replaced by more performance-oriented schemes.

It is generally held that one of the major reasons for ineffectiveness and inefficiency in the public sector has been corruption. Several definitions are in use, such as:

- corruption is the misuse of public office for private ends
- corruption is moral inferiority of a person related to a measure of average probity
- the essential aspect of corruption is an illegal or unauthorized transfer of money or an in-kind substitute. The person bribed must necessarily be acting as an agent for another individual or organization (this is the definition used by Rose-Ackerman, 1999).

Regardless of semantics, it must be clear that corruption is a term that covers several forms of misconduct (or quite frequently, simply crime) and it is not only observed among civil servants, but also among politicians in both the legislative and the executive branch. We will take a general look at three types of corruption:

- **bribery** and extortion
- **fraud** and embezzlement
- **patronage**.

BRIBERY AND EXTORTION

A bribe is a covert offer to enter into a mutually advantageous but illegal exchange. It is typically used in order to be favoured in public procurement or, likewise, public subsidies. It is also observed where valuable information has not yet been disclosed by an authority as is frequently the case in the course of amendments for zoning (where agricultural land is turned into building land etc.). A very important yet disturbing observation is that bribery *frequently causes more bribery*. To illustrate, when it is believed that one civil servant has observed the bribe and is likely to make a report an attempt will be made to keep that person quiet. However, this may as well give rise to extortion, a fact that clearly shows that the distinction between the two is blurred sometimes.

We should note, however, that according to prevailing regulations not everything a civil servant receives is automatically a bribe. Civil servants are allowed to accept gifts that do not exceed the value customary in the place. Clients who make presents to their officers (nice wine, good brandy, malt whiskey) not only express their gratitude but also intend to make them further inclined to provide a good service. However, the boundary between an innocent gift and a bribe can definitely be blurred. It has been observed, for instance, that in the course of the initiation of large foreign investments the value of gifts that were offered to foreign local authorities far exceeded what would have been customary value at home! Thus judges may have a hard time telling whether it was a bribe or just the local price for goodwill.

FRAUD AND EMBEZZLEMENT

These are misuses of public funds for private gain. Normally, this takes the form of secret payments, thus overcoming the problems that 'making gifts' in the sense of buying goodwill is carefully scrutinized. One way of handling such payments is known as 'kickback', where the contracting parties stipulate a price above current market value. Once the account has been settled the markup is split among the parties.

PATRONAGE

This involves showing an undue preference for relatives or friends where access is given to office or public benefits. While patronage is quite common, it is not always seen as unlawful! As a case in point, imagine a family in a developing country that has invested in the advanced education of one of their many children. The child fortunately finds employment in the highest levels of the country's bureaucracy. The family then expects a return on their joint efforts in terms of special privileges including patronage, thus putting the person of achievement under substantial pressure. Such circumstances can truly be a challenge for the establishment and enforcement of appropriate codes of conduct.

In what follows we cannot allow for all aspects of corruption. For illustrative purposes, we will confine ourselves to some legal and economic views of bribery.

As far as the analytical basics are concerned we can make straightforward use of what has been said in the chapter on law enforcement. Legal provisions are found in the sections on the duties and obligations of civil servants in public service law and related acts, such as salary law. One of the most important areas for withholding incentives for bribes is public **procurement**. This in turn entails auctions. Consequently, the appropriate acts on procurement and the 'rules of the game' of tenders contain provisions against bribery. We shall come back to these issues later in the paragraph on tenders.

Next, we deal with some general issues concerning bribery.

Notes on the law and economics of bribes

At the outset it is important to note that in a perfect market there can be no bribes. This implies that bribery is a consequence of market imperfections. Such imperfections are indivisible commodities, lacking competition and asymmetric information. It is for this reason that we find public institutions with varying but usually highly concentrated property rights mostly of the exclusive, non-tradable type (remember their properties?). We have procurement agencies, zoning authorities and the like. Their obligations are *res extra commercio* and this is exactly why they are susceptible to bribery, which boils down to an unlawful commodification of their functions.

Bribing has been termed a 'victimless crime', since the negative consequences of bribes do not immediately affect distinct people or groups, but rather their effect subtly shifts to become a burden to society at large.

It is not possible to deal with all the causes and consequences of bribery here. Nevertheless, it is useful to highlight some of the economic aspects, which, in turn, can help to establish and implement appropriate remedies.

First, recall that bribery implies that the bribed person is an authorized representative of the decision maker, but never the decision maker herself. One of the major questions then is under what circumstances the briber and bribed are acting unlawfully. Here are some tentative answers:

- Corruption in general and bribery, in particular, vary with the degree of heterogeneity of a society, that is to say, they reflect the asymmetry between power and income; this is reinforced if it is not apparent to the general public.
- Bribery may vary with fluctuations in the economy; more specifically, it will increase with decreasing utilization of capacity and anti-cyclical **budgeting**, since under these circumstances illegitimate practices of new order acquisition have been observed to increase.
- It is commonly held that negligent prosecution and low fines can even lead to an institutionalization of corruption, which in turn is a challenge for legislators and the executive branch.
- One must also be aware that the salaries of civil servants are frequently far below the value of the orders they handle. In addition, bribers frequently face high marginal tax rates, which in connection with high expected additional revenues could very well make it attractive to bear the avoidance cost.

The consequences of bribes are well known: virtuous citizens are discriminated against and trust in government officials is undermined. Misallocation of resources combines with undue profits, resulting in distributive distortions. These effects are sources of social costs and at the same time induce a rise in the cost of control. However, it is noteworthy that in centrally planned economies bribes occasionally lead to increases in allocative efficiencies, for example in cases where bottlenecks in inputs can be diminished!

It is almost superfluous to add that legal remedies play a predominant role in confining bribery. While there are several defensive strategies such as fines and other sanctions, it is important to see that there are offensive strategies as well. To illustrate: in order to increase the opportunity cost for misconduct of those civil servants who dispose of substantial amounts of public funds, salaries should be sufficiently high. Disciplinary measures in turn must include cuts of salaries as well as fines, which are so high that with a given probability of detection a deterrence effect occurs. For the briber, fines must increase proportionally to the expected additional gains, which is rarely the case when fines are administrative penalties rather than criminal penalties!

Moreover, it must be observed that the way in which civil servants make use of their entitlements is strictly detached from patronage by political parties. Patronage is characteristic for parties seeking political support in exchange for generous treatment.

The way in which civil servants are selected and trained to observe ethical standards must also be taken into account. One example is the esprit the corps imparted by French 'écoles', another example is the ever increasing number of 'codes of conduct' for civil servants.

Neither training nor codes of conduct can replace several other indispensable provisions such as:

- precise regulations for tenders and stipulations in public procurement
- maximum publicity in all decisions about public funds
- disclosure of goals and tasks of public agencies
- disclosure of funding of political parties.

Convincing as these measures might be, it must not be overlooked that such steps (with the aim of furthering public interest) are at variance with the private interests of some of the stakeholders. This is where the lessons learned from the application of the public choice approach come in. It may very well be the case that people who struggle for rents find that they will not end up as winners but rather as losers, so that under certain circumstances they are willing to submit themselves to common and accepted rules. We have had a look at such motivations in our brief review of constitutional issues.

(For further reading on issues of corruption you should turn to the end of this chapter.)

Some legal and economic reasoning: can we improve efficiency in public administration?

Section outline

In this section we will explore topics that are important but under-researched with respect to the role of public administration in the economy and in society. The selection is guided by a scan of the literature. Hopefully the following discussion will encourage more intensive research in the relevant fields.

We start with a short look at the controversial issue of a tenure track for civil servants, followed by another source of substantial disagreement, the feasibility of civil servants acting as politicians.

We then turn to **principles of budgeting**, which to the analytically oriented economists often appear as old hat, but which resurface even in the annual budget of the European Union. This is followed by reflections on the principles of public procurement by tendering, and the principles guiding the role of audit courts (general accounting offices). We conclude by looking at **ombudsmen**, who are appearing all over the world although they have so far seldom been analysed from a law and economics perspective.

Notes on public service law

Public service law is one of the essential premises for an efficient and effective public sector. But even if the prevailing legal regulations appear to meet the requirements, their realization is frequently weak and has seen continuous erosion (although the more general view is that they are simply outdated). As has already been pointed out, bureaucracies suffer from the principal–agent syndrome, which is characterized by divergent private interests and prohibitively high enforcement costs. It is frequently held that one of the main reasons for the lack of effectiveness in the public sector has been the fact that civil servants enjoy lifetime labour contracts, or 'tenure'. While nowadays this is judged as an undue privilege, it has rarely been asked why an employer would offer such a generous kind of contract. (It is certainly less difficult to see why employees appreciated it; can you explain?) Exceptions are only found in the field of university teaching for full professors.

Before continuing our exploration, we ought to stress that in a strictly legal sense, tenure is not part of a long-term labour contract, since civil servants and professors alike are appointed by decree on application. From the point of view of economics, however, these appointments boil down to contingency contracts with some peculiarities such as an obligation to work overtime, strictly to be sworn to secrecy and other additional requirements.

Before we can turn to an outline of a theory of tenure, however, an overview of types of employing labour for government is required.

In their SIGMA Paper No. 27, the Organization for Economic Cooperation and Development (OECD) describes the *Principles of Public Administration*, in which the legal structure for a professional civil service is stated. According to the paper, such a legal structure reflects two requirements. The first is responsibility for ensuring the efficient, professional and impartial performance of the public administration. The regulations concerning state employees need to meet the following tasks: staffing and career management policies, management systems for selection, recruitment, promotion and remuneration, 'all of which aim to guarantee the homogenous and high quality of the staff and its performance' (SIGMA Paper No. 27, 20).

A special feature of public administration is that it entails a notion of hierarchical delegation of state powers to individuals operating within the political system.

Consequently, public administration staff are not just employees but at the same time holders of state power (to some extent at least). This in turn points to a need for specific regulations concerning the labour agreements.

Details aside, two types of agreement can be distinguished:

- civil servants who are appointed (after a certain qualifying period)
- employees working on (temporary or open-ended) labour contracts.

The member states of OECD have adopted different approaches concerning the predominant mode of employment. One approach has been termed the 'broad concept of civil service', the other the 'limited scope of the concept of civil service'. The meaning of these notions is the following. Within the broad concept, almost all public employees are considered civil servants, since they are seen as part of the 'executive machinery'. Examples comprise France, Ireland, the Netherlands, Spain and Sweden.

Within the limited scope, a mix of civil servants and employees is found, with the former predominantly and increasingly working in so-called 'core functions' of the state, that is to say, functions that only the state is entitled to perform. Typical examples are Austria, Germany and the United Kingdom.

Where the limited scope prevails, for quite some time now, it is obviously the predominating belief among politicians that most areas of public administration can be handled by employees without special status or 'privileges'. Recall that the interior reform of public administration is inextricably connected with an ever increasing contracting out or even more rigorous forms of privatization. To illustrate from a more recent Austrian case, despite an ongoing discussion about the risk of violation of the rule of law, privatized firms which used to be government agencies – such as the civil aeronautics authority, now Austro Control – have been entrusted with authoritative power for some of their obligations. They are now carried out by private employees, not civil servants!

This may serve as an illustration for why it is sensible to ask whether such a peculiar type of employment as the appointed civil servant with tenure is indispensable.

To answer these questions two viewpoints should be observed. First, one may take the point of view of an impartial expert and see whether the specific requirements in the public sector render such contracts as efficient and what are – beyond legal provisions – the functions of civil servants, which warrant such privileges, as mentioned earlier.

Second, one may (and should, of course) ask, whether the extensive practice of giving tenure can be seen as a result of successful rent seeking on behalf of unions and, therefore, reflects allocative inefficiency and re-distributional goals, to some extent at least.

So let us start with the question: what could drive demand for tenured civil servants from a 'public interest perspective'?

Three (not necessarily mutually exclusive) answers come to mind:

1   (only tenured) professional bureaucrats generate positive externalities
2   a binding covenant with the state is honoured by a dividend on loyalty for the
      civil servants
3   tenure is a prerequisite for the exploitation of experience.

The first of these answers (or hypotheses, to put it more modestly) follows from
the views of Max Weber, who was optimistic about the role of bureaucrats in
democracies. To illustrate, consider instability in the political sphere, such as
unstable, frequently changing coalitions or temporary absence of a cabinet (government). Such instability most likely creates negative externalities for society and the
economy. The costs are borne by the citizens. An independent bureaucracy under
the protection of tenure could be useful in keeping that cost at a minimum, since
it would be able to temporarily continue operation of the system on the administrative level. Society might reveal a willingness to pay for such a bureaucracy in
the sense of an **option good**, as it is called in public finance (if you cannot recall
the meaning of this notion, see Box 5.1). Consequently, the cost savings from having
a bureaucracy which is continually ready to perform must be taken into account.

However, the familiar principal–agent model suggests different implications.
In the absence of substantial sanctions it predicts opportunistic behaviour of the
agent, if the principal shuns the cost of monitoring. In that case tenure can at best
be seen as the carrot at the end of the pole of a long career, where only good
performance prevents the employee from being dismissed. Stated differently, tenure
then becomes a dividend of loyalty. It is immediately apparent that it is a tricky
question for the employer, at what time the dividend ought to be paid!

Theoretically speaking, tenure allows for the maximum exploitation of
experience, which a civil servant accumulates during a lifetime of performance as
well as from on-the-job training. For the employer this experience appears to be a
valuable asset, so the employer would like to retain the civil servant, since the
benefits she can extract from her are (almost) always higher than the pay. This can
be inferred from the considerable barriers to exit that civil servant face. To illustrate,
a civil servant who wants to quit her job, will lose the claim to wage continuation
after retirement; moreover, she can be obliged to pay back the costs of training.

However, there has been some empirical testing of the covariance between
experience and tenure. The results indicate that this covariance is even higher in
the private sector than in the public sector! From this it could be inferred that tenure
is more likely rooted in the strength of the civil servants union than in experience
(which is part of the 'private interest perspective' that I address later)!

Given this perspective, doubts can be cast on the amenities of tenure and one
may ask if tenure could not be replaced by individual labour contracts, which still
warrant the appropriate properties, particularly in the field of law enforcement.
However, in order to be practicable, such contracts must allow for a certain degree
of discretion on both sides. Unfortunately, it is almost impossible to write out a
perfect long-term contract with discretion. Consequently, it can be predicted that
a system of individual labour contracts in the public sector might bring about
considerable costs from dealing with dissenting opinions. An objection to this is

that the prevailing code of conduct contains a variety of disciplinary procedures, thus indicating the potential for misconduct and its ensuing costs under a tenure system as well. Which of the two regimes will be better in terms of the minimization of social cost can hardly be assessed on a theoretical basis, but it is also not a straightforward empirical task.

Interestingly enough, in cases where a high amount of human capital is required and/or an employee is required to be a leader, these days temporary contracts with the option of renewal in the case of satisfactory performance often come into play. There is a general belief that this type of contract has a higher potential of creating incentives towards efficiency. However, a necessary condition for this kind of arrangement to work is a clear definition of measures of performance. Neither in the important field of law drafting nor in the enforcement business are such measures readily available. While it thus is difficult to assess performance, this type of contract might also be flawed if the probability of being renewed is low. In this case it can be predicted that the employee will try to maximize the rent from her temporary employment; moreover, towards the end of the contract, she might become less effective due to the fact that she will expend considerable efforts on finding another job, thus externalizing her cost by shifting it to the employer (or, ultimately, the taxpayer). As a matter of fact, beyond a certain age, say 50, search costs increase with the age of the employee. This implies that limited contracts with a low probability of renewal will be more inefficient the older the employee gets, unless there are more frequent audits or, alternatively, additional payments which are made with strict dependence on performance. Both measures will add to the cost of employment, of course.

For the sake of the improvement of performance, one may think of additional incentives such as measures of customer satisfaction. Clearly such measures are restricted to service-oriented branches of the administration. They will add the flavour of competition to working – conditions, inasmuch as they are determined by the degree to which services are valued by the public. Given such possibilities, one may ask why contracts need to be temporary at all. The contract could be made open ended and subject to revocation, if some predetermined **performance measures** are repeatedly not met (provided that such measures exist).

There is still another perspective, which I have so far only touched on implicitly: when addressing special properties of means of production including skills of human resources, this has eventually been labelled 'factor specificity'. In bureaucracies that are organized in a traditionally hierarchical way, civil servants are generally highly specialized and therefore provide a good example of factor specificity. Their expertise results from both training and experience. If investments in expertise are undertaken without a subsequent extraction of rents (returns) then considerable sunk costs will arise. Consequently, a fundamental change in policy concerning staff, such as a more flexible approach to recruitment, would require a fundamental change in the qualifications that provide proof of skills and knowledge. However, such a change does not automatically warrant more efficiency or lower overall cost. In that respect, a standard contract would be desirable that takes into account the problem of factor specificity, provided that the argument about sunk costs matters at all. Taking into account the likely disadvantages of the alternative, unlimited contracts or even tenure could very well turn out to be superior.

It would be short sighted not to take into account that bureaucrats form a strong interest group, represented by labour unions (although the right to form such associations has been questioned occasionally). This presumption is used in the seminal theory of the 'cost disease' of the public sector by William Baumol in the following way. Starting from the assumption that, contrary to the private sector, there are no increases in productivity in the public sector that would justify increases in pay, he assumes that in collective bargaining the union of civil servants will demand increases in pay equivalent to those of private sector employees. In doing this, they might have a hard time since they can only rely on their bargaining power. However, if they succeed – which they evidently have done, at least in the past – this results in a mere transfer of purchasing power from the private into the public sector. This seemingly powerful explanation must be complemented by another aspect, however: a standard assumption is that a union's main task is the enforcement of equally good working conditions for their members. In the case of the union for civil servants, this could boil down to equal opportunity to achieve tenure for all members, not just those who for the reasons stated earlier enjoy such special appointments. In accomplishing the task, the representatives of the union may be assumed to be under pressure to maintain loyalty among existing members and to recruit new members. Consequently, a valuable asset such as lifetime employment will be promoted as long as there are no more attractive alternatives. Distinctions by function would cause severe problems for the pursuit of the union's understanding of equality, although it can be inferred from recent statements by representatives in the public that they are well aware of these problems. However, given the constraints for their policies, unions are more or less locked in. One may predict that they are not really ready to comply with emerging types of employment.

Vote-maximising politicians, in turn, have realized for long that the abolishment of tenure is quite popular among citizens, since it is viewed as a privilege rather than a functional necessity. Following Downs' hypothesis on the creation of political programmes for electoral campaigns, the marginal increase in terms of votes on that issue is very likely considerably higher than the marginal loss. Therefore, from the perspective of politics the option is basically an 'all-or-nothing' solution to the future employment of civil servants, not gradual reform. That is to say, the intention is to abolish tenure on a large scale, as can currently be observed in most countries with few exceptions. Neither the bargaining power nor the voting power of civil servants appears to be strong enough at present to effectively reverse this trend.

Such tendencies in politics notwithstanding, lawmaking in the sphere of public employment ought to take into account that the application of a merely fiscal argument in favour of reform falls short of the broader but also more subtle scope of overall efficiency. Given this postulate, the incentives, risks and transaction costs associated with the intended change towards limited contracts instead of tenure ought to be assessed against the same criteria associated with overall efficiency. Stated differently, a careful comparative examination should stand at the beginning of such substantial changes, for which the general trend in public employment is a good example.

Civil servants as legislators?

It is an interesting observation that there are countries in which civil servants have a substantial number of seats in legislative bodies. According to my own investigations in the Austrian national assembly, for example, up to 57 out of 183 delegates were civil servants on leave from their posts during the last ten election periods. The situation is quite similar in Germany and still remarkable although not as astonishing in other democracies. Interestingly enough, this phenomenon is rooted in public service law. Austrian civil servants are explicitly allowed to run for office and enjoy special leave from their work if they are successful. This indicates that running for political office should be quite popular among bureaucrats. Now, recall the main three arguments of the bureaucrats' utility function, as they are frequently quoted in the literature, namely power, prestige and pay, and recall the favourable conditions for leave. From this one can infer that for the bureaucrat the opportunity cost of being on temporary leave from her job is fairly low (even claims to old-age pensions are not affected!). It may be noted in passing that becoming a delegate is sometimes the first step in becoming a member of the cabinet subsequently.

Several observations are in order: first, countries with high rates of participation of civil servants in politics are subject to a factual erosion of the separation of powers. Moreover, citizens may face an increasing lack in the transparency in the preparation and resolution of policies.

Furthermore rent seeking is encouraged. And last, the cost of control for both the legislature and the executive branch can rise substantially. Such reservations notwithstanding, making it easy for civil servants to become politicians might be beneficial in some instances. Civil servants are certainly knowledgeable in their respective fields and they may also have a head start in acquiring information. Therefore, it can be expected that they can substantially contribute to appropriate decision making. Unfortunately, there are no empirical investigations into these issues yet. Although national regulations might provide some evidence of the benefits of bureaucrats entering politics, unfortunately, they differ considerably from country to country. While France and Germany have regulations that explicitly permit candidacy along with release from duties and obligations, in Great Britain, a civil servant cannot become a member of parliament before she stops working for the state. Similarly councillors in Swiss cantons must not concurrently be senior officials. Although these were just a few examples, they clearly indicate that the legal permissibility of civil servants entering politics is an open problem, despite the fact that there are some countries where this is customary.

Increasing efficiency and effectiveness of bureaucracies: instruments and institutions

Overview

The last paragraph addressed an essential issue in civil service law for obvious reasons: the employees of the public sector play a crucial role in the functioning of the state. Given the individualistic approach to the issues at hand and the underlying assumption of a *homo oeconomicus* the constraints and incentives contained in the code for civil servants are of utmost importance for investigations into the performance of public administration.

However, the efficiency and effectiveness of the administration does not only depend on the capacity of the said constraints and incentives to guide utility-maximizing bureaucrats for the sake of common welfare. There is a diversity of instruments and institutions which are indispensable for the accomplishment of that task. In the remainder of this chapter, I discuss several topics that are at the forefront of the desire to enhance efficiency, such as regulations and procedures in budgeting as well as those for procurement.

Regulations and procedures in budgeting have a fairly long history dating back to medium term fiscal planning from the end of the Second World War onwards. They quickly went out of fashion and were replaced by other means such as planning programming budgeting systems, zero-base budgeting and so on. Cost–benefit analysis, cost–effectiveness analysis and, more recently, regulatory impact analysis have been established by legal acts (such as the law on the federal budget, the *Bundeshaushaltsgesetz*, in Austria). Another well known attempt was sunset legislation, which was followed by an abortive attempt to adapt overhead cost evaluation methods for the public sector. Controlling and instruments growing out of new public management such as the balanced scorecard are now found in the recipe books for better efficiency. Budgeting has also undergone substantial change inasmuch as the old cameralism has been left behind for quite some time in favour of an **expenditure budget**, multiperiod budgeting or accrual accounting which means that future burdens of public budgets are made more transparent than in the typical annual budgets. Intergenerational accounting is a further step to shed light on the dynamics of modern budgeting.

Interestingly enough, some seemingly old-fashioned ideas still play their role in the public sector. More specifically we still find 'principles of budgeting' that are, for instance, explicitly stated in the budgets of the European Union. And we find general accounting offices or **courts of audit**. These are generally in charge of ex post control, although their competences have been somewhat extended to ex ante examinations (in case of public borrowing) as well as concomitant control for larger undertakings for some time.

Procurement is important for obvious reasons: governments are still contractors for commodities and capital investments amounting to billions and billions of euros (or pounds or dollars). It seems quite natural that the OECD has picked this issue as the topic of numerous publications and that the EU has established an appropriate framework of rules and recommendations.

But there are also institutions that have not yet attracted much attention, although they are spreading continuously, such as ombudsmen. Originating in Scandinavia back in the nineteenth century, these public attorneys are established to take care of citizens' grievances and complaints about maladministration by institutions and bodies of (national) governments. They typically come into play when there is no (further) option of turning to a court or launching an official appeal. Since

1995 even the European Union has had its own ombudsman. Having shaped the schedule for this section we can now set out to work on our list.

Notes on the economic analysis of budgeting

In these notes, two somewhat contradictory aspects of modern budgeting are addressed. One is on its role in the struggle for and distribution of power between government and the parliament on the need for a comprehensible and efficient use of funds. The latter touches on the efficiency of politics and not on the efficiency of bureaucracy alone, since it is the principal's approach that can substantially influence the way in which a problem is treated (in analogy to the importance of briefing in the conformance of a mandate in the private sector).

Note that with some minor reservations our reasoning could be extended to budgetary problems in downstream subdivisions as well as problems of taxation and fiscal federalism. Because of limited space we have to abstain from addressing these issues, however.

The discussion surrounding public budgets centres around three major issues: struggle against public debt; struggle against structural deficits (roughly speaking, deficits caused by expenditure programs in excess of revenues from regular taxation); and a (still) oversized public sector as measured by the ratio of GDP to public spending (in real terms). These issues affect the three main purposes of the state: allocation of resources for the provision of goods and services; re-distribution; and the duty to maintain a stable and steadily developing GDP. In envisioning these grand missions it is frequently overlooked how important it is to have a structured and balanced design of procedures and incentives, which is laid down in the legal regulations concerning budgeting.

Before we look at these issues more closely, let us come back to the distribution of powers between the government and parliament. If we go back in history, we could replace the government with individual rulers (kings, emperors) and parliament with the pre-parliamentary state of concerned and emancipated citizens. With the move from absolutism to constitutional monarchies, these emancipated and concerned citizens struggled to achieve transparency in the ruler's use of funds. Originally there were frequently 'purses' for the royal household, including diplomats, and purses for military purposes where the latter were kept strictly secret. One of the problems then was that citizens suffered from the extraction of taxes but had no information let alone control over spending. It was a milestone in the process of democratization for citizens to get a voice when they were subject to direct taxes, as for the first time laid down in the Bill of Rights in England 1688. It was as least as important that first the purse for the royal household and subsequently that for military purposes were laid open and finally the two separate budgets merged into one at the time of Empress Maria Theresia in the Habsburg monarchy of the eighteenth century. At the same time a right of approbation was given to the empire's council (*Reichsrat* – the preliminary state of a parliament). Thus, the rights and obligations in setting up the annual public budget were entirely restructured. However, this did not happen without the establishment of basic principles, which were followed in restructuring the budget. The main purpose of these fundamental principles of budgeting was to guard against the misuse of loopholes in the way announcements as to the intended use of funds were made and in the way these funds subsequently were used. A budget is a declaration of political intent cast in figures. Information is provided on both allocation and (re-)distribution during a fiscal year. By the same token, a comprehensive, systematic and standardized overview of the authorisation for the use of these funds is given to the administrative bodies. Since the forecast of revenues is usually a tricky and highly uncertain task, the law by which budgets are enacted also contains the right of the treasurer to act in certain ways if financial gaps appear. Finally, the legal act of the budget lays the basis for administrative as well as political control.

Interestingly enough, the legal acts concerning budgets are more or less explicitly underpinned by basic principles, not by reference to techniques for the optimal allocation of funds. These principles are supposed to serve as guidelines in the composition of budgets. To illustrate, the budget 2007 of the European Union contains a section (addendum to part A – introduction) (www.eur-lex.europa.eu/budget/data/D2007_VOL1/DE/nmc-grseqN70091660751-2/index.html) in which the principles are explicitly stated and defined! We will explore the major principles. This entails an interesting exercise inasmuch as it shows the possible starting point for an economic analysis of the budget act. It turns out that some of the principles imply certain tradeoffs between conflicting goals, such as the requirements of precision and flexibility. Where this applies the question arises of what the effects are and how these can most easily be protected from exploitation by the private interests of officials. Such protection would require incentives and control at a reasonable cost.

The first two (complementary) principles are 'unity' and 'completeness'. This is reminiscent of the struggle of the citizens against the sovereign for transparency concerning secret parts of the budget for military purposes and other possible 'side budgets' for hidden activities. Unity and completeness are indispensable for the visualization of the full share of the public budget in the overall economy. Note that these principles also incur the obligation of recording only gross expenditures. The importance of this point can be seen from a serious problem, namely the recent trend of privatizing certain entities to the effect that only prospective surpluses and outflows of the privatized entities appear in the federal accounts! By requiring gross expenditures the cast of accounts is ruled out. It is held that such practices are obstacles to the transparency of the full burden of running the state. Is there one of the aforementioned tradeoffs? Of course, since more advanced techniques of accounting would call for balancing accounts and thus the application of a principle of net expenditures accruing to each entry in bookkeeping. The rejection of such standard techniques is one of the sacrifices of maintaining utmost transparency in politics.

The next principle is that of 'lucidity'. This requires that the budget follows standardized and easily accessible guidelines. Thus the origins and purposes of entries both for outlays and receipts can be made explicit. However, a purpose in economic terms would mean the accomplishment of a certain goal, allocative, re-distributive or stabilizing. The content of such goals normally is given in appropriate economic measures, which might be at variance with lucidity. Hence, budgetary laws are complemented by additions, which can be quite voluminous as in the case of the supplements to the Austrian federal budget, which contain the detailed materials needed to fully assess the economic intentions of the entries and figures listed in the budget act itself.

Also of substantial interest is the principle of 'precision'. This means that outlays and receipts should appear precisely as the amount which is most likely in the fiscal year ahead. Now, you will probably know the old joke among economists that 'making predictions is a difficult task, especially for the future'. Consequently, given the uncertainty about external factors that may substantially influence the need for funding (such as disasters, or unexpected rises in traffic levels, political crises and so on) the demand of precision is not easily met. However, the main focus of the principle is again politically motivated: at the time the budget is voted on in the legislative body, its entries must not be specified so low that delegates get hoodwinked by the alleged thrift of the government! Otherwise, they would soon realize that they have been tricked when a supplementary budget is applied for later in the fiscal year. This illustrates why precision is not just an irrelevant instruction!

Finally, we review the principle that has most come under attack in the course of public sector reform: 'specification'. According to this principle the funds must be used only for the purpose specified in an entry, i.e. 'qualitative specification'; moreover, the funds expended must not exceed the proposed amount, 'quantitative specification'. Finally, the sequence of spending is also binding according to this rule.

The rationale behind such stringent rules is that they are assumed to stabilize expectations concerning these expenditures (which can amount to thousands of pounds' or euros' worth of purchases in private markets) as well as to facilitate control.

However, there is a considerable price attached to this kind of specification. They are a potential source of inefficiencies. First, even if it were justified on economic grounds, a re-dedication of planned expenditures is prohibited – thus it is not possible to compensate shortages in one area by surpluses in another one. Moreover, there is no incentive to economize. One of the immediate consequences are actions known as 'December fever', when accounts are cleared towards the end of the (fiscal) year, since neither re-dedication nor stockpiling is allowed (to illustrate: there are legends that some offices have enough copying paper to last several years).

Recent reforms of public administration have substantially curbed the principle of specification. It has been replaced by flexibility. Chief bureaucrats have certain amounts of money at their disposal and then decide about their most effective use – a step towards **global budgeting**, as it is widely called nowadays.

This change in the practice of budgeting is matched by another recent trend which is worth mentioning here. To start with we need to remember the main weaknesses of bureaucracies. One of them is the tendency of bureaucratic entities to maximize the size of their shares in the overall budget. This is done by abusive utilization of the principles of precision as well as specification. More specifically, the demands made by chief bureaucrats are as high as possible. However, such strategies will only work where we employ bottom-up budgeting, which until recently was the typical way of establishing the annual fiscal budget (even if more sophisticated methods of budgeting are employed such as PPB techniques or zero base budgeting). It comes as little surprise that finance ministers or departments of budgeting etc. have turned to top-down methods to avoid the inefficiencies associated with earlier procedures!

The new methodology rests on targeted measures and the assessment of how well they have been accomplished. Thus it is output oriented or even outcome oriented, where the latter means that the execution of the measures does not suffice but that they must have an impact on well-being (to illustrate: the measure could be speeding fines issued per policeman per day, but the impact would be a subsequent substantial decrease of speeding).

The section may be concluded by a general statement as it appears in OECD Policy Brief No. 1 on Anatomy of the expenditure budget: 'An effective organic budget law provides the indispensable legal base for all key roles and relationships . . . as well as creating the competence and conditions necessary to establish key tools of the expenditure management system.'

This brief section should have aroused your curiosity for a field in the economic analysis of law which is as yet grossly underdeveloped, despite having a substantial impact on the overall performance of governments and the economy at large.

Procurement

Public procurement comprises purchases of goods and services as well as investment by governments and subunits such as departments, agencies, authorities, public funds, public enterprises but also self-governed social insurance institutions (which are a peculiarity of some European countries). All these institutions are contractors for a broad range of purchases that absorb about 11.5 per cent of the European Union's GDP, to give an illustrative figure, which is certainly impressive.

For well-known reasons, efficiency of public procurement is not automatically assured: commissioning and contracting is in the hands of civil servants, who are acting as agents and thus not trading for themselves. This may lead to the familiar problems we addressed in the paragraph on sources of inefficiency (see pp. 145–53). Therefore, the usual standards of efficiency, effectiveness and expediency are complemented by specific rules which are intended to mimic competition in public commissioning.

Given the importance of purchases for private entrepreneurs these rules are also meant to ascertain fair and non-discriminatory conditions for the assignees.

Since the typical way in which public procurement is maintained is through a **tender**, regulations tend to concentrate on this procedure. In its simplest form, a tender is meant to find the **bidder** who offers delivery at the lowest cost. Unfortunately, lowest bids tend to contain disadvantages, since they may fall short of certain quality standards, entail a lack of certainty in their performance or be subject to delays in delivery. Consequently, the regulations are designed to prevent such shortcomings.

There are several typical problems that need to be managed:

- undue preference of local bidders irrespective of the relative high cost of their offers
- bribes associated with undue preference for selected bidders
- the problem of collusion among bidders in order to extract rents from an order.

It must be pointed out, however, that the special regulations do not apply to all tenders. Rather, only those with a certain threshold value are covered.

Moreover, there is a gradation in the degree of competitiveness that is envisaged. Three grades are usually found:

- The strictest form of public procurement is that of a public tender (which in the terminology of the Austrian federal act on public contracts is called an 'open procedure'). A public tender typically contains no territorial restrictions, which, in turn, allows bidders from everywhere to make their offers. To illustrate, for the European Union this means that a contract from a local authority ought to be offered in the entire area of the EU provided the value exceeds a certain threshold. Similar regulations are found in the United Nations Commission on International Trade Law (**UNCITRAL**) as well as in the WTO Government Procurement Agreement (GPA) of 1996. We address these later.
- There are also restricted public tenders (in Austrian parlance a 'non-open procedure'). Their main feature is that (only) firms that economically perform well are invited to make bids. The reason for this restriction is that it secures efficiency where it is important to avoid any risk of poor performance. More specifically, it could be expected that there are bidders who seek entry to the market as newcomers without reputation, thus making the review of their qualification unduly costly.
- Finally, there are certain circumstances in which there are no restrictions on whom to contract (again in Austrian parlance, a 'bargaining procedure'). Imagine a situation where an innovative solution to a problem is sought, which cannot yet be specified in much detail – in such a case, the most specialized provider would be asked for her offer. Similarly, unrestricted contracting is applied in cases of high urgency. Note, however, that even in these cases the Austrian federal act on public contracts strongly recommends that alternative offers are obtained.

The procedural steps of tendering are subject to very detailed regulations. The most recent substantial amendment of Austrian law comprises 341 articles and additional supplements!

Let us look at one of the details to illustrate the application of economic reasoning here. §14 para 3 of Austrian law on public procurement states that in case of a non-open procedure the firms who are invited for bidding ought to be changed as frequently as possible. There are two contradictory observations concerning this rule. First, every contract with an enterprise constitutes a principal–agent relationship. While the resultant problems are well known, it could very well be that the enterprise at hand, which fulfilled an order, is interested being chosen again at a later occasion. However, in this case the management, contrary to the findings of the standard situation, will definitely try to gain the trust of the principal (a government agency). Thus it could be expected that the deviation from the principal's requirements will be small and consequently the cost of surveillance will also be low. Under these circumstances, the rule of §14 para 3 does not appear to be particularly wise!

Therefore we look at the converse argument, which runs as follows: the more frequently a specific principal–agent relationship is obtained, the more likely is it that the partners share rents from collusion (you may try to recall kickback as one form of corruption here). Clearly this would cause losses in social welfare.

The legislators appear to believe that the second consequence is more likely than the first or else that the second argument is more serious than the first – hence the requirement of the rule. In fact, only a theoretical and empirical investigation could provide a sound solution to the issue at hand.

The more fundamental problem underlying these considerations is that of strategic behaviour, which is frequently present in public tenders. Imagine the incentives for vote-maximizing politicians that are present where procurement is at stake. Some fields of contracting are of special interest for particular groups of voters. One illustrative example is provided by public construction projects. In this industry, the share of unskilled labour in total employment is particularly large. Moreover, the workers are very susceptible to dismissal. Therefore, tenders in the field of civil engineering can be tempting in pre-election periods! For some regions this can be replaced by shipyards or steel mills. What they have in common is the attractiveness of the use of public contracting as a political tool. Clearly, this can also be true if the task is to assuage strong labour unions. Needless to add, unrestricted contracting or at least restricted public tenders are particularly favoured in that respect. It is difficult to shape legal norms in a way that minimizes the temptation to misuse them. So they are complemented by monitoring and controls. Following the rationale of the economic analysis of law, it is required to check the additional cost against (potential) savings of such measures.

Strategic actions on behalf of the bidders are at least as problematical as those of the contractor. One typical option here is collusion. Interestingly enough, collusion can even be encouraged by some of the regulations. Imagine the attempt to mitigate the problem known as the **winner's curse**, which can result from applying the widely used principle of selecting the lowest bid (see Box 5.2). To overcome this problem tenders are made so as to encourage offers at a commensurable price. But it is not hard to predict that, in this case, bidders are induced to collude tacitly, in order to achieve the conditions which are most beneficial for an industry. Such collusions turn out to be quite stable since it would become immediately obvious if one colluding party violated the agreement. As a remedy, experts may be engaged in order to prove the economic case for bids. The Austrian act explicitly arranges for a federal placing council (*Bundesvergabekommission*)!

In lawmaking about procurement, there is one further discussion that is worth closer examination. The question is whether centralized tenders or decentralized tenders are more promising in terms of efficiency. How controversial the issue is can be seen from two facts: the recent formation of a (central) 'federal procurement limited liability company' in Austria (Federal Law Gazette I – 39/2001) and a paper published by OECD at almost the same time: SIGMA Paper No. 29 (Generalized and decentralized public procurement, Paris, 2000).

Article 2 of the Austrian act states that the objective of the mentioned act is to 'safeguard the goals in the field of procurement with the aim of bundling both volumes and needs so that the conditions for purchases by the federal government are optimized according to economic and qualitative criteria' (my translation).

In the OECD publication the advantages of centralized and decentralized procurement are listed.

Advantages of centralized procurement are:

* a significant cut in prices for goods as well as services
* a better service for potential bidders at lower costs
* higher purchasing power for the central agency
* the need for standardization for goods and equipment to be purchased regarding both technical issues as well as issues such as environmental compatibility
* several intangible advantages such as more alertness in the management of contracting and performing
* low cost of training for centrally pooled staff
* better performance measures for staff
* a high degree of transparency in processing together with lower monitoring costs.

Advantages of decentralized procurement are:

* lower amounts of purchases decrease the susceptibility to corruption
* goods and services can better be adapted to local or regional needs and performance requirements
* it is possible to reduce unnecessary excess expenditure, since sometimes large batch sizes are only theoretically advantageous
* shorter time limits cause less bureaucracy
* competitiveness of small and medium sized firms is higher
* use can be made of better value for money from local providers
* smaller units leads to higher contentedness of employees and thus better motivation.

Not surprisingly, the authors of the OECD paper conclude that there is no unambiguous winner among the competing options for organizing procurement.

Box 5.2   The principle of the lowest bid and 'the winner's curse'

Imagine the typical situation of bidders in a tender. Ideally, each of them must submit a bid with a fixed price, p, at which the bidder promises to perform if she gets the contract. If all bidders are equally qualified, it may well be the case that they are capable of performing at equal costs. They then would all bid at an equal price. However, there is uncertainty ex ante about the costs that ultimately will accrue ex post. So some bidders may be optimistic and some pessimistic to the effect that some bids are particularly low and others fairly high depending on the ex ante assessment of ex post costs by independently (!) acting bidders. Given this initial situation, who is most likely to win? Well, it will obviously be the bidder who is too optimistic, that is to say who underestimates the true costs. The more cautious bidder will thus miss out. But the winner will very likely not necessarily enjoy the victory if:

- additional claims are ruled out by contract (no recontracting)
- and it turns out ex post that her bid was too optimistic overall.

This is called the winner's curse.

Redress is possible by a markup on one's own offer for safety reasons. However, this should apply to the offers of all bidders. And, in fact, it can be expected that it will be the case if in the course of repeated participation in tenders bidders learn from their (bad) experience. Alas, processes of this kind take a lot of time.

At that time it must be pointed out that, for the contractor, the problem is serious as well. To picture this, imagine that a fixed price were stipulated in a deal that could later not be maintained by the winning bidder, whereas at the same time the contractor successfully defended herself from additional claims (through legal measures). This, in turn, constitutes a substantial risk for the bidder, who not only may go bankrupt but at the same time jeopardizes the whole undertaking. The welfare gains are thus withheld. Consequently, the contractor (a government agency) will concentrate on finding a solution and this is also what experts in the field of auctions and tenders would do. One cure for the winner's curse is widely known as the 'Vickrey rule'. According to this rule, the lowest bid is accepted . . . at the price of the second best. Thus the winning bid is cushioned by a safety net, but the bidder cannot consider the size of the safety net in her strategy since it is determined exogenously. This, in turn, creates a strong incentive to make the bid at the true computed cost. We cannot go through all the advantages and disadvantages of the Vickrey rule. We must be aware, however, that it definitely has some problems that might arouse our curiosity towards alternatives. Here is one: the contractor starts an auction, which starts with the highest bid. Then lower and lower bids are invoked until one of the bidders accepts the deal – this is called a Flemish auction (in contrast to the British auction which starts with the lowest bid). The effect here is similar to that of the Vickrey rule, since, ultimately, there will be only a small difference between the actual price at which the deal is accepted and the price previous to that (which was still more than one bidder was willing to accept).

It suggests considering a mix of options and not to forget about the potential of e-commerce.

For the purpose of this book, these notes are once more intended to demonstrate the wide range of applications of an economic analysis of law. And this may serve as a stimulus to look at other areas of research that have as yet by no means been fully explored.

At the end of this section, we should take a look at the institutional forms we find in procurement on a multinational level.

First of all, there is a directive by the council of the European Union, which can be downloaded from their website (www.europa.eu.int/eur-lex/index.html). There is also a prototype regulation by UNCITRAL (www.uncitral.org). These regulations have some similarities but also differences – they reflect different 'philosophies' concerning tenders.

The main differences between the two norms concern procedural issues in tenders, procedures in purchases and contracting including the obligations of the contract. Moreover, differing remedies for consignees are specified. There are also striking similarities. To illustrate, both cases of urgency and those with national security implications are addressed.

As far as the philosophy behind the regulations is concerned the following observations can be made. The EU regulation allows for both open tenders and restricted tenders; UNCITRAL, by contrast, is much stricter (and more competitiveness oriented) since departures from public tenders are only allowed as an exception to the rule. However, since the intent of the EU is harmonization among member states, differences at the state level are not tolerated. Here UNCITRAL is more flexible. It allows for adaptations at the state level according to need as long as they are comprehensible.

Finally, it must be pointed out that within the World Trade Organization (WTO) preparatory steps for an agreement on public procurement are underway. A multilateral task force is examining the need for more transparency in the light of a wide range of customs for procurement by national governments. The purpose here is obviously the reduction of asymmetric information in the light of future worldwide procedures. In the course of the General Agreement on Trade in Services (GATS), which is currently arousing considerable international concern, the WTO is very much concerned with purchase orders by national governments for services (www.wto.org).

Public procurement absorbs substantial parts of the GDP. Since politicians and bureaucrats are involved, it is a source of familiar weaknesses, such as losses in efficiency and effectiveness. Since public purchase orders are of utmost importance for quite a number of industries, the struggle for orders may tempt them to make use of unfair or even criminal means such as corruption. Hence, economic analysis can contribute substantially to an understanding of the problems at hand as well as the development of tools to help overcome the lack of incentives, prohibitive transaction costs and risks.

Exercise of control and the court of audit or comptroller's office

DIVERSITY

Whatever happens in the public sector, happens in three major steps: planning, performing and review.

This section is about review, with an emphasis on courts of audit, such as the Austrian, European or German courts. In some countries, a similar function is held by a comptroller (it appears that the term is an amalgamation of the French term *compte* for account and the English term *controller*). However, courts of audit or comptrollers are not the only institutions which are in charge of review, neither are their function always unambiguously defined. Therefore, before we start the investigation into the function and performance of courts of audit, let us look at the options for review in more general terms:

- Review can be undertaken by internal audit or external experts.
- It can be voluntary or obligatory.
- Review can and normally will be ex post, but it can be collateral, as is characteristic for **controlling**; there are instances, however, where review can be performed ex ante, such as in cases where the court of audit is engaged in financial decisions with an impact on public debt by the minister of finance.

Several institutional forms of review are in use:

- **Internal audit**, the focus of which is on financial affairs. It is supportive for the management to the extent that it serves as a means of control of a principal over an agent; internal audit is part of governance, both in private enterprises or entities of public administration and is voluntary in nature.
- Controlling, with a broader scope than that of internal audit inasmuch as it is supportive in planning and performance of the enterprise. Therefore, controlling is based on appropriate performance measures that exceed pure accounting. When there is potential for changes to plans for the future, controlling is strategic, whereas when it is limited to performance this is called operational controlling. Controlling can be carried out by an independent subunit of an enterprise (or public entity), but frequently the function is outsourced to an external expert.

- Audit by self-employed experts, as it is typically the case in the compulsory audit of corporations.
- Audit by a special court or 'comptroller's office', which will be our concern in the remainder of this section.

Before we start our detailed investigation, we should find out about the peculiar role of courts of audit in the economic and political dimensions of democracies. At first sight they appear to be indispensable parts of the public economy. Taking the Austrian court of audit as an illustrative example, its competences are tremendous. However, irrespective of the many functions they ought to carry out, they are poorly equipped with means of enforcement. While their work certainly attracts interest, the realization of recommendations following from their findings usually depends on the outcome of a struggle between politicians, parties, interest groups, bureaucrats and – of course – the media.

LEGAL STATUS AND FUNCTIONS

For illustrative purposes, we will concentrate on courts of audit in Austria, the European Union and Germany. For Austria, appropriate regulations are laid down in the Austrian Constitutional Act, Articles 121–8 as well as the Court of Audit Act of 1948. The 1997 version of the Treaty of the European Union contains regulations concerning the court of audit in articles 246–8. For Germany, the relevant sources are Basic Constitutional Law, Article 114, as well as Federal Accounting Rule, Articles 42–6.

For comparison, a comptroller and auditor general was also established by India's constitution; the first known mention of the exchequer in Great Britain was in documents from 1314; and the agency that is home to the **comptroller general** of the United States was founded by Congress in 1921.

The basic functions of courts of audit are:

- compilation and submission of the annual federal balance of accounts (to parliament)
- scrutiny of the accounts, management and achievements of the federal government and its subunits according to legal and economic standards (which are not necessarily uniform)
- scrutiny of single policies and projects, performed by government and its subunits
- scrutiny of public enterprises and firms in which the state holds a significant share
- prudence of government borrowing.

In what follows, we take a closer look at the problems entailed by the second point, scrutiny of the accounts, management and achievements of the federal government (including all state-owned agencies, funds and foundations).

I will first demonstrate that there are three principal–agent relationships that are relevant here. I will then address the issues of the efficiency and effectiveness of courts of audits.

The rationale of outlining these relationships is to point out that the court of audit may be seen as a specific institutional solution for the problem of how to exercise control in the complex setting at hand.

This is first characterized by the relationship of the constituency and the legislative body. Here, the body of voters stands for the principal and the delegates of the legislature are the agents. Inasmuch as voters are interested in politics, they seek information about the current political agenda. However, it is costly to get such information without distortions. Delegates pursue their own interests and therefore they will most likely provide information that appears beneficial or at least not detrimental to them. This may make a difference in the content of information but not in the underlying strategy, whether a delegate represents the majority or the minority of the legislative body.

Note that the media will not automatically be able to fill in the gaps, because they will most likely act with commercial success in mind (circulation and audience ratings); they will thus select and present the news in the most suitable way for this goal.

What follows from this situation is that it is perfectly rational for voters to remain uninformed. Correct information obviously becomes very costly and thus 'rational ignorance' comes as no surprise. For the delegates this facilitates the opportunity of moral hazard (exerted as hidden action) at the cost of the voters (what has been said concerning problems of contracting in Chapter 3 applies here – I am sure you remember!). Since delegates possess hidden information, they tend to adverse selection as well (associated with hidden information, imagine the handling of election pledges . . .).

And courts of audit? Given the situation from earlier, they might be most welcome since in order to accomplish their tasks they are usually allowed to inspect accounts and other documents, which means that they have access to original information. Moreover, they are not only entitled to process data, but also publish their reports subject to certain qualifications.

The next important relationship is that between the legislature (as represented by delegates, MPs or congressmen) and the government, where the former jointly act as principal and the latter as agent. For the government, the situation provides the opportunity to make use of their head start concerning information as well as to perform hidden action to their own advantage.

One remedy for such undesirable states is the request to submit the annual budget ex ante and the entitlement of approval on behalf of the legislative body. However, given the likely opportunistic behaviour of governments, which is in line with our general assumptions concerning human nature, it seems wise to also have some ex post control. This takes the form of review by the court of audit. By the entitlement to prepare and present the nation's balance of accounts, this independent body sees to the publication of details about the government's actual performance. This can be taken as an efficient and effective means of control.

Let us turn to the third relevant relationship: the relationship between the government and the bureaucracy, this time with the government as the principal and the bureaucracy as agent. From the economic theory of bureaucracy, we know that both sides will most likely pursue divergent interests. The politicians forming the government are mainly interested in staying in office and maintaining their power, which requires providing benefits to supporters. To accomplish this task, governments can make use of the expertise of bureaucrats – and at a low cost, too. But bureaucrats are basically interested in power, prestige and pay – and acceptable working conditions. Thus, authorities and agencies might seek excessive budgets or tend to be overstaffed, making use of their head start in information and their principals' high cost of monitoring. Now, it cannot be denied that in principle the interests of governments and bureaucracies are in harmony at times, particularly when a government pursues a policy of expanding the public sector. However, the contrary is more likely. A peculiar situation can emerge where governments try hard to cut back on budgets – be it voluntarily because of a belief in liberal economic ideas and/or guided by the need to curb deficits and debt, as in the European Union in our days – since bureaucracies may try to maintain their influence by proposing excessive regulation, which would at least stabilize their power.

Such circumstances will find the government ready to accept means that help keep the bureaucracy under control. This is what courts of audit can do, since they are entitled to scrutinize both the organization and the output of bureaucracies.

The effectiveness of courts of audit (and comptrollers) depends finally on their institutional status within the state as well as the chance to realize their findings.

As far as institutional status is concerned, a court of audit could be:

- an agency of the legislative branch
- an agency of the executive branch
- a special type of court within the judiciary.

Interestingly, many courts of audit are of the first or the second type. This in turn directs our attention to the procedure by which officeholders are selected and established. Such procedures need to ensure the independence of both staff and the head.

Highly qualified staff must be protected from backlash when investigations are incriminating. One way of accomplishing this is to give them tenure with special protection from dismissal.

The heads ought to be deterred from opportunistic behaviour that most likely is caused by political pressure. This task usually is accomplished by long terms of office and the exclusion from reappointment!

While such desiderata are quite obvious from a public interest perspective, it is interesting to ask why courts of audit and comptrollers are affected by the private interest point of view. We have seen that under various circumstances the key players in a democracy can be interested in a body of scrutiny. Whether they succeed in getting an appropriate vote will depend on the intensity of preferences and tactical skills. Alternatively, we may think of a sort of constitutional act, since all the players are behind 'a veil of ignorance' concerning the probability of being the persecutor or the victim of cases of misconduct – so that their best strategy is just to agree in the establishment of a body of review.

ON THE EFFICIENCY AND EFFECTIVENESS OF COURTS OF AUDIT

The main purposes of scrutiny are to ensure efficiency (that the unit under examination performs at minimum cost), effectiveness (that the unit performs so as to match the target level of performance) and productivity (that the ratio between output value and input value is as large as possible, but definitely larger than one).

In order to accomplish this task, (at least) three requirements should be met: there must be adequate measures for inputs and – more importantly – for outputs. These measures must be recorded over certain time spans in order to allow for the observation of performance over time. Finally, there must be clear-cut targets or performance levels for all units under investigation. These requirements are by no means generally met! In fact, public sector reform has for a long time struggled against the difficulties (technical, economic and of course, political), which thwart experts and players alike.

Two illustrative examples of the type of reform that is undertaken everywhere in order to meet the needs of a well-structured and comprehensible public administration are the 'program for innovation in administration', which was launched by the Austrian government in 2003 (www.bka.gv.at/site/5123/default. aspx) and the German counterpart 'a modern state – a modern administration' (www.staat-modern.de). Also noteworthy is the European Public Administration Network (EPAN), which serves as a common platform for the exchange of experiences. Within the OECD the public governance committee assesses and analyses reforms such as those in Austria and Germany and the other OECD member states, of course.

With respect to our topic, courts of audit and comptrollers, two observations are appropriate: first, there is a certain antagonism between the clear yardstick for audits and the still not fully developed measures for the performance of the entities under investigation. Second, and even more important in this case, with respect to courts of audit and comptrollers (and their staff), theory predicts several peculiarities, which can give rise to inefficiencies of these institutions. In particular, given the usual assumptions about rationality and constraints, it follows that the incentives of staff members of courts of audit to perform effectively in their business are rather weak.

Granted, there are no empirical tests with respect to this issue, but observations are at variance with the theoretical assumptions. Presidents and staff members alike appear to be rather unselfish and ambitious in their struggle for success. This observation may have something to do with the esprit de corps which has been attributed to public administration, particularly where staff is especially trained to adopt the service for the common good, as in the special *écoles* in France. Thus the employees of the respective institutions may approach the type of devoted civil servants that Max Weber had in mind (and which is at variance with results from economics of bureaucracy, of course). Some work needs to be done to shed more light on these issues.

However, there are some practices that have been seen as detracting from efficiency (I follow the 1990 paper on courts of audit by Frey and Serna here):

- Where shortcomings are identified in the course of review, quite frequently one consequence is to blame employees for not observing prevailing regulations appropriately. Consequently, an accentuation of the surveillance of compliance will usually be recommended. To illustrate, let us take adherence to the principles of budgeting that we went over earlier in this chapter. As an example, assume that a violation of the principle of specification was found. Consequently, strict compliance will most likely be demanded. However, in the spirit of more recent trends in government, this can give rise to higher inefficiency instead of improving performance, since it does not tolerate funds to be shifted to areas with greater shortage than in the areas of intended use!
- Sometimes courts of audit demand strict economy where this in fact can lead to a decrease in welfare. To illustrate, consider a case where there is criticism of road repairs being undertaken at night, thus causing excessive costs due to extra pay. However, in this case the abandonment of the admittedly expensive way of carrying out public works would cause negative externalities and social costs: deferred repairs would cause unnecessary traffic jams and increase the risk of accidents. Such considerations require the reviewer not to look just at the activity at hand but to take a broad economic view.
- Reviews sometimes follow strictly formal procedures. While the employees under review may thus be blamed for inefficiency, it is not taken into account that prevailing constraints give few incentives to background private interests in favour of public obligations. Where this is the case the courts of audit forbear the possibility of making clear-cut distinctions between shortcomings rooted in private interests and those that are due to weakly implemented public interests (for example, because of imperfections in labour contracts).
- Last, it has been found that criticisms of details outnumber criticisms of general failings. One obvious reason for this is that, in general, it is easier to prove details than systemic problems. That is to say the yardsticks applied can then show deviations from achieved performance measures and the agents can be blamed for allowing these deviations, but this obscures the view of underlying serious fault in planning in the past.

Our final point in this section deals with the fairly low potential to initiate economic and political action following negative results. In fact, the heads of courts and chief comptrollers are rarely given powers to take appropriate action.

For illustrative purposes, let us have a look at the situation in Austria, which is absolutely representative here. Following Federal Constitutional Law Article 126d, reports of the court of audit ought to be submitted to the National Council first and then be published. Moreover the court's president is entitled to participate in relevant sessions of the National Council and committees. If she demands it, she has the right to be heard when relevant agenda items are at stake. That is not very much – the publication of the reports in particular is far from spectacular! If it arouses public reaction at all this is maintained by the selection and propagation of certain points in the reports by the mass media. As a consequence, the heads of the affected previously reviewed entities may take a stand. This, in turn, mobilizes politicians of both the ruling parties as well as the opposition, which rarely leads to an objective discussion of the issues at hand; mostly, appropriate arguments are abandoned in favour of tactical point scoring! For the court of audit's concerns this is not supportive at all.

Such observations have two possible ramifications. The first is a legal one: besides her entitlement to participation the president (or the head of an equivalent institution) could be vested with a right to present motions (in legislative bodies). Such motions require formal treatment and settlement. This will give extra publicity to a court's critical reports and thus lead to greater pressure for a more substantial debate. Unfortunately, this can lead to action only when the forces of political control are activated in the course of debate.

The possible second ramification is pragmatic in nature, which means that the president herself turns to the public. Note that this fits into public choice theory inasmuch as it contributes to the profile of the agency and increases its prestige. However, the advantage of immediate and open criticism also entails a risk inasmuch as a president might be blamed for partisanship just because of the selection of the propagated deficiencies.

Although the topic is still far from being exhausted, we will end with one final remark. There is an ongoing debate on whether part of the business of public audits can be relinquished to certified accountants, thus 'contracting out' part of the agenda. The proponents claim that this could lead to a substantial increase of efficiency of review since certified accountants have specific knowledge that will be mobilized for the sake of better audits, thus disencumbering the courts and at the same time gaining latitude for high-profile cases.

Interestingly, there is not much literature on the law and economics of courts of audit, but the gist can definitely be found in the *European Journal of Law and Economics*, 1, 1994!

Some law and economics points about ombudsmen and citizen protection

The ombudsman poses interesting questions. Long before 'citizen proximity' became a favourite concept for politicians all over the world, the Scandinavian countries launched an institution that quickly became a byword for an institution that handles complaints concerning maladministration – the ombudsman.

Ombudsmen or public advocates (also *provedor* or *médiateur*) represent an institution of **grievance control**. Given the conditions under which ombudsmen can be engaged, they have an exceptional position at the intersection of political control, the protective function of appeals as well as the supervision by special administrative entities and the courts. Legal acts by which ombudsman-like institutions are established for the sake of the protection of citizens are typically **soft law**.

Grievance control is a particular type of measure in public administration. While investigations into reasons and impacts from the legal, sociological and political viewpoint appear quite natural, there is also an economic perspective of the issue. Before we start a necessarily short inspection of the issue we must make a qualification. The reason is that nowadays there are not only ombudsmen at a national level all over the world, even the European Union has its own European ombudsman and they are mushrooming in provinces, communities, even in hospitals, and in universities, prisons, the army, and social insurance institutions. It has, incidentally, also become fashionable for popular newspapers or radio stations to no longer have a letterbox for complaints, but rather an ombudsman . . . which would definitely not fit the requirements of grievance control in the sense we have in mind here.

Generally speaking, ombudsmen can be engaged when neither a regular nor a special legal remedy can be apprehended. It can also be the case that a legal remedy is not (or not yet) available. So from the economic point of view the employment of an ombudsman is rooted in insuperable high transaction cost and/or alleged, expected or effective uncompensated welfare losses.

On first sight, the economic theory of bureaucracy seems to provide adequate explanations for the occurrence of grievances. Still, existing theories fall short of answering some of the questions posed by the observations and findings just examined. For example, this can be inferred from annual reports of the Austrian public advocacy (as the ombudsman is called here) to the National Council. Frequently, it is not the misconduct of bureaucrats that is the reason for a complaint, but rather a severe lack of information on behalf of the citizen. This, in turn, is either generated by the inaccessibility of instructions and regulations or by the legal terminology and wording of the regulations, which is then denounced as user adversarial.

It is interesting to note in passing that the apparently new fields for research that emerge from these observations have already been taken up by scholars who advocate a 'new law and economics' (see the remarks on critical reflections in Chapter 6). They have pointed out that simplifying the semantics and semiotics of legal parlance can effectuate lower asymmetries in information and subsequently also transaction costs, which, in turn, makes public administration more accessible for the clients.

This definitely fits into the field of grievance control, of which ombudsmen are the predominant institutional form. Let us take a brief look at the history, the forms of appearance and conclude with the sketch of an economic explanation for the existence of ombudsmen.

The ombudsman is an institution with an astonishingly long tradition. Ancestors of our institution are found in the time of the Greek city states already. In Athens, ten *euthynoi* supervised the civil servants in their enactment of the decisions made by the parliament. In Sparta, it was found that in about 750 BC, the influence of the supervisors became so strong that they effectively took governmental power!

The first ombudsman of our time was established in Sweden in 1810. Nowadays, we find ombudsmen even in most of the European transition countries and the European ombudsman has been in office since 1995 (www.ombudsman.europa.eu/ guide/pdf/en/guide_en.pdf).

As always, there are noteworthy exceptions. One is found in Germany, where a committee on petitions, which is part of the parliamentary institution, takes the role of the ombudsman. In the United States, there is no statutory ombudsman. Some states have similar institutions that act on a voluntary basis. In the sketch of an economic explanation that follows we will address the exceptions again.

FORMS OF APPEARANCE

The competences or property rights of ombudsmen are quite dispersed. They are rather narrow where they comprise the receipt of complaints and advice as far as public administration is concerned. They are broad where they comprise the pursuit of complaint via the courts, the entitlement to make recommendations even to the legislature and they even enjoy the same rights as conferred by a successful petition. Morcover, they have the entitlement to information of all kinds: to access records as well as to summon witnesses and to conduct hearings.

Ombudsmen may be contacted directly. Occasionally, this has to be in written form. Direct address is prohibited in Great Britain and France. In Great Britain, the parliamentary commissioner is only allowed to act if a citizen submits a written complaint through a member of parliament. In France, the invocation is via a member of parliament, the national assembly or the senate.

Since the means of appointment can indicate the intended independence of an ombudsman, it is worth looking at the regulations in selected countries (see Table 5.4).

Besides competences and the means of appointment, the position within the structure of governance might be of interest. In most of the member states of the European Union the ombudsman is an independent, court-like administrative entity. Under Anglo-Saxon influence, it is rather an auxiliary attachment to the parliament. In France, it is an attachment to public administration, despite the filter in approaching it.

From an economic perspective, one may first ask what kind of property rights ombudsmen hold, since this together with the constraints (pay, possible achievements) will determine the incentives to perform effectively. Applying the distinctions of Chapter 2, the relevant type here is 'exclusive and non-transferable'. As has been noted already, the competences are rather dispersed. This, in turn, would support the suggestion that the performance might also differ considerably, which, in turn, could very well reflect the intentions of stakeholders in politics and administration. These conjectures demonstrate that there is room (and need) for further research!

Table 5.4 Regulations relating to parliamentary ombudsmen and respective country

Way of selection/peculiarities	Country
Election by parliament for one term of office	Iceland
Election by parliament/one re-election possible	Sweden, Denmark, Norway
Election by parliament through an absolute majority/ one re-election possible	Portugal, Hungary
Election by parliament with absolute majority	Finland
Appointment by the crown – following proposal by the government/function ends at the age of 65	Great Britain
Appointment by parliament after separate votes in the lower and upper house or alternatively by proposal from one top executive agency	Spain, Netherlands, Poland
Appointment by the president/renewal possible	Ireland, Cyprus

Source: Adapted from Michael Mauerer, *Die parlamentarischen Ombudsman–Einrichtungen in den Mitgliedstaaten des Europarates* (Parliamentary Ombudsman – Institutions of the Member States of the European Council).

TOWARDS AN ECONOMICALLY INSPIRED THEORY OF THE OMBUDSMAN

A brief anecdote: a friend of mine who is a professor of administrative law on the occasion of a conference on consumerism noted that public law is, by and large, ultimately inspired by a kind of *consumerism*. Looking at administrative procedure as it is understood in civil law countries, one immediately can see the point my friend was making. It specifies and limits the rights of officials and by the same token shapes the entitlements of citizens.

In case of an authority's ruling citizens are entitled to appeal. When citizens claim to be infringed by an authority in Germany, they can turn to special administrative courts. In Austria they may turn to the independent administrative senate when the possibilities of appeal have been exhausted; there is also the extraordinary remedy of appeal to the federal administrative court.

Moreover, citizens may turn to informal means such as complaints to relevant bodies. It is noteworthy that for quite some time agencies have run separate offices to handle complaints.

A special form of grievance is to turn to a member of parliament; this is a sort of political grievance control. However, this remedy has hardly been investigated. That is to say, very little is known about its efficiency and effectiveness. At the same time we do also know nothing about the efficiency and effectiveness of ombudsmen. The question whether such institutions can lead to overall net increases in welfare can only be answered if we can assess the savings in welfare losses due to the performance of ombudsmen as compared with the additional costs for staff and other resources stemming from these institutions.

A further preliminary question concerning the overall welfare effects of ombuds-men is why choose ombudsmen at all in order to accomplish the task of supporting citizens in case of complaints. An answer to this question is suggested by applying public choice theory, where the subjective interests under the assumption of utility maximization are investigated. Let us follow this approach.

First, we must identify the stakeholders (limiting our analysis to the level of a federal state). Here they are the citizen voters, the elected members in the legislature and the bureaucrats in the executive branch. Now we can readily assume that citizens (inter alia) will try to keep welfare losses in the course of claiming benefits as small as possible. Such welfare losses can follow from wrong decisions by the bureaucracy or from transaction costs associated with consultations; the reason could be queuing, misleading or missing information and so on. In general, the remedy of appeal can be employed in case of wrong (unfavourable) decisions. These can usually not be compared with other drawbacks such as undue opportunity costs due to queuing, lacking information etc. Here one natural remedy would be to employ the local delegate. It is the deputy who is obliged to not only take decisions but also to exert political control over the executive branch. However, this may precipitate the delegate into some kind of dilemma. Why? The main concern of the delegate is the pursuit of power and prestige (a standing assumption in public choice). Being political entrepreneurs, delegates attempt to accomplish the tasks by staying in power, i.e. by being re-elected. This can be effectively done by using capacity, time and physical strength to act as a broker for special demands of interest groups. From this, the deputy can expect both financial support for campaigns and votes at the ballot. The marginal gain is thus most likely much higher than in case of the pursuit of the requests of individual citizens. There is an obvious way out of the dilemma and that is to externalize the cost of **mentoring** for citizens. The deputies might thus be supportive for a special institution for handling grievances. Note that the prevailing voting system will most likely facilitate such an under-taking. With list voting, the candidates for the constituencies are frequently hardly known to the electorate since they are nominated by the political parties. There are severe barriers to the performance of a mentoring function on behalf of the delegates. There is, in fact, a failure of mentoring. Consequently, a special institution can be very attractive for both citizens and delegates. Inasmuch as the function of political control by the legislature is thus softened, the ombudsmen may even be accepted by the bureaucracy.

From this the hypothesis (or at least the proposition) follows that ombudsmen are surrogates for certain distinct functions of the delegates, particularly in countries with a list-voting system!

The fact that most ombudsmen are seen as subsidiary institutions to the legislature supports our view. Moreover, it is also widely observed that they enjoy a rather generous endowment with all kinds of entitlement concerning investigations and access to information. The case of Germany is not really contradictory. The com-mittee of petitions has been vested with rights and obligations that are equivalent to those of a fully fledged ombudsman. At this point you may suspect what the explanation could be for the deviating regulation in Great Britain: it could, of course, be the system of majority voting, which traditionally is held to result in greater 'closeness' of elected delegates to the citizens of their constituency. And France? Well, as could also be seen from the literature it came rather as a surprise for the experts when the *médiateur* was established there. The firm organization of public administration together with a high level of allegiance were seen as reasons why some sort of 'public advocacy' was not so desirable. So it might be a contribution to the Zeitgeist after all.

Key terms

administrative law
agenda setting
anarchy
bargaining
bidder
bottom-up budgeting
bribery
budgeting
bureaucracy
bureaucratic inefficiencies
bureaucrats as politicians
bureaucrats as voters
bureaucrats in politics
cameralism
campaign funding
citizens' rights
civil servants
comptroller general
constitutional act
constitutional economics
constitutional law
consumerism
controlling
coordination
corruption
courts of audit
D'Hondt rule
direct democracy
division of powers
e-government
expenditure budget
externalities

fiscal federalism
formal constitutional acts
formal privatization
fraud
functions of the state
general administrative law
global budgeting
grievance control
hybrid organizations
impossibility theorem
incremental budgeting
infinite regress
internal audit
Leviathan
lobbying
logrolling
majority rule
median voter
mentoring
merit goods
natural monopolies
near unanimity
NGOs
ombudsmen
one man one vote
one-shop stop
option good
Ordnungspolitik
oversupply
passionate minorities
paternalism
patronage

performance measures	soft law
petitions	sovereign administration
preference intensity	specific administrative law
principles of budgeting	status quo
prisoner's dilemma	subsidiarity
private interest perspective	tax burden
procurement	tender
proportional representation	theory of market failure
public administration	tit for tat
public choice	top-down budgeting
public interest perspective	unanimity
pure collective goods	UNCITRAL
QUANGO	undersupply
rationing by waiting	voter turnout
regulation	voting rule
rent seeking	winner's curse
representative democracy	WTO
rule of law	

Recommended reading

Axelrod, Robert, *The Evolution of Cooperation*, New York, 1984.
Baldwin, Robert and Cave, Martin, *Understanding Regulation*, Oxford, 1999.
Bartel, Rainer and Schneider, Friedrich, Efficiency and effectiveness control based on economic analysis: the example of the Austrian Court of Audit, *European Journal of Law and Economics*,1, 1994, 237 passim.
Bishop, W., A theory of administrative law, *Journal of Legal Studies*, 19, 1990, 489–530.
Black, Duncan, *The Theory of Committees and Elections*, Cambridge, 1958.
Blankart, Charles B., *Die öffentlichen Finanzen in der Demokratie* [Public Finance in a Democracy], 4th edn, Munich, 2001.
Blankart, Charles and Mueller, Dennis (eds) *A Constitution for the European Union*, Cambridge, MA, 2004.
Breton, Albert, *The Economic Theory of Representative Government*, Chicago, 1974.
Buchanan, James, *The Limits of Liberty – Between Anarchy and Leviathan*, Chicago, 1978.
Buscaglia, Edgardo, An economic and jurimetric analysis of public sector corruption in *Essays in Law and Economics*, Cheltenham, 1997.
Buscaglia, Edgardo and van Dijk, Jan, *Controlling Organized Crime Linked to Public Sector Corruption: Results of a Global Trends Study*, New York, 2003.
Diderisch, Nils, Cadel, Georg, Otmar, Heidrun and Haag, Ingeborg, *Die diskreten Kontrolleure – Eine Wirkungsanalyse des Bundesrechnungshofs* [Discreet Controllers: An Assessment of the German Federal Court of Audit], Opladen, 1990.
Engel, Christoph and Morlok, Martin (eds) *Öffentliches Recht als ein Gegenstand ökonomischer Forschung* [Public Law as an Issue of Economic Research], Tübingen, 1998.
Farber, Daniel A. and Frickey, Philip P., *Law and Public Choice*, Chicago, 1991.

Frey, Bruno S. and Serna, Angel, Eine politisch-ökonomische Betrachtung des Rechnungshofs [Court of audit from the viewpoint of political economy], *Finanzarchiv*, 48, 1990, 244.

Furubotn, Erik and Richter, Rudolf, *New Institutional Economics*, College Station, TX, 1991.

Johnson, Ronald and Libecap, Gary, *The Federal Civil Service System and the Problem of Bureaucracy*, Chicago and London, 1994.

Lane, Jan-Erik, *The Public Sector*, London, Newbury Park, CA, and New Delhi, 1995.

Locke, John, *Two Treatises on Government*, Cambridge, 1980.

Marshaw, Jerry, *Greed, Chaos and Governance: Using Public Choice to Improve Public Law*, New Haven, CT, 1997.

Matscher, Franz (ed.) *Ombudsmann in Europa*, Strasbourg and Arlington, VA, 1994.

Mayer-Maly, T., *Rechtswissenschaft* [Jurisprudence], Munich, 1999.

Montesquieu, Charles de Secondat, Baron de, *The Spirit of Laws* [translation of *De l' Esprit des lois*], Cambridge, 1989.

Mueller, Dennis, *Public Choice III*, Cambridge, 2005.

Nozick, Robert, *Anarchy, State and Utopia*, New York, 1974.

OECD, *Budgeting for Results*, Paris, 1995.

Ogus, Anthony, *Regulation – Legal Form and Economic Theory*, Oxford, 1994.

Ott, Attiat F., *Public Sector Budgets – A Comparative Study*, Aldershot, 1993.

Posch, Willibald, *Introduction to the Austrial Legal System*, Vienna, 1993.

Peters, B. Guy, *The Politics of Bureaucracy*, 4th edition, White Plains, NY, 1995.

Richter, Rudolf, and Furubotn, Eirik G., *Institutions and Economic Theory*, Ann Arbor, MI, 1997.

Rose-Ackerman, Susan, *Corruption and Government*, Cambridge, 1999.

Schotter, Andrew, *The Economic Theory of Social Institutions*, Cambridge, MA, 1981.

Stacey, Frank, *Ombudsman Compared*, Oxford, 1978.

Voigt, Stefan, *Explaining Constitutional Change*, Cheltenham, 1999.

6 There is still a lot to say on . . . applications, alternatives, criticism

Preliminaries and an interim result

This book is deliberately called a primer to the economic analysis of law. Its emphasis is on accessibly introducing economic reasoning in the field of law. Detailed descriptions or in-depth analysis of the legal acts themselves have to be omitted for the sake of brevity. In fact, the introductory nature of the text is best reflected by the fact that the fairly comprehensive *Encyclopaedia of Law and Economics*, which starting in the year 2000 was published in five volumes, covers more than 4,000 pages!

We, however, started with the theory of property rights, thus distinguishing between commodities by the ways in which by agreement they can be used in a legitimate way instead of just their quantities. We learned that property rights, broadly understood, are the building blocks of institutions, which gave rise to the observation that the economic analysis of law can be grasped as part of the so-called new institutional economics. This rapidly developing approach to the economy and society at large covers important fields of economics such as 'public choice' or non-market decision making, which, in turn, is essential for the better understanding of the emergence and stability of legal regulations and any future changes.

The specific viewpoint economists take on legal rules is that of efficiency. Consequently, we spent some time discussing the ways in which this yardstick can be adapted to the assessment of legal rules – be it existing ones or those for which a blueprint is sought. We saw that in order to assess the actual or intended efficacy of a law it should pass the test of Pareto efficiency. However, the exigent conditions of the Pareto criterion are hardly ever met in practice. Therefore the conditions are substantially weakened in the so-called Kaldor-Hicks compensation test. Whatever the criterion is, the value of entitlements and obligations (which are cast in legal terms) to the individual must be measured somehow. Ordinal utility theory does not allow for an immediate operational measure. Therefore, several measures, which are meant to be means of relief, are in use. The most prominent among them is willingness to pay. When willingness to pay is applied in a Kaldor-Hicks test, we end up with the familiar cost–benefit calculus.

Turning to the fundamental task of legal rules, guiding mutual consent (by settlement in case of conflicts and by contract in case of potentials of mutually gainful cooperation), we started with a benchmark for the accomplishment of the latter tasks – the Coase theorem. This was preceded by a review of the major ingredients of the toolkit, the notions of 'externality' and transaction cost. While the Coase theorem demonstrates how mutual consent can be achieved in a perfect world, the identification of failures in this achievement gives rise to liability rules and ways of handling imperfect or incomplete contracts. However, where incentives and deterrents are created via liability rules and obligations to compensation for damages do not suffice, trials have to be sought and in cases of severe wrongdoing punishment has to be threatened. For the sake of trust in the effectiveness of the legal system, they also have to be imposed. In the course of these considerations, we learned about the influence of fees on litigation, judges, lawyers and legal aid as well as the peculiarities of fines versus imprisonment. That is the point where we will now stop.

As I have already said, we have only very briefly dealt with the application of the tools to distinct branches of law. Apart from this, the economic analysis of law has seen such widespread application that it is barely possible to cover all fields even just approximately. To get an impression of the uses besides that of the *Encyclopaedia of Law and Economics* mentioned just before you are referred to Richard Posner's – already quoted – impressive text *Economic Analysis of Law* (now in its fifth edition) and the *Bibliography of Law and Economics*, although some years have passed since it came out. Even a random search of the literature will show you applications in family law, the law of adoption, divorce, even assisted suicide, moreover, in internet regulation with its peculiar problems of the protection of intellectual property. Corporate governance, finance, insurance and taxation are widely addressed fields in law and economics.

In order to give you at least a glimpse at typical fields of application, this chapter starts with sections on **labour law** and **business law** respectively. You will see that the knowledge you acquired in preceding chapters can readily be applied to those fields. They rest on the same model of human action and, consequently, make use of incentives and deterrents, as they are present in liability rules and obligations for compensation in the theory of (imperfect) contracts. Public choice plays its part as well as considerations about punishment for wrongdoing (i.e. crime and punishment).

I will continue with a little detour: interestingly enough, there is a remarkable and widely respected approach to the analysis of legal rules, which was actually developed somewhat independently of our subject matter. For some time, however, this **regulatory impact analysis** converges to the methodological approach at hand. Since it is widely advocated in the USA, by organisations such as OECD (Organization for Economic Cooperation and Development) as well as the European Union it is worthwhile to summarize it here.

Finally, I will review critical viewpoints, which will reveal why the economic analysis of law, despite the wide range of issues covered and the high level of sophistication it has reached, is still not fully acknowledged among scholars and practitioners alike.

Application to labour law

At the outset we ought to make a distinction between individual labour law and collective labour law. The former deals with the rights and duties of the individual employee and employer respectively. The latter refers to collective action for the pursuit of employees' interests and their limitations. Note that this distinction follows good continental European practice, where **labour relations** in general and organized labour in particular are subject to legal **regulation**. However, even if labour relations are more voluntary, the gist of the economic reasoning remains valid.

I must emphasize that what follows is just a sketch of the existing literature. Moreover, I should point out that even the literature in the realm of (applied) economic theory frequently touches on issues of the institutional framework in general and legal issues in particular. To illustrate, one intense discussion is about the anticompetitive effects of so called non-wage labour costs. These in turn are rooted partly in labour protection measures and partly in social benefits. As these are either granted voluntarily by **works council** agreement or enforced by law the closeness of labour market economics to the economic analysis of law becomes quite obvious.

Let us turn to individual labour law and one of its principal elements: labour contracts. Such contracts could either refer to a specially assigned task, which frequently has a distinct date of completion or else lasts until the service is completed, but they could clearly also establish a lasting employment relationship. Contracts with an assigned task – **service contract** for short – could comprise expert advice, the illustration of a book or other straightforward issues. In case of an employment relationship, the employee commits herself to the accomplishment of orders by the employer according to the firm's needs and under the command and guidance by the employer herself or by an authorized person; presence and availability at certain predetermined hours is included.

What both cases have in common is a familiar principal–agent relationship, which we have already addressed when we discussed (imperfect) contracts in Chapter 3. (You surely remember the three major flaws in imperfect contracts?) What we will see shortly is that the problems arising from the second type of labour contract are gradually greater than those of the service contract. At the outset, however, we can use our toolbox of general results concerning imperfect contracts. To illustrate, we can predict that the performance and its quality on behalf of the agent are likely to be defective when there are neither incentives to comply with the stipulated contents of the contract nor appropriate efforts to monitor the agents' activities on behalf of the principal. In a longlasting employment relationship, the problem of insufficient performance can be reinforced by opportunistic behaviour, not only be the employee (the agent) but also by the employer! To picture this, imagine an employer who takes advantage of asymmetric information between her agent and herself concerning certain risks inherent in a job and attempts to save on costs for safety devices. Opportunistic behaviour is facilitated in long-term contracts that are contingency contracts in nature. Such contracts are characterized by the fact that it is difficult to determine in advance what kind of work ought to be done at a certain point in time in the future so that only willingness to work during certain hours can be stipulated for sure. This appears to require the provision of appropriate legal conditions in which there are specifications, for example, of what kind of work is expected and what is not in case of a conflict. However, conflicts of this type are generally not discharged on an individual basis. Usually the work council will be employed, which in turn stipulates operating agreements. If settlement still cannot be accomplished, the courts will be invoked (in Austria, for example, there are special **labour courts**). A lot of transaction costs could be saved, however, when even contingency contracts specify how conflict situations will be handled – ex ante of course.

We need to talk about qualifications next. An employee can be characterized by certain qualifications. Some of them she will bring along and some of them result from special on-the-job training or further education. Performance hinges on qualification. Qualifications, in turn, determine how easy it is to replace an employee. The specific skills that determine the ease of replacement have been labelled **factor specificity**. To illustrate, where no specific qualifications or skills are necessary to carry out a job, replacement (substitution) of one employee by another is fairly easy. This, in turn, makes it easier for the employee to quit in case of a better offer. However, when the employee is an expert who is well acquainted with special work conditions, replacement can become very costly and it is therefore in the interest of the employers to avoid premature departure. This in turn gives a strategic advantage to the employee over the employer. So in this case, the employer will be interested in stipulating conditions which prevent her from disadvantage. This is equivalent to saying that there are situations where the labour relationship is equal to bilateral monopoly, which in turn can be anticipated and therefore stipulated in appropriate provisions.

One of the more prominent sources of factor specificity is investment in human capital on behalf of the employer. However, such investments may arouse the interest of a competitor, who consequently will try to poach employees. Labour law therefore contains clauses that forbid changing jobs and immediately working for some competitor – in the case of high factor specificity only, of course. Employers can counteract such changes of job by offering wages well above the equilibrium wage rate – thus increasing the **opportunity cost** of change of job for the employee ('efficiency wages'); the rationale here stems from the likely extra costs of training a new employee.

Sometimes it is not the primary interest of the employer to establish a longlasting labour contract. However, shorter contracts also give rise to problems, particularly when they are interconnected. If an employer cannot make strong predictions about what will happen in the future, she will prefer (a series of) short contracts. Labour law rules out such a series of contracts ('chains') in the sense that once they have been stipulated the resulting contractual relationship is inferred to be of an open-ended type (thus granting the employee a certain amount of security). Still there is another aspect of short-term contracts, which implies a disadvantage for the employer. Short-term contracts create no incentive for the employee to improve her skills – and thus her productivity. This in turn may lead to lost rents; she may thus be inclined to bear a part of the cost by awarding extended contracts.

So far we have concentrated on such perspectives of labour law, which aim at the reduction of transaction costs as well as the minimization of risks from opportunistic behaviour.

These are, of course, by far not the only relevant fields for an economic investigation. For example, one of the most important issues is incentives from remuneration, particularly when there is division of labour. It can be shown that in this case remuneration of the individual employee does not depend on the overall result of production. The contribution to the overall result by the individual employee might be barely perceptible ('inframarginal'). Consequently that individual could take a free ride, thus keeping her contribution to the collective efforts to a minimum for her own comfort. Interestingly enough, this could serve as one explanation for the prevalence of hierarchies within firms. These are effectuated via directives and sanctions, which, in turn, are necessary to stop opportunistic behaviour once more.

Clearly, this could be seen as a special case of hidden action in a principal–agent relationship. However, being a special case it points to details that are present in the well known general setting for asymmetric information.

Our framework allows for some considerations of wage setting. Let us start with an ostensibly unusual case. In a software development firm, an employee might show high factor specificity. Hence her principal might suffer from a lack of information (since he might lack appropriate knowledge). In this case the employee would be able to dominate bargaining over the wage rate and an inefficient high wage would be the result. Needless to say, contracts should contain provisions to get around such deficiencies. For example, they could stipulate that employees must not set wage levels. Unfortunately, the employer also has motivations that would induce him to set wages at an inefficient level. Given profit maximization, wages would definitely tend to be too low. However, specifically with unskilled workers (low specificity, easily replaceable) an employer could make use of the head start in information concerning the true economic performance of the firm and simulate a need to lower wage rates (although the performance of the firm is perfectly satisfactory). If workers disagree they will be dismissed and then offered a new contract with lower wages, of course. From this one can infer a mutual benefit of official wages by agreement. Unfortunately, official wages have the disadvantage that in this case cost savings are only possibly by dismissals. From an overall economic perspective this could give rise to a further inefficiency: imagine that the dismissed workers either remain in a state of complete inactivity (resulting in a productivity of zero) or get employment at a lower productivity than in the previous firm. Wages and employment thus create a two-edged problem.

Rigidity is as detrimental here as asymmetry in information. An interesting option to overcome the latter is to incorporate a worker representative in the management or – as is the custom in so-called **two-tier systems** – in the advisory board. While at first sight this seems to improve the (fair) distribution of powers, it is interestingly enough a contribution to the improvement of efficiency, since information flows foster a more efficient management.

Let us look at official wages once more. We have noted that one-sided competence to **wage setting** would lead to inefficiencies in terms of too high or too low wage rates. One way out is official wages – but why are these usually negotiated on a collective and not on an individual basis? One possible and plausible answer is that the employer who negotiates individually with each of her employees faces cumulative transaction costs. From this an interesting proposition emerges: **collective bargaining** between social partners can be quite efficient. However, this can be a matter of degree. Agreements are in use on both the level of enterprises as well as the level of industries. The bargaining parties are, in any case, representatives of the employees and of the employer, respectively. Where industries are affected, the representatives are generally elected or nominated by a professional association.

Note that we have now arrived at issues of collective labour law. We shall stop here only for a moment, however. First, we observe that the delegation of bargaining in the case of wages (but also for other work conditions such as work hours, safety conditions etc.) enhances efficiency. It requires the establishment of associations, which, in turn, has been a delicate problem involving the formation of citizens' rights in the past. Given the strength associated with a coherent association, governments are naturally reluctant to concede unrestricted property rights to such associations. To illustrate: unions and their conditional entitlements to strike are the most prominent example of the kind of problems at hand. What we can see from these observations is that regulations such a collective labour law are a matter of logic, for which the economic theory of collective decision making provides appropriate tools.

Let us now move to a final aspect of individual labour law, liability. Where employees are exposed to risk or damages, they are exempt from liability. The reason for this is that the employer usually has better information about the dangers associated with a certain workplace and that she has extracted the rents from employing people on such dangerous jobs. They are basically both the cheapest cost avoider as well as the cheapest insurer. (Can you explain why this is true – or not?) It has sometimes been asserted that the employer has a fiduciary duty to her employees. However, as we have just indicated, beyond any moral arguments there are substantial economic reasons why under normal conditions liability rests with the employer. She will be exempt from liability, of course, in case of gross negligence or intent by her employee! Unfortunately, safety regulations can give rise to rent-seeking behaviour, and can thus become a source of inefficiency. Note that at the outset we find workplaces that are not equally exposed to risks of danger.

Consequently, from the perspective of efficiency we will find regulations that necessarily differentiate among groups of employees. However, it may well be that a union (or a strong works council) is urged by some groups of employees to negotiate for an expansion of the privileges of those in the more risky positions. For the sake of loyalty and stable memberships, the unions or works councils follow such requests (resulting, for example, in administrative staff in the mining industry getting breaks as long and frequent as those of the much more exposed miners or equal benefits for train engine drivers and their assistants and so on).

Application to business law

The economic analysis of business law is a booming field. Mostly, it is corporation law and related fields which attract scholars. These are in turn closely related to industrial economics. But it is definitely no exaggeration to claim that modern industrial economics in general and the literature on (corporate) governance have benefited from transaction cost economics, one important tool of the law and economics approach. To support this claim, we can go back to the seminal contribution by Ronald Coase, On the theory of the firm, in 1937(!). The question Coase sets out to answer is why there are enterprises with various manufacturing levels and departments, thus being vertically and horizontally structured, although economists usually start with atomistic competition among small units.

The question appears to be trivial but it turns out to be as prudent as it is witty!

In answering the question, Coase makes use of the concept of transaction costs (as they are called nowadays – surely you remember the notion from Chapter 3 (pp. 44–50)). He argues that it can be advantageous for an entrepreneur to unite several manufacturing levels and lines of action under a common organization. This implies having employees under someone's command, thus creating a hierarchical structure. The negotiations with various vendors will thus be replaced by an integrated system of interior relationships. Note that we are essentially addressing the question 'make or buy' that is so prominent, particularly in the field of public utilities nowadays.

At the same time we are also approaching the issue of standard types of enterprise that are thought to meet the requests of varying degrees of complexity.

In line with our approach, we may readily assume that the resulting complex organizations will hardly be stable without an adequate institutional framework. They face all kinds of imperfections resulting from a multiplicity of relationships among self-interested rationally acting agents. To illustrate, property rights and liabilities will be specified in mutually binding contractual relations. In fact, the approach that is characteristic for the economic analysis of corporate law is the **contractual approach** to enterprises. (You may try your skills here by making use of the theory of contract, which was offered as part of the toolkit of law and economics in Chapter 3 (pp. 76–80).)

Box 6.1 Economies of scale

Before we proceed it must be stressed that it is not always a saving in transaction costs that gives rise to the formation of larger and more complex units. Economies of scale or decreasing average costs are well-known phenomena, but where they appear there can be a tendency towards a market-dominating position taken by the enterprise at hand ('natural monopolies'), which even hinders entry of new firms and which, in turn, entails the need for regulation and competition (law).

Now let us move on from these general observations to more specific ones. One starting point is the distinction between the type of enterprise where ownership and management are in the same hands, in contrast to separate ownership and management.

In the first case, contractual relationships will pertain to sharing duties and responsibilities as well as the risks associated with these fields among the owners, who at the same time form the management. In legal terms, we are dealing with firms according to civil law or trade law! Peculiar questions emerge from undertakings, where ownership and management are separated, i.e. corporate entities.

However, taking into account only owners and managers, may fall short of other people taking an interest in the corporation since they are economically affected in one way or the other. People or groups of this kind are usually termed **stakeholders**, a term that may include employees, customers, creditors and contractors. They all have in common that their economic well-being is affected by the corporation. Consequently, they will have an interest in certain entitlements with respect to the firm. This, in turn, gives rise to the establishment of an appropriate institutional or legal framework (since these stakeholders may lobby for such regulations depending on their skill – and power, of course – at political bargaining). We will not go into all these emerging complexities. Having pointed them out, we will, rather, return to the core problem: the relationship between owners and management. We are thus moving into the field of **corporate governance**, which entails a number of complex issues related to principal–agent relationships, where shareholders are the principals and boards of directors are the agents. In a simplistic view, their main problem here is to ensure a fair return on their money to the shareholders and to keep them from being taken advantage of by the board of directors.

In order to accomplish this task the following four aspects deserve special attention:

- choice of the type of enterprise: applying the contractual approach, a set of optimal entitlements and obligations is sought that minimizes transaction costs
- search for structures that give rise to minimal transactions costs leads to the attempt to establish standardized types of enterprises

---

Box 6.2   Corporate governance

Here is a concise view of the problem at hand (Shleifer and Vishny (1997, 737–83): 'Corporate governance deals with the agency problem: the separation of management and finance. The fundamental question of corporate governance is how to assure financiers that they get a return on their financial investment . . . the agency problem is serious: the opportunities for managers to abscond with financiers' funds, or to squander them on pet projects, are plentiful and well documented.'

- special emphasis is given to the obligation for financial statements. From the economic perspective two aspects are stressed here:
  - the issue of the efficiency of the availability of information and the incentives this entails
  - the disclosure requirement (which has hardly ever been doubted or even questioned in the German-speaking world) generally held that is essential for the protection of interests of creditors and investors
- there is an ongoing debate on the economic rationale for the need of additional supervisory boards besides the option for control given to the shareholders via the shareholders' meeting. The discussion is about the merits of a two-tier system versus a **three-tier system** (i.e. board of directors + shareholders' meetings or board of directors + shareholders' meetings + supervisory board). This dispute is as yet not settled.

Two more points should be made. First, what is the likely effect of the disclosure requirement on the competitiveness of the corporation? Note that by law, disclosure of the balance sheet ought to take place by publication in a newspaper. However, given that competitiveness in the marketplace is fostered by a winning margin in information, one could very well believe that rigorous disclosure requirements are detrimental to innovation. Alas, in economics there is rarely an argument without a counterargument. So it could be argued that disclosure of information helps avoid uneconomical parallel research and development operations.

The second detail worth mentioning here is the issue of **minority rights**. That is to say, when minority shareholders enjoy veto power. Thus they can enforce minimum distributions of dividends and block investments that they assume to be too risky. The problem is, however, that successful investments push up the value of assets and eventually pay extra dividends. This, in turn, would be quite a strong incentive for the majority shareholders to buy out the minority. The amount of the indemnity or market price would then be contrasted with the expected gain from additional dividends.

One of the resulting tricky questions is whether a veto power should be part of governance at all, because it can have a negative impact on the efficiency of the enterprise, since it will not, for instance, solve the issue of risk bearing in an optimal way (recall the problem of the cheapest insurer!).

The role of managers as shareholders and the problem of so-called management buyouts along with the closely related and controversial topic of insider trading are much debated issues nowadays. Interested readers are referred to the relevant literature. However, we ought to stop here in order to avoid needing a second volume for this brief introduction.

A digression: regulatory impact analysis

Interestingly enough, the economic analysis of law is not the only current economic approach to legal norms. For quite some time regulatory impact analysis (RIA) has been developed without reference to the rapidly growing literature on law and economics. RIA deserves attention for at least two reasons. First, and most important, it finds substantial support and promotion by the US government, and the Organization for Economic Cooperation and Development (OECD), where it is embedded in two major subprograms, 'Support for improvement in governance and management in Central and Eastern Europe' (SIGMA) as well as 'Public management service' (PUMA); moreover, it is advocated by the governing institutions of the European Union and many countries all over the world.

Second, RIA has a slightly different focus than the economic analysis of law inasmuch as it starts exclusively from the viewpoint of 'public interest', thus being applied in normative ways only. Stated differently RIA has not been applied to the identification of flaws in legal regulations stemming from misguided subjective interests, as is characteristic for the economic analysis of law. However, more recently it has tended to converge with the familiar subjective-based approach that is pursued here!

This section, therefore, provides an overview of RIA.

Definition of RIA

Let us start with some quotations from a guideline published by OECD (in SIGMA Paper No.13, 1974):

> The purpose of RIA is to improve the quality of government interventions. It operates on familiar principles and seeks first to ensure that the impacts both intended and unintended of proposed legislation and regulations are assessed in advance, and form an input into decision making. RIA begins by answering the questions: Will the proposed intervention actually cause welfare to increase? What are the economic effects, i.e. how do the benefits stack up against the costs?

> Next, RIA highlights the strictly redistributive impact of proposed government intervention and establishes precisely who wins, who pays and how much.

> A RIA is simply a way of gathering and organising information about the expected impacts of a law or regulation and its major feasible alternatives.

It is important to note that the term 'regulation' here is not meant in the narrow sense of imposing government constraints on private undertakings, as public economics and the theory of regulation might suggest. In fact, regulation is understood as a particular kind of **incentive mechanism**, namely, a set of incentives established by the legislature, government or public administration that mandates or prohibits the actions of citizens and enterprises. Regulations are supported by the explicit threat of punishment for non-compliance. Finally, regulation here includes the full range of legal instruments and decisions – constitutions, parliamentary laws, subordinate legislation, decrees, orders, norms, licences, plans, codes and often even 'grey' regulations, such as guidance and instructions.

So, in short, RIA deals with the analysis of likely effects on net welfare of rules and that makes it appear a close relative to, if not even a subset of the economic analysis of law, broadly defined.

However, this was not the case from the very beginning.

Short history of RIA

To see why the similarities between RIA and the economic analysis of law have been stressed already, one must be aware that RIA's focus underwent a substantial change over time: originally, it was invented to meet needs of macroeconomic policy. At that stage, the only characteristic, if any, that RIA shared with the economic analysis of law was a 'consequentiality' point of view. The origins are in the United States of America. It was initiated by the administration during the presidency of Gerald Ford after the 1974 oil crisis. There was concern about the impact on employment levels and inflation of the sharply increasing prices on spot markets, along with the implications of this impact on government policies. This led to the foundation of the Council on Wage and Price Stability, which was obliged to cooperate with the Office of Management and Budget (OMB). A directive stated that each newly established regulatory act had to be analysed primarily with respect to its impact on the rate of inflation.

However, in the course of time, the scope of RIA was continuously expanded and with good reason, of course: according to one estimate, the aggregate compliance costs of regulation both in the private sector and all levels of government amounted to US$668 billion in 1995 (approximately 10 per cent of GNP). In another estimate, regulation was blamed to cut GNP growth rates by 0.5 per cent annually, mainly due to obstacles to innovations and to productivity.

So the conclusion was that regulation (ranging from maintenance of high employment to environment protection) had severe unintended consequences in terms of lost welfare improvements. As a consequence, RIA was adapted to accomplish the task of either securing a certain level of welfare at lower costs or improvements in welfare at constant costs. RIA underwent the change from a macroeconomic device to a tool rooted in welfare economics.

This change was initiated and subsequently reinforced by two directives, one enacted by President Reagan (Executive Order 12.291 of 1981) and the other, even more influential, by President Clinton (Executive Order 12.866 of 1993). The latter led to a number of studies aiming at a more rigorous application of cost–benefit analysis in the field of regulation, which were carried out by prominent economists. In Great Britain, a similar initiative was launched in the mid-1980s and basically was intended to reduce regulatory burdens on business. This regulatory appraisal concentrates on compliance cost assessment (CCA) and has recently been complemented by a risk assessment.

At some point in the early 1990s the idea obviously had been carried to OECD. In June 1993 a SIGMA workshop on improving the quality of new laws and regulations was held at the Joint Vienna Institute in Austria.

Next, on 9 March 1995 the OECD council released the reference checklist for regulatory decision making. (For further sources see Recommended reading at the end of this chapter.)

Notes on the methodology of RIA

Basically, two things underpin a RIA, one being an almost exhaustive checklist for regulatory undertakings, and the second a rigorous cost–benefit analysis. The gist of the reference checklist is the following:

1 Is the problem correctly defined?
2 Is government action justified?
3 Is regulation the best form of government action?
4 Is there a legal basis for regulation?
5 What is (are) the appropriate level (or levels) of government for this action?
6 Do the benefits of regulation justify the costs?
7 Is the distribution of effects across society transparent?
8 Is the regulation clear, consistent, comprehensible and accessible to users?
9 Have all interested parties had the opportunity to present their views?
10 How will compliance be achieved?

This list obviously requires full-scale considerations of economic analysis, procedural rules (cf. point nine) as well as typical issues of compliance and enforcement respectively (cf. point ten).

As point six suggests, a major focus is on the cost–benefit analysis (CBA) and cost–effectiveness analysis respectively (where in the latter indicators of performance replace measures of benefits, where they are difficult to measure).

Now, remember that the basic structure of every CBA is to secure that $B(x) - C(x) > 0$, where B are the benefits (appropriately measured) of an act such as lowering the degree of regulation to some desired level x and C are the (social) costs. In the case of a continuous variation of x the criterion requires that $\delta B/\delta x = \delta C/\delta x$, constraints and contingencies notwithstanding.

The benefits B accruing from some project (level of regulation) x are captured by the (consumer) surplus brought about at the prevailing virtual price of some regulations. As you know, consumer surplus requires the knowledge of the willingness-to-pay schedule, which in turn is the opportunity cost of a particular action in terms of the next best action.

C in turn is the costs that have to be borne by people, who are not necessarily identical with the beneficiaries.

Consequently, in general, the formula implies that the Kaldor-Hicks test will hold, since otherwise the application of the Pareto criterion, i.e. the goal of net welfare gains through x is rarely achieved.

After first inspection, then, the main tool of RIA is identical with the main tool of the economic analysis of law!

However, there are obviously considerable differences that spring to mind immediately. As I pointed out in the introduction to this paragraph, the most important of these differences seems to be that, in the course of a RIA, typically no analysis is made of how a single representative individual would react to a norm; that is to say, how this person would calculate expected benefits and expected cost, so as to make the inherent incentives and likely transaction costs (broadly defined) of some regulation more visible. Instead, an aggregate measure is sought from the outset.

It is beyond the scope of this note to treat the steps of a RIA in detail. However, some of the requirements, as laid down in several guidelines as well as the previously noted Clinton Directive, deserve mention. One such requirement is the 'statement of need', which is supposed to justify government intervention. The following types of market failure are acknowledged as justifications for government action: natural monopolies; market power caused by collusion, which lead to welfare losses due to pricing, or to barriers to entry; externalities and spillovers; inadequate or asymmetric information.

Moreover, the possibility of overregulation due to preceding rent seeking is stressed.

Nevertheless, the directives point out that different standards of safety and quality of commodities are legitimate according to specific demands; even the legitimacy of barriers to entry for distinct professions is stressed, one example being pilots.

To summarize, evidently RIA seems to have been developed for a distinct field of government policy. The economic analysis of law also started from peculiar policy issues originally. With respect to the theoretical underpinning of both approaches a convergence can be observed. Still there are considerable differences. To illustrate: while RIA neglects transaction costs as well as the role of courts, it is definitely true that the economic analysis of law may be less conclusive on the aggregate level than RIA. This might follow from a typical way of reasoning within the law and economics framework: frequently, the generalized consequences for resource allocation emerging from the way in which a judge handled a particular case are at stake. The famous Learned Hand formula may serve as an illustrative example. Here, the problem at hand – the liability of the cheapest cost avoider – is worked out by induction, that is to say by the generalization of considerations in the course of handling the case *United States vs Carroll Towing Co.* (159 F2d 169 [2d Cir 1947]), where RIA, with its flavour of pragmatism, takes a different approach.

It may be the case that the loss of such subtleties is the price one has to pay for the explicit intention of both the US government and OECD to provide a tool for a standardized treatment of a very broad range of issues.

Critical reflections and an afterword

Directions for use: jurisprudence and economic analysis of law differ in scope

In general, jurisprudence is oriented towards cases, whereas economics draws advice from a general principle (efficiency). Jurisprudence is concerned with objects of legal protection; economics focuses on the consequences of human action. This makes the two approaches somewhat incompatible. However, jurisprudence cannot elude the creation of general and purposive norms. Economics, in turn, must regularly examine the empirical application of its norms for single cases. It must be checked whether they fit the efficiency criterion and if not, why not. The strength of economics lies in the availability of a clear-cut measure for social well-being as well as a tool for the explanation of observed phenomena and the resulting re-design of the measure. The strength of jurisprudence, in turn, is in the rigorous semantic as well as substantial detection of contradictions between a case and the demand. However, when a prediction is needed, jurisprudence is dependent on an ancillary science (economics or, as a variant of econometrics, jurimetrics). It is therefore evident that an interdisciplinary approach such as the economic analysis of law is mutually gainful.

For the economist, Box 6.3 is an act of exchange, which entails no particular sophistication. It is just a question of mutual advantage and it is therefore the case that irrespective of the composition of the (relative) price of the commodity at hand, the exchange will take place voluntarily, since it gives rise to rents on both sides thus increasing overall welfare (you might check Figure 1.1 on this). Following

---

Box 6.3   Jurisprudence

For those who have made it to this point, the fairly abstract statements we have just read ('the strength of jurisprudence in turn is in the rigorous semantic as well as substantial detection of contradictions between a case and the demand') will be illustrated by an example (which relates to civil law, of course).

In legal norms, the matters of fact T are paraphrased. Then it is stated that the legal consequence R should follow that which applies to T. In order to prove whether this is true, it must be verified that case S fits T. If this holds then the consequence for S is R.

But now look at this: the price for a new car may be €40,000. The car can be purchased by abandonment of the old car plus €25,000 in cash. Now, in order to find out if act S fits some T (on the purchase of a new car) it must be clear whether the deal is really a purchase or, rather, a barter. Or does it comprise two different and independent acts of purchase or two contingent acts?

Moreover, the lawyer will scrutinize what is relevant and what is irrelevant to the deal; and what is disputable and what undisputed.

The consideration of evidence thus refers to the actual circumstances, not the matter of fact. Consequently, the question of an action must be kept separate from the legal rule. The latter embodies 'what ought to be' and thus contains the intended essence of the legal norm at hand – which is the realization of justice.

this, rationale economic analysis postulates that it is also a matter of justice when by the exchange the rights to commodities are directed to where they create the relatively highest utility. You will immediately recognize the underlying principle of social efficiency or welfare. This once again is why the Chicago School at least has emphasized that a legal norm should mimic the market solution or that courts should be given a sufficient degree of discretion to accomplish the same task. This is by no means undisputed by economists. One strand in the discussion questions the significance of institutional economics when the neo-classical approach is adopted. Another strand picks up the much debated welfare criterion. Professors Kaplow and Shavell from Harvard are critics of the bias towards market solutions in the Chicago tradition and point out that contrary to the former a criterion of social welfare comprises moral preferences, which gives rise to their proposal, called 'welfarism'. Unfortunately, digging deeper into this highly interesting and sophisticated debate is beyond the scope of the book. (Further reading is listed at the end of the chapter.)

In continental Europe, at least, legal scholars seem to be much more defied by the application of economics to their subject issue than economists by jurisprudence. There is a simple reason for this, which has already been pointed out at the very beginning of this book: 'orthodox' economists have always assumed legal norms as part of the framework for economic analysis, notwithstanding a critical attitude towards the content of this framework. Recall the strong impact of the 'Freiburg School of economic thought' and the work of Walter Eucken! 'Orthodox' lawyers instead basically have two kinds of **objection**. One more general claim is that an economic approach to the law can at best cover certain aspects of the law, but never be comprehensive. The other claim originates from difficulties with some of the details of the analysis. Here is a sample:

- Legal scholars are more concerned about the **out-of-pocket cost** than opportunity costs. To illustrate, let us look at the assessment of care and reliance (on behalf of partners in contracting). Opportunity cost of time will definitely have a stronger influence on the performance of the contracting parties than out-of-pocket-cost, although the former hardly tear a hole in the wallet!
- Legal scholars sometimes have difficulties with the strong emphasis on ex ante considerations and the entailed incentives
- There are strong objections to the attempt to value the consequences of all actions in money terms. Particularly the valuation of health and life meet with fierce opposition. The problem with the latter point is what is frequently overlooked is that there is no immediate valuation: economists are well aware of this. Therefore, they frequently concentrate on the assessment of the likeliness to prevent damages or to restore health.

Review

Let us have a closer look at some of the objections that are raised against the economic analysis of law. In order to accomplish our task, I will make a distinction between three types of objection, 'discourse', 'clash of paradigms' and 'interdisciplinary discourse':

- *Discourse*. This is a traditional way of putting to test scholarly work among scholars within the same field of research. Thus, shortcomings, errors as well as the strength and novelty of research are examined.
- *Clash of paradigms*. A paradigm is simply a certain approach within a field of research, to which so many scholars adhere that it can go as a self-contained view (contrary to dissenting opinions of single scientists). Even within the economic analysis of law, there are already several paradigms, such as the Chicago School, the New Haven School and the Michigan School. (This distinction is taken from Mercuro and Medema, 1997). Discussions of that sort can be very fruitful in making strengths and weaknesses of the different approaches visible.
- *Interdisciplinary discourse*. This is what happens when one field of research is critically addressed by scholars from another field of research. It can be observed whenever traditional legal scholars criticise the economic approach to law and vice versa.

Let us look at some illustrative examples. From these we can learn a lot about the perception of the economic approach in both theory and practice.

A downright classical example of discourse is the critical review by Mitchell Polinsky of Posner's seminal book (1974). Mitchell Polinsky, himself one of the leading scholars and a professor at Stanford University, starts with the observation that in Posner's approach the structure of law becomes redundant as soon as the assumptions of competitive markets are met. The effects of the law are then merely distributional. But, in the absence of transaction costs, even these effects can be changed by other means of redistribution at no cost.

The fact that the strong assumptions are hardly ever met in practice renders analysis both more difficult but also more important. However, according to Mitchell Polinsky, the strong assumptions are not observed throughout by Posner, an illuminating example of this assertion being the occasional disregard of the convexity of preferences, for instance, when someone is said to enjoy swimming in a clear river, but after learning about the actual level of pollution of that river loses interest in swimming altogether.

Mitchell Polinsky concludes that is not the problem of weaknesses the reader must be concerned about in the first place but rather the missing 'buyer's guide' for the handling of the peculiarities.

A good example of a clash of paradigms is the review of Posner's seminal book by Peter A. Diamond, one of the creators of the theory of optimal taxation, thus being a prominent member of mathematically oriented mainstream economics. Diamond points out that a broader use of mathematics in the presentation could have avoided most of the ambiguities and errors (Diamond, 1974).

Our third example of discourse refers to a more fundamental problem. As Malloy and Brown (1995) point out, the orthodoxy of law and economics with its orientation

towards welfare maximization or the minimization of welfare losses cannot cope
with a variety of problems in reality. The legal problems entailed in ethnic riots
after the Rodney King case in Los Angeles or the war in former Yugoslavia
demonstrate that standard welfare maximization might fall short of the practical
needs (the authors claim).

Their basic argument is that the seemingly objective standard used in orthodox
neo-classical theory tends to engender illusions. Therefore the authors postulate a
'new' law and economics, which is discursive and subjective in substance. It is
embedded in context and a subjective perception. Moreover semiotics (the science
of symbols) plays a crucial role in the perception of certain situations. The notion
of an equilibrium is contingent on such symbols and their interpretation. Once this
view is accepted it can help to overcome the traditional view on incentives towards
efficiency. To illustrate, the authors point out that the likelihood of a confession in
a hearing can be quite different depending on the picture hanging on the wall over
the chair. The picture can show the head of the court, a clergyman or the hangman,
thus most likely evoking different reactions from a defendant.

Malloy and Brown (1995) stress the need for a new comprehensive and
interdisciplinary approach, which supports a better understanding of narrative,
metaphor and linguistic conventions, since these elements shape both the law and
the economy to a considerable extent. Going back to Los Angeles and former
Yugoslavia, the authors express their belief that their comprehensive new approach
would help to avoid misapprehensions caused by cultural or ethnic differences
and would ease mediation.

Let us switch to interdisciplinary discourse. Bearing in mind that we are using
economics as a methodology here, it will be interesting to look at the reactions of
some prominent legal scholars. At this point I will refer to critics from the civil
law countries Germany and Austria, where the reception of the economic approach
to law is still a controversial issue.

I start with a taster from the accessible chapter on the economic analysis of law
in the book *Fundamental Principles of Law* by the well-known Austrian lawyer
Franz Bydlinski (1988). He writes:

> Some of the basic ideas of economic analysis of law appear to be almost trivial.
> To illustrate: With respect to the notion of expediency it is mundane to require
> a legal norm to be an appropriate means for the furtherance of the underlying
> purpose . . . As a matter of fact it would strictly contradict the notion of
> expediency to adopt fairly unerring means at a cost which amounts to a multiple
> of what could have been accomplished by much cheaper measures.
>
> (my translation)

He continues with a subtle examination of utilitarianism as a means for interpersonal
comparisons of well-being and the inadequate functions of markets and prices to
assess objective measures for the intrinsic value of commodities. In concluding,
he points out that cost effectiveness is just one of several legal principles and that
the economic analysis of law is of limited use specifically for intangible rights and

their valuation. Therefore, Bydlinski asserts that it can neither be claimed nor demanded that the analysis at hand is the only rational approach to normative reasoning.

Much more severe criticism comes from the German lawyer Karl-Heinz Fezer of the University of Konstanz (1986). As a matter of fact, he is one of the most severe critics – in the German-speaking world at least. This can be illustrated by three quotations from the essay just cited (all my translations):

- With respect to the Coase theorem he notes: 'If certain conditions of the model hold then the law does not influence the allocation of resources. Economic rationality emerges from factual economic action: it will result in a Pareto-optimally efficient allocation. This is an astonishing assertion! If the economically sensible in reality would forge ahead, then all efforts by lawyers would in fact be in vain: The law as a strategic game over the sand-pit, jurisprudence as a game of marbles.'

- With reference to the *homo oeconomicus* he writes (thereby using a popular description of utility maximization with a basic endowment and a budgetary constraint, the notion of resourceful-evaluating-maximizing man (REMM): 'Legal scholars are acquainted with the insight that the image of a human being, which they adopt, will influence their legal reasoning . . . the alignment of the rules for human action towards optimal allocation of resources discloses the image of man as that of a mere utility maximizer. REMM is the abbreviation for the human being in the imaginary world of theorists of economic efficiency. As a lawyer this idea makes me shiver! In my view to make REMM the central notion of legal reasoning spoils the essential purpose of the law, to provide the order for compensating justice.'

- And finally, as a matter of principle he observes: 'The key objection against a reception of the economic analysis of law as well as the property rights approach in jurisprudence is in short the ideology [emphasis in the original text omitted] of that economic theory of law. And this applies to the entire range of the law: parliamentary legislation, judicial decisions, legal execution by the public administration, private contracting as well as scientific work in jurisprudence. But the application of economic analysis of law inevitably has fatal consequences: it will end up in an economically determined reduction of the complexity of the law. This approach actually reduces the multiplicity of tasks of the judiciary to just one reason. Thus the law is curtailed of its essential objective! To be even more outspoken: Economic analysis of law and liberal legal reasoning are incommensurable!'

I leave it up to you, the reader, to judge the acceptability of such radical denial. However, I also hasten to add that these quotations are just tasters for the wide range of positions taken in the discourse about the subject matter. Besides such dichotomous views there has also been a sufficient amount of integrative contributions. To illustrate, two examples might suffice. Norbert Horn states: 'The economic analysis of law is an attractive doctrine, although . . . it has little chance to be fully accepted as a comprehensive theory of law in German jurisprudence of today' (On the economic rationality of private law – the utilization of economic analysis of law in theorizing about private law, *Archiv für die civilistische Praxis*, 1976).

Finally the well-balanced assessment by Martin Morlock is worth mentioning here. For illustrative purposes, it is sufficient to quote just the title of his exhaustive article, which reads: About the appeal, the use, the difficulties and the risks of an economic theory of public law (sic!) (Engel and Morlok, 1999).

Outlook

If you have made it to this point, you should by now have an idea of the use, the richness and the still controversial aspects of what can truly be seen as one of the most rapidly developing branches of applied economics.

Nothing can underline this better than one example given in the very beginning of the book. If it is true that shoplifting amounts to damages of equal to 2 per cent of GDP (an estimate for Austria), it seems strange that both the legislator and the executive branch hesitate to reinforce deterrence by replacing flat rate fines with a tariff which progressively rises with the average value of theft. As the economist would point out, flat rate fines will drop out in the thief's (marginal) calculus of the benefits and costs of her wrongdoing, thus not affecting her at all, the probability of being detected and, of course, convicted notwithstanding. Economists would probably go one step further by claiming the need for punishment. But they will definitely also consider the business's side and their cost–benefit calculus of how easy it is to handle the problem, as often seems to be the case.

Where, then, is the point of departure for discrepancies between law and economics? Well, one such point of departure is in the issue of whether negligible wrongdoing should be made the subject of efficient deterrence or, by way of contrast, an approach of 'commensurability' should apply, where due to standards of justice no ex post sanctions are encompassed. Lawyers see exposing people to the risk of becoming criminals problematic in any case, even if their intentional wrongdoing only leads to minor damages. At this point, economists will claim the departure from an efficient system of law enforcement unless it is proven that the tertiary cost of maintaining an effective legal system exceeds the benefits of deterrence.

You may read this, lean back and concede that the solution even of such fairly simple problems is far from straightforward. However, economists have never claimed to be able to simplify and subsequently solve problems; they try rather to make them more transparent and more calculable. The virtues of this claim are by now increasingly being acknowledged.

In any case, reading this introductory volume has given you, I sincerely hope, some useful insights and triggered your curiosity for further study.

Key terms

business law
collective bargaining
contractual approach
corporate governance
factor specificity
incentive mechanism
labour courts
labour law
labour relations
minority rights
objection

opportunity cost
out-of-pocket cost
regulation
regulatory impact analysis
service contract
stakeholders
three-tier system
two-tier systems
wage setting
works council

Recommended reading

Arrow, Kenneth J. et.al., *Benefit-Cost Analysis in Environmental, Health and Safety Regulation – A Statement of Principles*, Annapolis, MD, 1996.
Baldwin, Robert and Cave, Martin, *Understanding Regulation*, Oxford, 1999.
Bydlinski, Franz, *Fundamental Principles of Law*, Vienna and New York, 1988.
de Geest, Gerrit (ed.) *Law and Economics and the Labour Market*, Cheltenham, 1999.
Diamond, Peter A., Posner's *Economic Analysis of Law, The Bell Journal of Economics and Management Science*, 5, 1974, 294.
Engel, Christoph and Morlok, Martin, *Public Law as a Subject of Economic Research*, Tübingen, 1999.
Kaplow, Louis and Shavell, Steven, *Principles of Fairness versus Human Welfare: On the Evaluation of Legal Policy*, Discussion Paper No.277, Cambridge, MA, 2000.
Fezer, Karl-Heinz, Aspekte einer Rechtskritik an der economic analysis of law und am property rights approach, *Juristen Zeitung*, 817, 1986.
Malloy, Robin Paul and Brown, Christopher K., *Law and Economics – New and Critical Perspectives*, New York and Vienna, 1995.
Mercuro, Nicholas and Medema, Steven G., *Economics and the Law – From Posner to Post-Modernism*, Princeton, NJ, 1997.
Morrall, J., *Assessing Costs and Economic Effects: Improving the Quality of Laws and Regulations: Economic, Legal and Managerial Techniques*, Paris, 1994.
OECD, *Budgeting for Results, Perspectives on Public Expenditure Management*, Paris, 1995.
OECD, *Assessing the Impacts of Proposed Laws and Regulations*, SIGMA Paper No. 13, Paris, 1997.
OECD, *Law Drafting and Regulatory Management in Central and Eastern Europe*, SIGMA Paper No. 18, Paris, 1997.
Polinsky, A. Mitchell, Economic analysis as a potentially defective product: a buyer's guide to Posner's *Economic Analysis of Law, Harvard Law Review*, 87, 1974, 1655–81.
Shleifer, Andrei and Vishny, Robert W., A survey of corporate governance, *Journal of Finance*, 52, 1997, 737

www.oecd.org//subject/Products/index.htm
www.aei.brookings.org

Further recommended reading

For economists who feel not adequately acquainted with jurisprudence, legal reasoning and the legal system, a range of helpful textbooks is available.

For residents of civil law countries, a compact introduction to jurisprudence is Theodor Mayer-Maly, *Rechtswissenschaft* [Jurisprudence], 5th edition, Munich and Vienna 1991.

Moreover, it is useful to have readily at hand a volume on the legal system. For the United States of America, that could be:
Peter Hay, *Law of the United States*, 2nd edition, Munich, 2005.

For Austria, Germany and Switzerland:
Hermann Avenarius, *Die Rechtsordnung der Bundesrepublik Deutschland* [The Legal System of the Federal Republic of Germany], Berlin, 1995.
Martin Lendi, *Rechtsordnung: eine Einführung in das schweizerische Recht mit Tafeln und Beispielen* [Legal System: an Introduction to Swiss Law with Tables and Examples], 3rd edition, Zurich, 2001.
Willibald Posch, *Einführung in das österreichische Recht* [Introduction to Austrian Law], Darmstadt, 1985.

For lawyers looking for a brief and convenient introduction to microeconomics, one choice could be Robert H. Frank and Ben S. Bernanke, *Principles of Microeconomics*, 3rd edition, New York, 2004.

For those who are familiar with German, an alternative is Aldfred Endres, *Moderne Mikroökonomik – erklärt in einer einzigen Nacht* [Modern Microeconomics – as Explained in One Single Night], Munich and Vienna 2000.
Clearly there are textbooks in various degrees of difficulty. An excellent text building on simple examples is A. Mitchell Polinsky, *An Introduction to Law and Economics*, 2nd edition, Boston, MA, and Toronto, 1989.
Frank H. Stephen, *The Economics of the Law*, Ames, IA, and Brighton, 1988, is divided into two parts: methodology and applications to the law.
Similar to Stephen's text but with a slightly different emphasis is Anthony W. Dnes, *The Economics of Law*, London, 1996.

A more comprehensive text, which is among the most widely used in the field, is Robert Cooter and Thomas Ulen, *Law and Economics*, 3rd edition, Reading, MA, 2000.

Those who are interested in more rigorous formal analysis will like Nicholas L. Georgakopoulos, *Principles and Methods of Law and Economics – Basic Tools for Normative*

Reasoning, Cambridge, MA, 2005, and, perhaps, more especially Thomas J. Miceli, *Economics of the Law – Torts, Contracts, Property, Litigation*, New York, 1997.

Special emphasis on game theory is contained in Douglas G. Baird, Robert H. Gernter and Randal C. Picker, *Game Theory and the Law*, Cambridge, MA, and London, 1994.

If you are interested in the seminal books on the subject and at the same time want to get an exhaustive idea about the fields of application, then this will be the right thing: Richard Posner, *Economic Analysis of Law*, 5th edition, New York, 1998.

More recently another pioneer of law and economics published a voluminous textbook: Steven Shavell, *Foundations of Economic Analysis of Law*, Cambridge, MA, and London, 2004.

A groundbreaking book for civil law countries, and Germany in particular, is: Hans-Bernd Schäfer and Claus Ott, *Lehrbuch der ökonomischen Analyse des Zivilrechts* [A Textbook of the Economic Analysis of Civil Law], 3rd edition, Berlin, Heidelberg and New York, 2000. It has also been translated into English.

Finally, an attempt to shape the existing paradigms or schools of thought within the law and economics movement might be worth having on the shelf: Nicholas Mercuro and Steven G. Medema, *Economics and the Law – From Posner to Post-Modernism*, Princeton, NJ, 1997.

The pertinent academic journals are (an ever increasing number of publications in almost all academic journals in either economics or the law notwithstanding):
American Law and Economics Review
European Journal of Law and Economics
International Review of Law and Economics
Journal of Law and Economics
Journal of Law, Economics and Organisation
Journal of Legal Studies
Review of Law and Economics

Last, if you want to be up to date, you are well advised to become a regular user of the following websites, where original and most recent scholary work can be checked and usually also downloaded:
Berkeley Electronic Press at www.bepress.com
Social Science Research Network (SSRN) (especially the Legal Scholarship Network (LSN)) at www.papers.ssrn.com

Well, this is more than just a start! You are, however, also referred to the recommendations for further reading at the end of each chapter.

Index

Note: *italic* page numbers denote references to Figures/Tables.